PEAK
PARENTS OF ESTRANGED
ADULT KIDS

PEAK
PARENTS OF ESTRANGED ADULT KIDS

A Resource for Recovery

Updated and Revised Edition

Fe Anam Avis

PEAK

Parents of Estranged Adult Kids: A Resource for Recovery
Copyright © 2022 Fe Anam Avis. All rights reserved. No portion of this material may be reproduced or distributed in any manner without written permission.

peakrecoverytogether@gmail.com
Registered trademark pending PEAK™

Eighth Printing

Scripture quotations are from English Standard Version Bible. (2001). Unless otherwise noted, all Scripture quotations are from The ESV® Bible (The Holy Bible, English Standard Version®), copyright © 2001 by Crossway, a publishing ministry of Good News Publishers. Used by permission. All rights reserved.

Cover image ©Heather Clark.
Published by Magi Press
ISBN: 978-0-9977687-6-3

Dedicated to Dr. Azaria Akashi

Table of Contents

Acknowledgements ix
Preface xi
Introduction 1

Part I - The Estrangement Experience
1. Parental Estrangement—There's a Name for It 17
2. A Pattern of Reactions 35
3. Drama and Trauma 45
4. Our Starting Point 53
5. Understanding One Another—Types of Estrangement 65
6. Two Stories 77
7. Ghosting and Shunning 89
8. After the Fire 103
9. The Pain of Ambiguous Loss 119

Part II - The Journey Toward Recovery
10. Recovery and the Unwelcome News 133
11. Parental Estrangement and a Spiritual Perspective 145
12. The Sharing Drug 159
13. Doing the Work 169
14. A No-Fault/No-Cause Perspective on Recovery 181
15. Powerlessness 193
16. Our Spiritual Source 205
17. Forgiveness 215
18. Getting to Acceptance 227
19. Here There Be Dragons 237
20. For Adults Only 249

Part III - Bringing Life Back Online
    21. Living in the Estranged Parents Community 267
    22. An Estranged Parents Bill of Rights 277
    23. Rethinking Family 293
    24. Seeing a Larger Life 303
    25. On Friendship 311
    26. Fearless Relational Audit 319
    27. Practical Concerns 327

Conclusion 335
Appendix A: Key PEAK Affirmations 339
Appendix B: PEAK Life Review 345
Appendix C: Letter to Friends 355
Appendix D: Estranged Parents Bill of Rights 359
About the Author 361

Acknowledgements

The underlying premise of this book is that pain shared is pain eased. In isolation, the burdens of this life bear down with a weight that brings many of us to the brink of the intolerable. I am hopeful that these pages will serve to connect soul to soul and through that connection some light will break through the darkness. I believe that this is possible because I have experienced it through this writing with the support of colleagues, friends, and loved ones.

In particular I would like to thank Amy Fondroy Eich who made a careful first reading through the manuscript and made many helpful recommendations. Michelle Snyder is a continual source of encouragement for projects such as these. Mark Acker was a patient and supportive listener as I shared with him thoughts that would eventually make it into the book. A special thanks goes to Richard Brantley for his reading and suggestions, to Linda Karlovec for her insights on trauma, and to Lyndon Harris for his contributions to the chapter on forgiveness. Other readers included Jim Hanna and Tim Johnson.

The editor of the first edition, Susan Niemi, has become my tutor for better writing, but also cheers me on by affirming the important contribution the writing will make. Once again, I want to thank Heather Clark for the original cover design, and for the PEAK logo which has helped give name recognition to this work of mercy.

Thanks also to my wife, Shawn, for her emotional support combined with the very practical gift of proofreading the manuscript.

Last, but by no means least, I must not fail to acknowledge the vast, collective wisdom that has been offered me through hundreds of interactions with estranged parents over the last four years. The reason this second edition of the book is roughly double the number of pages of the original edition is a testament to what I have learned through their generosity of heart and mind.

Strangely, there is a beauty in sadness to which the poets and mystics point. I have seen this star and I have followed it to its Source whom I have come to adore.

Preface

I can trace the origins of this book to three discoveries.

The first was that suicide is a major risk for divorced men, more so than for women. Divorced men are as much as eight times more likely to kill themselves than divorced women.[1] This is partly due to the fact that divorcing fathers are much more likely than divorcing mothers to become estranged from their children. Men often lose the role of being a father in a way that women do not lose the role of being a mother.[2] In either case, father or mother, loss of contact with one's children is a risk factor for a range of self-destructive behaviors.

Having worked in the field of suicide prevention for nearly 25 years, I have also learned that diagnosed mental illnesses are factors in only about half of the suicides in the United States. The other half involves stressors like divorce and parental estrangement, which are often ignored or, in the case of antagonistic parties, purposely exacerbated to secure an emotional or financial advantage. From my experience in working with estranged parents, I estimate that at least a third of them have had thoughts of suicide. Among other purposes, this book will hopefully become a suicide prevention resource. My work with estranged parents has led me to believe that we must rethink how we deal with these stressors if we are ever going to make headway curbing a disturbing suicide rate among older adults.[3]

The second discovery was that many of our personal problems are reactions to issues within our families of origin where there were struggles with alcohol, substance abuse, or other family dysfunctions. Some of the problems we have in relationship with our own adult

---

[1] https://www.fatherly.com/health-science/psychological-effects-divorce-fathers-men-suicide/
[2] http://www.divorcereform.org/mel/amensui.html
[3] https://www.cdc.gov/media/releases/2018/p0607-suicide-prevention.html

children can be traced back even further to a bundle of issues passed down from generation to generation and finally through us to them. In most cases of parental estrangement, there is a pattern of behavior going back generations that uses relationship cutoff as a means of dealing with anxiety. Healing in our relationship with adult children requires us to keep our focus on how issues from previous generations and our childhood continue to affect us and the relationship with our children today. I continue to believe that that approach has merit.

However, I have also concluded that when the relationship becomes estranged—an adult child has severed or severely curtailed communication with the parent—an additional set of tools needs to be brought to bear in addressing the problem. That's because parental estrangement has its own particular characteristics, including extreme emotional pain, that need to be addressed directly as a primary issue and not simply as a reflection of issues cascaded from a previous generation.

The third discovery was the prevalence of parental estrangement in Western societies, particularly the United States and Europe. At the beginning of this project, I did not know there was such a thing as parental estrangement until I did an online search. And while it was clear that the research on the topic was sparse, I was surprised to discover how often parental estrangement was occurring among older adults, with the adult child almost always responsible for making the break.

These three discoveries, combined with my own personal experience, have made major contributions to my navigation through this painful world of parental estrangement. I have done the work of conducting my own thorough and fearless relational audit. I understand how my failures have had serious consequences for others. However, as we say in PEAK, everyone deserves to recover.

This book is not about me. I do not tell my personal story in these pages. My ultimate purpose is to help estranged parents navigate through the pain of parental estrangement and into recovery of a life worth living. The quotes in text boxes are all from actual communications with estranged parents, though the details have been altered to protect their anonymity.

The goal is not to eliminate all sadness. Since life is a journey, every morning must bid a small farewell to the path walked the day before. Losses, large and small, are perpetual in life, and we will always carry a wisp of sadness in our hearts. Sadness is like the small tears of wax flowing down the candle of love that lets us know that the wick is still lit. Real joy is not possible without it.

Fe Anam Avis
July 26, 2022

Introduction

This book is written to serve as a resource for parents with estranged adult kids. If you are an estranged parent, little more needs to be said about the need for this book. You have likely been wandering about in a silent wilderness with little to comfort or guide you. You may have talked with friends or consulted with a physician, clergy person, or even a professional therapist and found little help. Or you may have browsed the internet only to find a confusing cacophony of competing voices with fingers of blame pointed in both directions.

"I'm an estranged parent. I'm hurting." Every week I receive desperate messages from estranged parents like this one. These pleas from complete strangers remind me that there are few situations more agonizing in life than to find that your adult child has cut off communication with you and possibly you from your grandchildren. Personally, I have experienced the loss of a best friend in war, the tragic death of my only sister in a car accident, the murder of my sister-in-law, the death of a 34-year-old son, the total loss of nearly every financial asset, and despair so deep that I nearly took my own life. I can say without qualification that parental estrangement is more painful than any of these other experiences. Many estranged parents would express similar sentiments. I can say with equal conviction that estranged parents can find hope and healing.

As the author of this book, I make four assumptions about you as an estranged parent.

1. I assume that intense pain and confusion is your starting point. Therefore, it will not help to simply dive into quick answers that ignore the feelings you are experiencing as a result of parental estrangement.
2. I assume that parental estrangement is interfering with your ability to live a full and productive life. Parental estrangement

has multiple impacts ranging from psychological to medical to relational.
3. I assume that you are ready to enter a process of recovery. In other words, you are ready to begin taking responsibility for your own well-being and take steps to emerge from the negative impacts of parental estrangement.
4. I assume that you are open to new information and perspectives about your relationship with your adult kids. As in many other situations in life, much of what keeps us trapped in the pain of parental estrangement are patterns of thinking that are unhelpful. Key to recovery is the ability to change our minds, that is, the way we perceive what is happening to us. As Einstein put it, "We can't solve problems by using the same kind of thinking we used when we created them."

Understanding the Estrangement Experience

These pages take you on a journey, a journey that begins with understanding the estrangement experience. In spite of the fact that they have already lived three-quarters of their lives, most estranged parents have had little exposure to parental estrangement. Other family members or friends don't speak of it, even if it has struck their adult-child relationship, a silence usually borne out of guilt or shame. Unless a parent goes searching for it, there is not much in the media that addresses parental estrangement, especially when compared with the family-soaked coverage of holidays, Father's Day, Mother's Day, and Grandparent's Day, etc. Simply understanding what is happening to you, and why you are feeling the way you do is an essential part of the healing process. It is also important to know that someone else understands what you are going through.

A key understanding of the estrangement experience is that parental estrangement is a trauma. Trauma is an emotional response to an unexpected, deeply distressing event. One of the common characteristics in the stories of estranged parents is the element of shock. Beginning with the day of their child's birth or adoption, and continuing through all the seasons of their nurture, it never occurred to most parents that one day the relationship with that child would come to an end, either suddenly or after years of on and off communication. Dealing with parental estrangement engages us in a process of *trauma recovery*.

We are familiar with physical traumas like automobile accidents. The recovery from the trauma of an automobile accident may require surgery, medication, physical therapy, and rest, all engaged over a period of months. Similarly, recovering from the psychological trauma of parental estrangement also requires commitment to an intentional program over a period of time. Even reading several pages of this book every few days for several weeks can make a substantial contribution to your recovery process.

Overcoming Isolation

As an estranged parent, hearing others talk about their children and grandchildren is like being blind and hearing how beautiful the world is. While other parents are engaged in the expected ritual of swapping photos and catching up on the latest communication, estranged parents are left with meager attempts to try to cover up the fact that they have neither. They feel they must hide their estrangement given the substantial amount of stigma and shame surrounding parental estrangement. Because this discourages open, honest conversation, it fosters the mistaken belief that parental estrangement is rare. This has the effect of isolating parents in their pain and confusion. In fact, parental estrangement is a common experience in both the United States and

> *I feel ashamed and all alone. Help me not feel so alone in my grief.*
> M.T. from Portland, ME

Europe, affecting millions of parents, along with their adult kids and grandkids.

Just because estranged parents are not talking about their experiences does not change the fact that estrangement is having a profound impact on their lives. Those impacts are similar to any other major family dysfunction that renders life unmanageable, including addictions to drugs, alcohol, or gambling. Many of the lessons learned by those living with an addicted loved one are applicable to parents dealing with an estranged adult child. While parental estrangement is extremely personal, and affects every parent differently, many of these characteristics are shared by all estranged parents.

Critical to the recovery process is the ability of estranged parents to speak honestly with one another about their experience. There are several obstacles to be overcome. First, it may be difficult to discover other estranged parents. As a partial remedy, I am also developing resources for a support network I am calling PEAK (Parents of Estranged Adult Kids). By joining a PEAK recovery group, parents can find others who are willing to talk about their experience. A second obstacle is the issue of family loyalty. Parents often feel bound by an unspoken code that forbids them from talking about problems with those outside the family. A final obstacle is the belief that seeking help for parental estrangement simply adds one failure upon another.

Overcoming these obstacles is part of the early work of recovery. Estranged parents must be able to talk about the multiple ways that estrangement is impacting their lives. Estrangement is a form of shunning, and estranged parents need to have an understanding of all the ways that they are impacted—emotionally, spiritually, even medically. Estrangement also involves loss, and loss triggers a grief reaction. In addition to the common grief reactions of shock, denial, anger, guilt, and bargaining, estrangement is characterized by something known as *ambiguous loss*. Because there is always the hope, however faint, that the relationship will be restored, estranged parents find it difficult to navigate through acceptance in a way that enables them to move on with their lives. Estrangement also threatens a parent's ability to make meaning of their lives. Raising children to adulthood represents the most significant investment of time, energy, and money that most people will make. Estrangement calls the value of that investment into question. In the words of Shakespeare's King Lear, "Is this the promised end?" (Lr.5.3.)

Practical Consequences

Beyond the substantial trauma symptoms of estrangement are the practical consequences for parents. Who will take care of them in their years of decline and eventual death? How will they handle their estate? What should they do on holidays when everyone else is celebrating with children and grandchildren? Estranged parents in recovery must be able to talk about all these impacts.

Parental estrangement is not only traumatic, but also touches upon some of the deepest questions of life such as:

- What is the meaning of my life?
- Am I loved?
- Am I forgiven for my failures?
- Do I deserve to be happy?

Because these questions cannot be addressed from a purely human perspective, I believe that recovery from parental estrangement requires assistance from a Spiritual Source that alone has the ability to restore us to lives that are full and productive. Not only does this Spiritual Source offer the unconditional love that heals us, but also the wisdom to guide our recovery process.

The Causes and Mystery of Parental Estrangement

The causes of parental estrangement are varied and complex. Behaviors in a parent that lead to estrangement from one child are easily overlooked by another child, even in the same family. In some cases, children are able to view a failure in a parent's relationship with a spouse as separate from the relationship of the parent with them. In other cases, a failure in the marriage of the parents is seen as a betrayal of the family, and children feel compelled to side with one parent or another. Personality differences between parent and child can form irreconcilable differences in spite of their best efforts. Cultural differences introduced by "mixed" marriages can also prove insurmountable.

In all cases, it is safe to say that human beings, parents and adult children alike, will be subject to human frailties. Mistakes will be made, sometimes a series of mistakes. It is not necessary to conclude that a particular failure "caused" the estrangement. What we can say is that we can never be fully released from the guilt and shame that keeps us stuck until we open ourselves to self-examination. We do this with confidence that there is no failure so irredeemable that can ultimately separate us from the love of our Spiritual Source, who some choose to call God. This introduces us to a quality of spirituality that many may never have experienced in their religion. As one person put it: religion is for people who are afraid of going to hell; spirituality is for people who have been there.

It is helpful for estranged parents to realize that we are not alone, and that our Spiritual Source loves us unconditionally. Taking steps to share with other estranged parents is courageous and healing. For many estranged parents, this is not enough. In the words of one author on parental estrangement, they are done with the crying and ready to move on.[4] This requires some new ways of thinking about the relationship with our adult children. This is the part of the book that runs counter to nearly every holiday commercial, Hallmark movie, and religious sentimentality. This is the part of the book where you, as an estranged parent are most likely to find yourself saying, "Yes, but . . ."

---

[4] Sheri McGregor, *Done with the Crying: Help and Healing for Mothers of Estranged Adult Children* (Sowing Creek Press, 2012).

Wrestling with these ideas is a normal part of the process, as long as you remain open. Ultimately, we all need to exhaust our best attempts to solve the problem on our own. When we reach that point, we become open to other possibilities.

Rethinking Parental Estrangement

First, we are going to have to rethink our understanding of the relationship between parents and children over the course of their lifetimes. Our assumption is that in a "normal" family, parents and children have a responsibility to stay in relationship until, like marriage, death do them part. Is that necessarily true? I have observed that it is not. By the time an adult child reaches 25 years of age, the essential work of parenting has been completed; I call these *completed children*. At that point a completed child has every right to move on with their lives totally independent of their parents. And many do.

Likewise, a parent has the right to move on as well into a time in their lives when they will have responsibilities and needs other than those of rearing children: retiring, relocating, reflecting on the past, and preparing for their eventual decline and death. This last quarter of a parent's life I call the *finalist stage*. Some adult children will feel ready to make the transition from being cared for to caring for their parents in that finalist stage. I call these *transitioned children*. Transitioned children are able to move beyond simply completing childhood, and enter into adult-to-adult relationships with their parents. Estranged parents need to accept that some of their children may make that transition, and some may not.

Second, we need to accept the fact that the relationships between parents and adult children are privileged and voluntary. It is beneath the dignity of any adult relationship that one should have to beg another for consideration. Whatever the shortcomings in either individual, a relationship is a privilege offered freely to another. When all the emotional power in a parent-adult child relationship has shifted to one or the other, neither benefit. In those cases, this stage of the relationship is over, and should be grieved as such. Another stage may be possible in the future, but it will be a different relationship built from a new starting point.

Third, in some cases, estrangement may be a solution rather than a problem. Rather than viewing estrangement as a problem to be solved, we may need to view it as a solution to an otherwise unsolvable problem. Unsolvable problems are created in situations like these:

- Relationships that force extremely different personality types into situations they otherwise would not choose. People with significantly different personalities sometimes only serve to make one another miserable. The requirement that they suffer through the inevitable, multiple clashes experienced at mandatory family gatherings makes little sense.
- Relationships that serve as a reminder to one or both parties of unforgiveable past failures. Contrary to what we would like to believe, some personal failures result in ruptures that are simply irreparable. In a relationship, each is reminded of the breach: One is retraumatized and the other is re-guilted. No one wins.
- Relationships that require people to deal with fundamentally irreconcilable differences in culture or core values. More than ever, we live in a global community, and adult children often choose partners who have very different views of family, the obligations of parents to adult children, and vice versa. When these differences are pressed with a low degree of appreciation or even tolerance toward others, a decision to part ways may be the better choice.
- Relationships that place either parents, children, or both, in loyalty binds that apply pressure toward exclusivity. Divorce is a major factor in estrangement, usually because adult children feel the need to blame or exclude one parent over another. Ending the relationship is often a choice that adult children feel they

must make as a way of avoiding ongoing conflicts with one or both parents.

It is always possible to try to simply avoid dealing with these problems, but the results—chronic conflict, deepening resentments, losses of esteem, and generational impacts on grandchildren—can be devastating. A decision that continuing the relationship is too high a price to pay for everyone involved can be a responsible, moral choice.

This brings me to the fourth change we must make in the way we think about estrangement: acceptance. Acceptance is not affirmation. It is adjustment. If we do not adjust to the reality of our adult child's estrangement decision, we will never be able to lay the foundation of a full and productive future. Whereas the ambiguous loss of estrangement prevents many parents from moving through the entire grief process to acceptance, fully recovered estranged parents have accepted that the relationship with their adult children, as they have known it, is over. This does not mean that it might not be reestablished at some future point, but if it is, it will not be a restoration to a past relationship but the creation of a new one on different terms.

Acceptance enables estranged parents to move on with their lives in ways that are essential to their well-being. This includes forming new relationships (sometimes with surrogate children and grandchildren); establishing new interests and opportunities for service; planning for their future care; and dealing with legal, financial, and logistical issues.

The fifth and final change of thinking has to do with nothing less than the meaning of life. There are many sources of meaning. Having adult children who desire to have a relationship with you is not the sum total of your life. Other sources of meaning include friendships, personal growth, vocation, hobbies, spirituality, service to others, education, even learning to "turn pain into gain." For most people, two-thirds of their lives will be spent doing something besides raising children. Jesus had no children. Buddha had one son that he named "impediment" indicating the concern that a child might impede his search for enlightenment. Only one of Muhammad's seven children outlived him. The Apostle Paul suggested it was good for the unmarried to remain single, (and therefore, childless). The significance of their lives was measured in other terms. Yet estranged parents are tempted to measure their significance based only on a continuing, positive relationship with their adult child. Changing the way you think about the meaning of your life requires nothing less than an intentional, counterculturul life review. This book will help you do that.

There is no intention in this book of diminishing the beauty of family relationships that endure across multiple generations. Hundreds of books and media productions have been written to dramatize, guide, and celebrate those relationships. Unfortunately, there are a large number of parents today whose children have indicated that they want no part of such relationships. Without passing judgment on their motives, it is important to face the impact of that decision and work to relieve the suffering of those parents who deserve to move forward in their lives with dignity, purpose, and even joy.

I also make no attempt in this book to analyze broader social patterns that are contributing to parental estrangement. Nor do I provide a laundry list of causes with ideas for fixes. I will leave that task to other authors who are more qualified than I. Parents who are looking for a moral case to be made against their children will not find it in this book. Likewise, children who are seeking support for breaking from a family situation will not find that in these pages either. Those books have been written and have value. There is no question that the behaviors of flawed parents in the early years of their childrearing can have serious, lifelong consequences on their adult child. It is equally true that the actions of an adult child upon their parent through estrangement can have a ruinous and life-shortening impact as well. The cycle of blame takes us nowhere. I am assuming that estrangement is a stubborn reality that parents need help addressing in order to move forward, whatever the cause or however justified it might seem in the eyes of others.

Practically Speaking

Now for some practical matters.

This book has been developed to serve as a resource for participants in PEAK recovery groups. PEAK recovery groups also make use of a script with a variety of sections that are read during each meeting. These can be found in Appendix A: Key Affirmations of PEAK, and include "Our Common Experiences," "The Way Forward," and "The PEAK Turning Points." The experiences and perspectives found in these affirmations are essential to the recovery process. For that reason, they are frequently referenced in the chapters that follow. Where a PEAK recovery group does not exist, readers may want to start a group in their community. I have designed some materials for a PEAK group that you might find helpful. You'll find contact information in the About the Author section at the end of the book.

Nonetheless, I have written this book with the hope that it might be beneficial in a variety of settings. Some will benefit from a book study format where the book serves to jump-start a discussion about parental estrangement. This could include unestranged parents as well who want to gain a better understanding of this experience that is likely affecting their friends and family members. To that end, I have included some questions for reflection and discussion at the close of each chapter.

Groups are not for everyone. I hope this book will also be useful for individuals to read and reflect on. For some parents, simply reading it will be enough to help them feel affirmed and less alone.

Another way of using the book would be to give it to friends or family members as a way of educating them about what you are going through. If you find the book helpful, you also may want to give it to any caregivers like clergy, physicians, or counselors who are supporting you. Alternatively, you can copy Appendix C: A Letter to Friends in the back of the book and give it to others as a starting point. I strongly discourage giving the book to estranged adult children. If you are an estranged child, this book might help you as a way to "listen in." While I have worked hard not to assign blame for parental estrangement, the needs of parents are quite different from those of adult children, and no one book can meet the needs of both.

Most important is that you find a way to use this book that will help you recover from one of the most difficult life experiences most of us will ever face. Your journey on this earth is too brief, and your life too precious to stay stuck in pain. We live in a day when we need older adults who can bring their skills, learnings, and energy to the table in addressing the problems of the world. To have several million people in our country alone who are sidelined by the impacts of parental estrangement is a waste we cannot afford. These people have not only accumulated a lifetime of skills and expertise, they will be the source of the greatest migration of wealth ever to hit humanity—the unprecedented flood of money, four times the size of the US gross domestic product, that will be passed along to a younger generation over the next half-century.[5] We need this generation to be as vital, energized, and positively engaged as possible. A generation of dispirited, guilt-ridden, disengaged, and emotionally crippled adults is simply not acceptable.

Questions for Reflection and Discussion
What led you to begin reading this book? What are you hoping for?

"...there are few situations more agonizing in life than to find that your adult child has cut off communication with you and possibly you from your grandchildren." As you think about other painful experiences in your life, how do they compare to your experience as an estranged parent?

---

[5] https://nypost.com/2014/06/22/top-1-percent-spreading-nearly-60t-in-assets-to-heirs-charities/

Review the four assumptions about you as an estranged parent listed near the beginning of the introduction. How do you relate to them?

How isolated do you feel as an estranged parent? Who have you attempted to talk to? Who has been the most understanding? The least understanding?

How did the introduction leave you feeling after you read it?

If you are using this book in a group discussion, what did you gain from hearing others speak? From speaking?

Is there anyone else it would be helpful for you to give this book to?

PEAK: Parents of Estranged Adult Kids
A Resource for Recovery

Part I
The Estrangement Experience

Chapter 1
Parental Estrangement: There's a Name for It

When I first began to do research back in 2018, I had no idea what I was dealing with. I started where everyone else does today: a Google search. My search term was "children divorcing their parents." What popped up at the top of the list was a legal process whereby a minor could be emancipated from their parents. While legal issues are occasionally an aspect of parental estrangement, that wasn't my primary area of interest.

As I scrolled down, I came across the phrase "parental estrangement." For the first time, I realized that there is a name for this painful thing. It is important that parents call this experience by name: *parental estrangement*. Some parents are hesitant to name it for fear that it will make it true, similar to the way alcoholics are hesitant to admit their addiction for fear that it might be true. Confucius wrote that the beginning of wisdom is to call things by their proper name. In their recovery process, it is important that parents call this experience by name: "I am the estranged parent of an adult child." Most parents find an initial sense of relief just by saying it out loud.

Struggling with the word, but saying it for the first time. That is a milestone in the estrangement experience.

What is parental estrangement?

Parental estrangement occurs when one or more adult children make the decision to significantly curtail or withdraw from the relationship with their parent. (As will be discussed later in this chapter, it is relatively rare that the parent cuts off the adult child.) The definition of the age of adulthood is going to vary from one situation to another. With parental consent, a seventeen-year-old can join the military, which certainly must qualify him or her for adulthood. Other children may remain financially dependent through their college education. The average age of marriage is now about twenty-eight years of age, and the average age of first birth is the same. Barring special circumstances, it is reasonable to define an adult child as any person who is twenty-five years of age or older.

This is also the point at which the brain development required for responsible decision-making is complete. As I will explain in Chapter 5, the decision of a young adult in their early 20's to cut off the relationship with a parent may be qualitatively different from the same decision made by a 35-year-old. Young adults possess an impulsiveness and fluidity in their decision-making that may be reversible with maturity. However, the traumatic impact on the parent is the same. That trauma must be addressed.

If we accept the average age of adult onset at twenty-five years, and add it to the average age of a parent at first birth, about twenty-eight years, it suggests that the window for a less recoverable estrangement opens, on average, around fifty-three years of age and can last to the end of their earthly sojourn, thirty years or more. Few things are sadder in my work than a conversation with an 80-year-old woman whose adult child has ended the relationship with her. Yet this seems to be happening with increasing frequency.

I have had many conversations over many years with folks in this estrangement window, early 50's to early 90's. Only once did a person confide in me that they actually had no relationship with one or more of their adult children (and consequently their grandchildren). I had to conclude that virtually no one else was wrestling with the problem of parental estrangement, and that the problem must be relatively rare. I was wrong.

Not Rare

Parental estrangement is not rare. Research suggests that 12 percent of parent-child relationships in the United States are estranged, which is likely a conservative estimate since the study only observed mother-daughter relationships.[6] This means that there are about five million estranged parents in the United States. Stated another way, for every eight parents you know, one is likely to be estranged from one or more of their adult children. They are simply not talking about it. When I tell friends I have written a book for estranged parents, their first response is that they have never heard of it. By our next conversation, almost without fail, they tell me with some surprise that they have encountered several parents whose children have stopped communicating with them.

As mentioned above, parental estrangement tends to occur among older parents in their mid-fifties and beyond. One might hope that the rate of estrangement would ease as parents get older and reconciliation becomes more likely. Unfortunately, this is not the case. Over one-third of estranged parents fall into the seventy-to-eighty age range.[7] This means that many parents are facing the permanent loss of the relationship with their adult children at the same time they are most likely experiencing other losses: spouses, friends, siblings, health, vocation, and financial security.

> *I am 79 years old. I am now estranged from my 46-year-old son and 2 grandchildren for a little over a year. It is absolutely devastating. I have no idea what I did.*
> P.D. from Birmingham, AL

It also suggests that a significant number of persons living in retirement communities are likely to be experiencing parental estrangement from one or more of their children. Again, this means that they are experiencing estrangement at the same time that a

---

[6] https://www.nextavenue.org/myths-about-estrangement/
[7] https://www.verywellfamily.com/when-adult-children-divorce-their-parents-1695810

geographic relocation is requiring that they start over again in building their social networks. Even in those networks, parental estrangement will hardly be mentioned. You are unlikely to hear a sermon in your faith community, a presentation in your senior center, or in an educational class for seniors that addresses the issue of parental estrangement.

Shame and Isolation

You think you are alone. You are not.

In our PEAK recovery groups, we say every week, "We are isolated from other estranged parents who might serve as sources of insight, support, and guidance. We feel alone."[8] This is an important part of understanding the estrangement experience. In spite of the prevalence of parental estrangement, most people are surprised by how common it is. This is largely due to the shame that parents feel in admitting that their adult children have broken contact with them. Sharing photographs of children and grandchildren, and catching up on what is happening in their lives is part of the ritual of older adult conversation. Admitting that there are no recent pictures, conversations, or updates to report because an adult child broke contact a number of years ago is painful. Since parents often believe that the work of raising children was the most important job of their lives, parental estrangement feels like a massive personal failure. As we shall see later, this is not actually the case, but the feelings are real and intense. Since admitting parental estrangement to others is so difficult to do, parents often feel isolated in the experience. They assume that the experience is unique to them, which deepens the sense of failure. The isolation deprives them of a proper perspective on the issue, that parental estrangement can occur in any parent's life regardless of their investment in raising children or the shortcomings their children may

---

[8] See Appendix A: Key Affirmations of PEAK, "Our Common Experiences."

or may not choose to forgive. In addition, estranged parents do not benefit from the experience of other estranged parents in dealing with an array of practical issues ranging from contact with grandchildren to planning for their own care in the years of their decline.

One-Sided Power

Healthy adult-to-adult relationships are characterized by elements of mutuality and commitment. Mutuality means that both parent and adult child hold equal responsibility for maintaining the relationship. Phone calls, text messages, emails, letters, and visits are initiated by both parent and adult child. Each express concern for the well-being of the other. Commitment means that both parent and adult child feel bound by a pledge, usually unspoken, to the long-term continuation of the relationship through good times and bad. Together, mutuality and commitment ensure that both parent and adult child have an equal stake in the relationship.

Parental estrangement destroys this essential balance. It is generally the case that it is the adult child who breaks off the relationship. Only five percent of those estranged from a son or daughter say that they made the move.[9] It is usually the case that the estranged parent is left longing for a relationship that they have no power to reinstate. They may resort to begging, pleading, bargaining, or unreciprocated attempts to reconnect. This "keep trying" approach is often prescribed by professional caregivers including clergy and therapists However, over time, this begins to erode the self-worth of the estranged parent. Unchecked this self-denigration can lead to a variety of serious psychological and medical maladies.

Even when a parent's efforts to avoid estrangement maintain the semblance of a relationship with an adult child, it often comes with a

---

[9] https://www.verywellfamily.com/breakdown-of-family-estrangement-1695444

price. They often feel that they are walking on eggshells. Frequently, an adult child will cycle in and out of the relationship with seasons of connection followed by seasons of estrangement. This leaves the parent wondering when the other shoe will drop during times of connection and wondering if the break is permanent during periods of estrangement.

Unfortunately, estranged parents often underestimate the severity of the break from their adult children. When asked to respond to the statement: "We could never have a functional relationship again," roughly 75 percent of the adult children agreed or strongly agreed. Only 14 percent of the estranged parents of those same adult children agreed or strongly agreed.[10] In other words, many estranged parents are hopeful for reconciliation in a relationship that their adult children have given up. This will be addressed at length in Chapter 10: Recovery and the Unwelcome News. As a result, many parents spend their days waiting for the call from their adult children that will never come. The impact can be devastating. As the proverb puts it: hope deferred makes the heart sick.

While it is difficult to get a handle on how fast the problem of parental estrangement is growing, it seems to be part of a larger pattern with older adults. Reports of domestic elder abuse (including neglect) to adult protective service agencies increased 150 percent between 1986 and 1996.[11] One of the reasons that estranged parents underestimate the severity of the break is differences in generational perspectives. An older generation tended to maintain a relationship with parents, even with difficult parents. They expect their children will eventually do the same. However, researchers have found that

---

[10] https://www.verywellfamily.com/breakdown-of-family-estrangement-1695444
[11] https://www.psychologytoday.com/us/conditions/elder-or-dependent-adult-neglect

members of the younger generation are initiating breaks with parents at a level some call a silent epidemic.[12]

Not Finding Help

Estranged parents often find little help, even from sources they have found useful in the past. This leaves them not knowing where to turn. Many estranged parents complain that social services were "useless" while the clergy's urge to be forgiving fell wide of the mark. A quarter of those who asked advice from a doctor said she or he seemed ill equipped to provide it.[13] When I spoke with my cardiologist about the death of my son, he said, "I'm sorry. Do you have other children?" When I said, "Yes, but they are estranged," he turned back to his computer screen without saying a word. Even physicians that I have spoken to about estrangement never ask how I am dealing with it in subsequent visits.

The puzzling question is this: Why is it so difficult for us as estranged parents to find real help? I believe the answer is basic: trauma. Most professionals who are called to meet the needs of estranged parents are failing to do so because they are not identifying and addressing trauma. Professional caregiver expectations of what traumatized parents should be able to handle are often unrealistic and misguided.

I am not a therapist, but from my extensive experience with estranged parents, I observe that they generally exhibit the symptoms of complex trauma similar to that seen in abused children. Whereas trauma generally refers to a single incident, like a car accident, complex trauma refers to a series of traumatic events that take place over an

---

[12] https://www.today.com/parents/parental-estrangement-silent-epidemic-cut-kids-1C9163139

[13] https://www.psychologytoday.com/us/blog/domestic-intelligence/201512/the-persistent-pain-family-estrangement

extended period of time, like months or years. This is the typical time frame of repeated episodes in the life of an estranged parent.

The effects of trauma are well-known. Among those is an impaired ability to make good decisions. As individuals, estranged parents are generally no less capable of making thoughtful decisions than any other adult. However, they are traumatized, and that trauma sabotages the decision-making of even the best of us. John McAloon, Senior Lecturer at the Graduate School of Health in Sydney observes that "people who have experienced complex trauma may display symptoms including poor concentration, poor attention, and poor decision-making and judgement. Complex trauma translates into a range of social, emotional, behavioral and interpersonal difficulties that can be life-long."[14]

"We Sometimes Act Crazy"

Estranged parents typically know this about themselves. In our recovery meetings, we recite these words to one another every week: "The intensity of our feelings sometimes boils over into behaviors that we are not proud of. We feel, and sometimes act, crazy." But when we ask for help from various quarters, what we may encounter is a focus on these behaviors instead of the underlying trauma that is contributing to them. We often feel judged and further shamed. How can we reasonably expect a person whose thinking is compromised in all the ways identified by McAloon to make sound decisions in response to an adult child who has cut off or severely curtailed the relationship with them? It is like asking a person who has been critically injured in a near-fatal car accident to play and win a game of chess.

Margot is a sixty-four-year-old divorced mother who works as a drug counselor. Her son, Anthony, is a nurse. Anthony became

---

[14] https://theconversation.com/complex-trauma-how-abuse-and-neglect-can-have-life-long-effects-32329

addicted, first to opioids, then to street drugs, about two years ago. Six months ago, Anthony cut off all communication with his mother. As a result, Margot is having a range of issues, insomnia, headaches, and depressed mood. When she couldn't get out of bed, she had to take several days off from work.

When Margot went to her priest for help, he advised Margot to track her son down, meet with him face to face, take his hands into her hands, look him in the eye and say, "Anthony, I forgive you."

When, Margot did what the priest suggested, Anthony jerked his hands away, and stormed off, shouting, "There's nothing I need you to forgive!"

Why would she make a decision that runs counter to all her expertise and training in dealing with an addicted loved one? Because Margot is traumatized by the estrangement. Her freeze response is making it difficult for her to function at work, and her approval-seeking response is leading her to abandon her own best judgement, and listen to the questionable advice of the well-intentioned, but ill-equipped priest.

The priest does not recognize that Margot is too traumatized to make a good decision about how to proceed. In her traumatized state, she is vulnerable to a childlike response to his authority. When the priest's approach fails, she may become angry at him, but she is just as likely to blame herself, which will simply add a heaping helping of self-reproach to the trauma load she is already bearing.

Margot's story is no exaggeration. I have seen people who are extremely competent otherwise, attorneys, financial planners, therapists, clergy, authors, marketing executives, and musicians, to name a few, make unfortunate decisions related to their estranged children. I place myself among them. We don't need judgement. We need compassion and help.

Here is another way of saying it: *addressing the trauma of parental estrangement is primary, fixing the relationship is secondary.* Without help, a traumatized person is likely to make mistakes that hinder any efforts at reconciliation, and make those same mistakes over and over again.

Even if the adult child makes serious overtures to reconnect, the trauma will still need to be addressed if the relationship is to be healthy and sustainable.

Parental Trauma Is Primary

A soldier serving in a war zone must deal with the daily reality that unexpected, loud sounds could signal serious injury, loss of a limb, or death. Even after those traumatic events are past, the startle response and other symptoms remain. We call it PTSD, post-traumatic (after the trauma) stress disorder. Simply returning to a safe environment with family and friends will not automatically address the symptoms he or she is experiencing, even after the source of the trauma is gone. Without help, the trauma can put family relationships and friendships at risk. Soldiers are often not healed by taking them out of unsafe situations and placing them in safe ones. They bring the unsafety with them, and recreate it.

Parental estrangement is similarly traumatic with similar symptoms. We might call it *parental trauma*. Without the right kind of help, parental trauma can seriously impair and even shorten the life of a parent. It can also make a healthy reconciliation less likely. It is for this reason that I believe parental trauma to be primary, and that it must be addressed whether reconciliation occurs or not.

The failure to recognize parental trauma helps explain why estranged parents may find so little real help. Time after time, estranged parents have shared with me their frustration and eventual exhaustion at the disappointing responses of professionals they have consulted. In the remainder of this chapter, I will briefly review the frequent response of three different helping professionals, clergy, therapists, and physicians, and explain why you as an estranged parent may not find help there.

Why is it important for you to understand this? It is not to discourage you from seeking help from the growing number of professionals who *are* gaining a deeper understanding of this problem. However, should you encounter some of the responses that follow, it is important for you to be able to step back and recognize where they are coming from.

But before I delve into specifics, I want to make a general observation about all helping professions that are asked to address the needs of estranged parents.

Training for most professionals in the area of parental estrangement is virtually non-existent. As a result, their effectiveness is hampered by several pieces of missing information. (a) Because they do not recognize parental trauma as primary, they not only fail to address trauma symptoms, they set impossibly high expectations for what estranged parents should be able to handle. (b) Because they do not realize that the likelihood of a healthy reconciliation is relatively small, they press forward solutions that are unlikely to be successful, leaving the parent even more demoralized and self-blaming. (c) Because they underestimate the degree of desperation estranged parents experience, they do an inadequate job of assessing the risk of self-destructive behaviors, including suicide. (d) Finally, because they do not realize the scope of the problem and the growing number of parents who are dealing with this issue, they are not highly-motivated to update their training. It is impossible to motivate someone to address what they don't know they don't know.

There are no villains here. People are generally doing the best they can with what they have. However, estranged parents are extremely vulnerable. Stories of reconciliation trafficked on the internet can be highly misleading. They may leave parents with the perception that their estrangement can be resolved through a relatively simple, though sometimes expensive, intervention. As a result, parents are often left with their trauma untreated, combined with feelings of failure to boot.

Clergy

In general, ordained clergy and lay pastors in the Christian tradition tend to focus on reconciliation as the solution to interpersonal conflicts. The flow of worship in many liturgical traditions is from praise, to self-examination, to confession, and through assurance of forgiveness to the passing of the peace. More informal faith communities still follow a similar train of thought. As we become self-aware (convicted of sin), admit our failings to God, and are forgiven, we are enabled to reconcile to one another. Following this theological thread, clergy and lay pastors are likely to suggest an approach to parental estrangement focused on forgiving and being forgiven, with confidence that reconciliation will result.

Unfortunately, most people do not have a clear understanding of forgiveness. As we shall see in a later chapter, forgiveness is an important aspect of healing, but it does not necessarily lead to reconciliation. More importantly, ordained and lay pastors have often paid inadequate attention to their own scriptures. The Bible is rife with examples of people who live with irreconcilable, estranged relationships. Paul writes, "If possible, so far as it depends on you, live peaceably with all."[15] But even the old apostle can't live up to his own teaching. He gets into a tiff with Barnabas, a disagreement so sharp that they parted company. They likely never recover.[16]

There are exceptions, of course. However, armed with an idealized, abstract understanding of reconciliation and forgiveness, untempered by the realism of sacred scripture, and devoid of the gospel emphasis on healing broken individuals, estranged parents are likely to be dealt a hand of holy expectations that leaves them hurting, confused, and burdened.

---

[15] Romans 12:18
[16] Acts 15:39

Therapists

Therapists do not routinely screen their clients for parental estrangement. As a result, they won't learn that a client is suffering from parental trauma unless he or she brings it up. And the stigma is of such magnitude that clients may wait months to share it, or never speak of it, even with their own therapist. This means that therapists may be misidentifying the causes of their client's symptoms, and failing to treat parental trauma at all. Therapists are generally trained to search for and identify a childhood trauma as the root of a person's symptoms, and may not be prepared to recognize the trauma in a sixty-year-old client that occurred only six months earlier in the rupture of the relationship between the parent and their adult child.

Articles in news media and professional journals that therapists read tend to support the assumption that some significant flaw in the parent is the source of the problem. The case studies most often recorded describe parents who are toxic, abusive, addicted, or mentally ill, rarely mentioning the corresponding fact that adult children are members of the general population who, statistically, exhibit the very same issues in their lives, with exactly the same frequency.

> *My son hasn't spoken to me in over 7 years. I am in therapy but it's not enough. Please tell me where to go for help.*
> A.H. from Tucson, AZ

Too few therapists adopt the perspective articulated by psychologist Joshua Coleman that "you can be a conscientious parent and your kid may still want nothing to do with you when they're older."[17]

Again, there are welcome exceptions. Many therapists, especially those trained in family systems, are providing real help to estranged parents. And we can realistically expect the incidence of parental estrangement will motivate more therapists to receive training. For now, estranged parents who encounter these kinds of attitudes will

---

[17] https://www.theatlantic.com/family/archive/2021/01/why-parents-and-kids-get-estranged/617612/

need to keep looking until they find a clinician, or other resource, that can help them recover. Above all else, they need to resist the temptation to internalize a clinical failure as a reason to give up on themselves.

Physicians

SSRI's (selective serotonin reuptake inhibitors) were first introduced to the market in 1987, and physicians, rather than psychiatrists, rapidly became the most frequent prescribers of these medications for mood disorders. It is natural that estranged parents would reach out to their physicians for help in dealing with the emotional components of trauma, and walk away with a prescription. However, research on anti-depressants has found that many perform little better than placebos in treating mild depression, and with significant side-effects.[18]

Physicians prescribe these medications after relatively brief conversations with the patient, who may, or may not disclose their estrangement. In a study posted by Health Services Research, it was found that the median visit length with a physician was 15.7 minutes covering a range of six topics, less than three minutes per topic.[19] Parental estrangement is extremely complex with multiple factors and impacts. In my experience, it takes at least an hour of listening to even begin to understand the unfolding of the estrangement, and all the ways the person is being affected. No wonder estranged parents rarely feel heard by their physicians.

Because trauma is stored in the body, a variety of physical symptoms almost always accompany estrangement. These emerge or are aggravated after the cutoff, and often result in referrals to specialists: dermatologists, cardiologists, pulmonologists,

---

[18] https://www.ncbi.nlm.nih.gov/books/NBK361016/
[19] Tai-Seale M, McGuire TG, Zhang W. "Time allocation in primary care office visits." *Health Services Research*. 2007 Oct;42(5):1871-94.

gastroenterologists, neurologists, orthopedists, to name only a few. These specialties tend not to communicate with one another. As a rule, they favor medical or surgical interventions rather than body-based approaches to deal with stress-induced inflammatory responses. These body-based approaches include nutrition, exercise, yoga, tai chi, meditation, massage, sunlight, a pet, and spending time in nature. Again, specialists do not have time to listen to the details of an estrangement experience, or to treat the patient wholistically. Parents often end up with a cabinet full of medications, salves, and supplements that do not address the root of all these maladies: trauma.

The final reason that professionals may not address the needs of estranged parents is the estranged parent themselves. It is important to remember that professional caregivers tend to respond to us at the level of our questions. If we express feelings of guilt, they will tend to assure us that we are all human and make mistakes, or suggest forgiveness as a remedy. If we speak of our bewilderment over why this has happened, they will tend to explore reasons why. If we express confusion about how to eventually reconcile, they will tend to offer suggestions on steps we might take. If we share our hurt over the unfairness of it all, they will tend to side with us and express disbelief at the way we are being treated. If we feel anxious that the estrangement might be long term, they will encourage us to keep the faith and stay hopeful.

If we articulate that we are suffering from a multi-dimensional form of parental trauma, with mental, emotional, physical, relational, financial, and legal impacts, and that we need help to recover, they are more likely to be able to help us. However, this requires that we, as estranged parents, accept that our primary need is for recovery, and, by extension, that reconciliation is secondary. While a healthy reconciliation is always a preferred outcome, the immediate goal of PEAK is to help parents experience significant reductions in trauma symptoms and enhancement of positive life experiences, even if their adult child continues to choose estrangement. What does this mean?

- We are willing to accept the current reality of our estrangement. Acceptance is not affirmation. It is adjustment (to reality).
- We are willing to admit that we are dealing with parental trauma, and that addressing this trauma is our priority.
- We are willing to release our minds from the relentless search for "why?" Chasing why is an alibi. It becomes a distraction from our recovery work.
- We are willing to embrace the fact that parental estrangement is not a measure of our love, competence, or mental health. We treat ourselves as deserving of worth, dignity, and respect.
- We are willing to adopt a no-fault perspective on our estrangement. Assigning blame to others or ourselves does nothing to advance our recovery.
- We are willing to stop revolving (around our pain), and start evolving (to become better people).
- We are willing to practice self-focus, self-care and taking responsibility for our own recovery, regardless of the choices made by our children.

All these are statements of intention. They indicate a willingness; learning how to actually live these intentions is a process that takes time. It is also important to recognize that mere intellectual assent is not sufficient for recovery. In order to heal, we must learn how to integrate our minds and our hearts so that they are in sync. It will be of no benefit to affirm that dealing with trauma is our top priority, if we rent out large amounts of our mental space to brainstorming various fixes to the relationship, fueled by anxiety about how long the estrangement might last.

We now have a few insights into why it is so difficult for estranged parents to find help. Many of the professionals we rely on most to help take care of us are not adequately trained to deal with a fundamental aspect of parental trauma. We do not have the power to change that in the short term. However, the most important insight is that our future well-being will largely depend upon our commitment to a recovery process that offers us real hope in arising from one of the most serious health issues we will ever face.

And that choice does lie within our power.

Questions for Reflection and Discussion

How disruptive to your life is estrangement from your adult child? How does the designation "parental trauma" fit the severity of your experience? Does it overstate the severity, understate the severity, or is it about right?

How difficult has it been to make decisions related to your adult child (or grandchildren) after their decision to cut off or severely curtail the relationship? How do you think trauma might be affecting your ability to make decisions that are good for you?

What professionals have you sought out for help? What was their approach? How effective were they in helping you?

In your own words, what does it mean to say that recovery from parental trauma is primary, and reconciliation is secondary?

When your adult child chooses to reconnect, why is it important to deal with parental trauma in order to experience a healthier reconciliation?

How difficult is it for you to commit to a process that gives priority to helping you recover from parental trauma?

If you are using this book in a group discussion, what did you gain from hearing others speak? From speaking?

Chapter 2
A Pattern of Reactions

My first professional job was working with spools of photographic film retrieved from reconnaissance satellites. These looked nothing like the small, plastic canisters produced for 35-millimeter personal cameras. The film webs were nearly ten inches in width and thousands of feet in length, and the spools that held them were massive. These were loaded into a machine that replicated their images by winding them from spool to spool in contact with a duplicating stock.

Since photographic film doesn't conduct electricity, the process of winding and unwinding such a large spool of film generates thousands of volts of static electricity. Such a charge can draw a six-inch spark from the hand of the unfortunate machine operator. The discharge is dangerous to the operator, but not for the reason one might assume. While the voltage is high and can be painful, the electrical current is much too small to do bodily damage. It is the startle reflex of the operator that can be harmful. Their reaction can cause them to hit their head, drop something on their foot, or even fall down. This unconscious, spontaneous reaction is much more dangerous than the spark itself.

Before we can begin to make progress recovering from parental trauma, we must come to terms with one fundamental principle: our prolonged reaction to the estrangement is more dangerous than the estrangement itself. As painful as the shock of estrangement might be, it is rare that our adult child is a direct physical threat. It is our extended reactions to the estrangement that become the problem. These reactions threaten our mental, emotional, and even physical health. They can shorten our lives.

The prime example of such a reaction is anger. Nearly every estranged parent has experienced anger about the way they have been treated. This is normal and understandable. Anger can be a useful emotion that motivates us to make positive changes. It can be particularly useful in helping us move forward with our lives. However, unmanaged anger can be harmful to ourselves and others. Some of the short and long-term health problems that have been linked to living angry include headache, digestion problems, insomnia, increased anxiety, depression, high blood pressure, skin problems, heart attack, and stroke.[20]

The 90 Second Emotion

It is one thing to *feel* devastated. It is another to *live* devastated. And it is one thing to *get* angry; it is another thing altogether to *live* angry. Being estranged may result in our getting angry. Living angry is our choice. In her book *My Stroke of Insight: A Brain Scientist's Personal Journey*, Jill Bolte Taylor reflects on the extremely brief lifespan of an emotion:

> When a person has a reaction to something in their environment, there's a 90 second chemical process that happens in the body; after that, any remaining emotional response is just the person choosing to stay in that emotional loop.
>
> Something happens in the external world and chemicals are flushed through your body which puts it on full alert. For those chemicals to totally flush out of the body it takes less than 90 seconds.
>
> This means that for 90 seconds you can watch the process happening, you can feel it happening, and then you can watch it go away.

---

[20] https://www.betterhealth.vic.gov.au/health/healthyliving/anger-how-it-affects-people#physical-effects-of-anger

> After that, if you continue to feel fear, anger, and so on, you need to look at the thoughts that you're thinking that are re-stimulating the circuitry that is resulting in you having this physiological response over and over again.[21]

Anger is like a campfire; it tends to go out on its own. In order to stay angry, our minds have to go looking for thoughts that will keep it burning. The only reason we experience feelings such as anger for much longer periods is that we keep choosing thoughts that reactivate them over and over again. And we don't have to look very far. "How could they have done this to me? Why don't they see how this is affecting me? How can they disregard all the things I have done for them? What about their grandparents and other people who have loved them?" Thoughts such as these are never far away. We don't have to go trapsing through the woods to find kindling for any emotion we want set afire.

Like any fire that is given enough fuel, anger can begin to spread into other areas of life. We become grumpy and irritable. People may begin to distance themselves because they have no idea what is really going on. They withdraw. We withdraw. We become more isolated and self-focused. We may begin to take on a negative view of the world, the particular life situations we face, and the persons in them. I have repeatedly observed situations where a parent's reaction to being estranged by their adult child actually increases the parent's tendency to withdraw from other relationships as well. To one degree or another, they begin to mirror the behavior of their adult child.

We Become What We Judge

Here we begin to realize what our friends in the addiction community learned years ago. In their prolonged reactions to an addicted spouse,

---

[21] Jill Bolte Taylor, My Stroke of Insight: a Brain Scientist's Personal Journey (Penguin Books, May 26, 2009)

parent, sibling, or child, families tend to take on the characteristics of their addicted loved one. Just as their addicted loved one lives at the mercy of their need for a drink or drug, families begin to live at the mercy of their feelings: shame, anger, anxiety, and despair. The wisdom of Jesus in urging us not to judge was the insight that we tend to develop in ourselves the very quality we judge in another—and become blind to it.

Appendix A: Key Affirmations of PEAK found at the end of this book provides a brief catalogue of prolonged reactions in the section "Our Common Experiences." These are descriptions of what frequently happens as we react to the estranging behavior of our adult child. Here are a few of the things found on that list:

- We waste precious time and energy focused on who to blame or what went wrong.
- Because we focus on what we cannot control, we feel weak and powerless.
- The intensity of our feelings sometimes boils over into behaviors that we are not proud of. We feel, and sometimes act, crazy.
- We feel alone.
- We get stuck in anger and feelings of unfairness.

These are some of the ways that our prolonged reactions to the estrangement are more dangerous than the estrangement itself. The reader may want to take a moment to review the entire list in Appendix A. Sooner or later, we must face the fact that the estrangement isn't doing this to us. We are doing it to ourselves.

This does not mean that recovering from anger or any of the other reactions is easy. Over time we have established a pattern of reacting to the estrangement that replays all the reasons we feel justified in holding on to that hostility, restokes the feelings of anger, and rewires our brains. There is a reason that the Bible advises us not to "let the sun go down on our anger." The more sunsets our anger survives, the more deeply it gets wound into the soul. In words that we repeat regularly in PEAK, we get stuck in anger and feelings of unfairness.

Distracted Living

Ever get distracted from driving by a bug in your car? According to a study conducted in 2005, researchers at the Virginia Tech Transportation Institute (VTTI) discovered that an insect in your car is really dangerous; a bug in your car increases your risk of a crash by more than six times compared to an attentive driver (without any insects in the car). That's a greater risk than dialing a phone, putting on makeup or reading a book.[22] Just as our reaction to a bug is much more dangerous than the bug itself, our prolonged reactions to parental estrangement become a harmful distraction from living full and purposeful lives.

These are the bugs in the brain of estranged parents. I find that many of us as estranged parents read through the common experiences list and are comforted to see that our experience is shared by others. "Of course," we say to ourselves, "this is what our adult children have done to us." Here is the truth. They may have put the bug in the car, but we are the ones that allowed ourselves to get so distracted that we have forgotten the one thing that our Spiritual Source asks of us: to live a life of love and to live it abundantly. We are the ones who have risked crashing our lives.

The Good, the Bad, and the Average

Earlier we saw how an emotion only lasts 90 seconds, and how sustaining that emotion requires that we keep stoking it with thoughts. Where do these thoughts come from? Memories.

The memory capacity of the human brain is reported to have the equivalent of 2.5 petabytes of memory capacity. As a number, a "petabyte" means 1024 terabytes or a million gigabytes, so the average adult human brain has the ability to store the equivalent of 2.5 million gigabytes of digital memory, approaching the number of grains of sand

---

[22] https://www.nhtsa.gov/sites/nhtsa.gov/files/100car_esv05summary.pdf

on earth. Memories of interactions with your child occupy thousands of gigabytes in your brain.

Do you need a thought to trigger feelings of profound sadness? There are hundreds of them. Think of the pregnancy, the day of their birth or adoption, watching them sleep at night, their first day of school. Do you need a thought to stir up feelings of inadequacy or to feel badly about yourself? There are probably a good number of those as well in that sea sand memory bank. Think of times you were short-tempered, got your priorities askew, paid too little attention—or too much. How about some thoughts that generate feelings of pride regarding your parenting, the things you did well, the ways you expressed love. Sure, it is all there.

It is the parents who were most conscientious, dedicated, and even sacrificial who may have the most difficult time with feelings of bewilderment, unfairness, hurt, and anger. They have an encyclopedic memory of all those parental responsibilities, some performed by sheer duty, but most from the deepest of loves. Here is the irony of parental estrangement: the better parent you were in the past, the harder it may be to let go of the hurt and anger that can steal so much of your future. But by choosing to hold on to hurt and anger, you are simply sacrificing more and more of your life on a different altar.

Then there are those of us on the other end of the spectrum. What rises to the top of our consciousness are feelings of guilt, self-blame, replaying past failures, not deserving to be happy or have fun, and not trusting that anyone can love us. In our minds, we have good reason to stay immersed in this sump of self-disgust. Do we have memories to stoke these feelings? Hundreds. They arise at the snap of our mental fingers.

So, there you have it. Whether we consider ourselves great parents, angry that our sacrifices have been forgotten, inferior parents whose failures can never be forgiven, or the average parent who bounces back and forth between the two from one moment to the next, we have the fuel to stoke our perpetual unhappiness.

Recovery requires that we find an alternative energy source to fuel our emotional lives.

Electric Souls

Several months ago, my wife and I bought an electric car. After more than 50 years of relying on fossil fuels to get from point A to point B, it is difficult to kick the mental habit of "getting gas." When I see a station with a good price per gallon, I am still inclined to turn in toward the pumps. This impulse abides in spite of the fact that the electricity I now "burn" in my car is cleaner, quieter, and cheaper. Actually, it is free.

Many of our thinking patterns are the equivalent of internal combustion engines that pollute our souls and our relationships in all the ways "Our Common Experiences" articulate. There is an alternative fuel for estranged parents besides the memories that stoke pride and anger, deficits and guilt, or a dozen other prolonged reactions. This alternative fuel is spiritual in nature. It is as different as electricity is from gasoline. It is clean. It is quiet. And it is free. It is the fuel of a different kind of being. I use the metaphor of an electric soul.

An electric soul is powered by an alternative mental fuel. It is energized by a Spiritual Source that is described in specific chapters of this book, but is present throughout. It affirms an unconditional love, an unshakable foundation of human dignity, a liberating forgiveness, an embrace of imperfection. This kind of thinking fuels love, serenity, and a zest for living.

Like the 70-year owner of a new electric car, there will be times when old mental habits of an earlier time intrude into our thinking. We will be tempted to pull into the pumps of unfairness, anger, and guilt. At those moments, we simply need to make the decision to drive on without self-recrimination. As Martin Luther said, "You cannot keep birds from flying over your head but you can keep them from building a nest in your hair."

It's Some of My Business

And so, we each have a decision to make regarding which thoughts we allow to fuel our lives. Yet, your decision is not simply about you. You may think, "What is it to you that I decide to remain sad, angry, or guilty for weeks on end? It's none of your business."

Actually, it is *some* of my business. Courage, faith, and positivity are contagious. Unfortunately, so are resignation, self-pity, and fear. Any decision you make that diminishes you, diminishes me also. If I feed on negative thoughts that debilitate me, it debilitates you in some small ways as well. In the words of the poet John Donne,

No man is an island entire of itself; every man
is a piece of the continent, a part of the main;
if a clod be washed away by the sea, Europe
is the less, as well as if a promontory were, as
well as any manner of thy friends or of thine
own were; any man's death diminishes me,
because I am involved in mankind.
And, therefore, never send to know for whom
the bell tolls; it tolls for thee.

Should any of us as estranged parents choose not to recover, but to inwardly die to the joy of living, the bell will toll for the rest of us as well.

Steps Toward Recovery

What steps can you take in your recovery from your prolonged reactions from parental estrangement?

- Turn to Appendix A: Key Affirmations of PEAK and read through "Our Common Experiences." Use a pen to mark all the reactions that have tended to become patterns of thought, feeling, or behaviors in your life.

- Journal some of the ways these prolonged reactions have become detrimental to you or others. Remember. Exercise self-compassion at every step of the way.
- What thoughts are fueling these reactions? What is one change you can make in your thinking that can fuel serenity in your life?

Questions for Reflection and Discussion

"…we must come to terms with one fundamental principle: our prolonged reaction to the estrangement is more dangerous than the estrangement itself." Give an example of how you have seen this principle at work.

What thoughts are fueling your most negative emotions (anger, sadness, guilt, etc.)?

Which memories are the most difficult for you to deal with? How do these memories make you feel? When they come to mind, how long do they last?

In your own words, what is an electric soul? What mental fuel are you running on?

How are the decisions that other estranged parents make some of your business?

If you are using this book in a group discussion, what did you gain from hearing others speak? From speaking?

Chapter 3
Drama and Trauma

Second only to being able to say, "I am an estranged a parent," is the ability to say, "I am experiencing parental trauma."

We have already defined trauma as an emotional response to an unexpected, deeply distressing event. Trauma is different from a stressful experience like being cut off in traffic or losing your keys. Eventually, that happens to nearly everyone. And while we might find ourselves ranting about these experiences, they are relatively short-lived and best understood as a kind of drama. I do not use the word in a negative way. Drama of various kinds, within limits, makes life rich and colorful. We all do drama.

The effects of drama quickly dissipate over time. After being cut off in traffic, I generally calm down shortly after I arrive at my destination. If I lose my keys, I have to go through the time-consuming experience of having to replace them. That's frustrating, and I may play out the drama of it all in conversation with friends as the story of my life. But it isn't trauma. A few days afterwards, I'll be fine.

On the other hand, if someone breaks into my home and steals my keys while I am on a jog, I feel differently. I still have to go through the time-consuming experience of replacing keys, and maybe changing locks. But in addition, I now feel unsafe every time I enter my home, a feeling that may last for weeks, or even months. I may have flashbacks to the original experience of approaching my home and discovering the broken door ajar. All the feelings of that moment, fear, apprehension, and anger come rushing back when I arrive at the door, even though there is no longer any threat.

That's trauma. Trauma symptoms diminish very slowly over time, sometimes not at all. They are retriggered by reminders of the original experience. Flashbacks become unwelcome intruders into one's mental space. There are some things you cannot unsee or unhear.

Complex Trauma

Then there is something known as complex trauma. Let's say that every few days when I come back from my morning jog, I discover that my house has been broken into, and something different is missing every time, always something important to me. Now, I not only feel unsafe every time I enter my home, I may not feel safe *anywhere*. Whoever is entering my home could be wherever I might go, work, shopping, school, jogging, etc. That's complex trauma. It is happening over and over and over again. It's expanding to take over other aspects of my life.

Parental trauma is a complex trauma. Life no longer feels safe. I have had the experience of receiving estrangement messages that left my entire body shaking to such a degree that I had no choice but to go to bed and shake it off. This is the result of the mind's perception of a lethal threat. The body dumps a large dose of the hormone adrenalin into the bloodstream to prepare the muscles for fight or flight. When neither can happen, the muscles shake uncontrollably.

Yes, there are painful memories of particular conversations, voicemails, text messages, emails, letters, and social media posts that were traumatic events. Reminders of these moments can create the same overwhelming rush of feelings and mental flashbacks as a person whose sense of safety was lost when their house was broken into. When one parent is reminded of a text message he received saying "You are dead to us," he still has a mental flashback of those words on his cell phone, the inner thud of feeling punched in the solar plexus, and the experience of freezing up and simply staring into space. This is a complex trauma response.

But a newly estranged parent awakens to a fresh experience of their estrangement on most mornings. In their case, it is not some uninvited burglar who has intruded into their physical space and stolen a valuable material possession. It is something more precious that has gone missing. Safety. It is the experience of a missing limb, an arm or leg, horribly ripped away in the latter years of one's life. And beyond that daily reinjury are those occasions, special for many others, when the blade of the knife feels particularly sharpened, holidays, celebrations, or seasons of vulnerability when no one calls. Imagine if there were holidays where the only people who were celebrated were those with all their arms and legs, and you lived without one. The emotional equivalent of this experience happens at celebrations several times a year, year after year. This is the complex trauma of parental estrangement.

Alone, Confused, Powerless

If some evil genius were to set his mind to inflicting maximum emotional pain in an older adult without doing anything illegal, it would look a lot like parental estrangement. Trauma specialist, Dr. Linda Karlovec, says that trauma is the experience of something excruciatingly painful, combined with feeling alone, confused, and powerless. These are precisely the agonized sentiments regularly expressed by estranged parents:

I am alone. This doesn't happen to other people. I have nowhere to turn. I am ashamed to talk with people about this. The ones I do share with do not understand what I am going through.

I am bewildered. I am stunned. I can't believe it. I don't understand why this is happening in our relationship. I don't know how to think about this. I don't know what to do.

I feel totally helpless. Nothing I try works. I can't stop these thoughts that keep popping into my head. I can't make myself feel better. I can't stop these annual holidays that tear me apart.

Alone. Confused. Powerless.

Avoidant Behavior

Another difference between complex trauma and a garden variety drama is that trauma often results in avoidant behavior on the part of the parent. A person who loses his keys doesn't avoid driving his car. But a person whose house was broken into might avoid going home. It can be painful to be in conversation with non-estranged parents who talk frequently about their kids and grandkids, so we avoid them. It can be painful to attend services at faith communities around the holidays, so we don't go. It can be painful to see pictures posted on our adult child's social media sites, so we close those accounts. It can be painful to visit friends and loved ones near the community where our adult child lives, so we avoid going there.

Sometimes our avoidant behaviors have no specific connections to our children. We are easily overwhelmed. We do not have any spare emotional energy, even for activities that may otherwise be positive experiences. Interacting with people at a party, even people we know may be difficult. Venturing into a new experience that others anticipate as enjoyable may demand more energy than we can muster. Uncertainty feels unsafe. As we retreat to feel safe, parental trauma can result in parental loneliness.

Related to the avoidant behavior is the tendency of trauma to metastasize into other parts of life that were previously healthy. Parental estrangement injects a significant amount of esteem-killing toxin into our inner lives. If someone so close, someone we love so much could abandon us, how bad must we be? This makes every relationship feel unsafe. One of "Our Common Experiences" we recite weekly to one another is "Because we see ourselves through the lens of our estrangement, it may be difficult for us to believe that we can be loved by others." A loss of confidence threatens to send us into a downward spiral. We lack confidence,

My daughter has not spoken to me in two years. I am in agony.
B.V. from Trenton, NJ

which causes us to hesitate. But that only makes us lose more confidence, become more hesitant, and down and down.

Triggering, intrusive thoughts, flashbacks, freezing/staring into space, avoidant behavior, metastasis into previously healthy areas of life, feeling alone, confused, and powerless, these are some of the ways we know that parental estrangement is a complex trauma rather than simply a difficult experience.

There are more impacts of parental trauma. Since human beings are an integrated whole, the rest of the impacts of parental estrangement do not fall into neat categories. For the sake of conversation, I will mention a few. Parental trauma impacts our thinking, the nature of thoughts running through our minds, and the quality of our decision-making. Parental trauma impacts us emotionally with an intensity of feelings that we may never have experienced previously. Parental trauma results in a whole range of new or aggravated medical conditions caused by an out-of-control inflammatory response and a depressed immune system. Parental trauma often results in problematic behaviors when we use ways of coping with our pain that we are not proud of. Parental trauma can impact our spiritual lives by triggering a crisis of faith and a reduced involvement with our spiritual practices or faith communities. Parental trauma can put us at financial risk by leading us to make decisions that are not the best. In the next chapter, I provide tools for assessing the impacts of parental estrangement in most of these areas.

Recovering from Parental Trauma

This book is focused on a process of recovery for those suffering from parental trauma. As mentioned in the previous chapter, expecting a traumatized parent to negotiate a healthy reconciliation with an adult child who does not want it is like asking the survivor of a head-on collision to win a game of chess that no one else wants to play. If you read this chapter, and believe that you are suffering parental trauma, I would simply ask you to change your focus from reconciliation to recovery. At whatever point your adult child is ready to reconcile, you will be in a much better position to do so if you have engaged in this process of trauma recovery.

There is no single magic bullet. However, a good summary statement might be that recovery requires a reversal of Karlovec's three contributors to trauma: feeling alone, confusion, and powerlessness. In PEAK, we turn isolation into companionship as we walk with one another in our recovery. We turn confusion into a better understanding of the estrangement experience along with some insight into steps that might be helpful. We turn powerlessness into potential and positive intention, which ends up empowering us in ways we might scarcely have imagined. If the reader can embrace actions moving him or her in the direction of these three stars, companionship, insight, and positive intention, we have every reason to believe that life will get better.

But this requires more than the passage of time.

As a boy growing up in the 1950s, I played outside every spare minute. There are a lot of hard surfaces in cities: asphalt streets, concrete sidewalks, gravel driveways, steel grates and manhole covers. Hard surfaces plus gravity plus skinny kid equals a variety of contusions, lacerations, and abrasions. I often wonder what my 72-year-old body would look like today if none of the scraped elbows and skinned knees of my childhood had ever healed. Fortunately, and miraculously they always did. Except for a thorough washing and those few splashes of methylate that would make a Marine beg for his mother, nothing was required for this miracle of healing…except time.

Thus, the phrase: time heals all wounds. However, parental trauma is not a skinned knee. And time doesn't heal all wounds. Time heals some wounds. Time gives us the opportunity to heal the rest. Time is grace.

Healing the wounds of parental estrangement requires more than the passage of time. In fact, passive inaction can cause our wounds to "set in" and harden like seasoned concrete. A deep cut that is not stitched becomes a scar; a broken bone that is not realigned becomes a deformity; a crushed finger that is not disinfected can be life threatening. Sometimes, we must actively engage in the healing process. Time gives us the opportunity to do that.

Steps Toward Recovery

What can we do to promote our recovery?

- We can be discerning about our own lives, which aspects are simply stressful experiences, and which are expressions of parental trauma.
- We can acknowledge to ourselves, and a few others that we trust, that we are experiencing parental trauma.
- We can become specific about the ways that parental trauma is impacting our lives.
- We can set an intention to take action, and not expect the passage of time alone to accomplish our recovery.
- We can search out others who are willing to be on the recovery journey with us.
- We can engage in the assessment process found in the next chapter.

Parents sometimes think I am asking them to give up. I am not. I am asking that we grow up. The problem with growing up and giving up is that they can both look the same. Giving up is embracing illusion, and letting go of things you *can* change. Growing up is embracing reality, and letting go of things you *can't* change.

It's never too late to grow.

Questions for Reflection and Discussion
Tell about a time when you had a full day of drama in your life, perhaps one big stressor, or one stressful experience after another?

In your own words, what is the difference between drama and trauma as defined in this chapter?

Below are listed some of the characteristics that distinguish parental trauma from a stressful experience. Which of these have you experienced?
- triggering
- intrusive thoughts
- flashbacks
- freeze response
- avoidant behavior
- estrangement spilling over into previously healthy areas of life
- feeling alone, confused, and powerless

Do you think you are suffering from parental trauma? Why or why not?

If you think you are suffering from parental trauma, say that out loud. How did that make you feel?

What memories did this chapter trigger?

If you are using this book in a group discussion, what did you gain from hearing others speak? From speaking?

Chapter 4
Our Starting Point

Several years ago, I had a consulting job with an organization headquartered in Salt Lake City. Though it is difficult to imagine now, it was before the days of GPS, and I was lost. I called up the client to get directions. The secretary asked, "Where are you now?"

"I don't know," I said. "I'm next to a tall, white stone building."

She responded, "Do you have any idea how many tall, white stone buildings there are in Salt Lake City?"

There was a pause. And then,

"Sir, if you can't tell me where you are, I can't tell you how to get here."

I have used that story many times in my work with organizations and individuals. Organizations may have inspiring vision statements articulating where they want to go. Individuals may be earnest about achieving personal goals. But if they don't know their starting point, I can't help them get there.

As we begin to recover from parental trauma, it is important to know our starting point. Some parents are at the very beginning of the recovery process. They are reeling from the shock and bewilderment of the experience, but the full impact may not have hit them yet. Intellectually, it is important that they acquire some basic information. What is parental estrangement? How common is it? Why does it happen? Emotionally, they need to know that they are not alone, that there are millions of estranged parents just like them.

I am devastated by the estrangement from my adult son.
L.L. from Barberton, OH

Other parents have descended deep into the agony of the estrangement experience. They have a depressed mood, and heightened anxiety. New medical conditions are developing in their bodies, or previous ones are worsening. Important relationships are being stressed. These parents need a more intense recovery approach that might include a family therapist specializing in estrangement, participation in a recovery group, and evaluation for a medication to get them over the hump.

Other parents show few trauma symptoms. They may be confident the situation is temporary and feel that a reconciliation in the near-term is almost certain. Alternatively, they may have been dealing with the estrangement dance for so many years that they are past the darkest days, and have adjusted to life alone. These parents won't relate to the emotional intensity of other estranged parents. They may find that listening to parents beset with a number of trauma symptoms is unnecessarily agitating. They need an approach that simply helps them maintain their equilibrium.

In each case, the severity of trauma symptoms varies from mild to severe. In the most severe situations, parents may feel so desperate that they begin having thoughts of suicide. Across the lifespan, the highest rates of suicide in the United States occur among men and women in their 50s, the same age as the onset of parental estrangement. In my experience, thoughts of suicide are common among estranged parents, perhaps as high as one in every three. If you are having suicidal thoughts, please get help. Call the National Suicide Prevention Hotline at 800-273-8255, or Text "HOME" to 741741. As someone who has gone through the experience of suicidal thinking, I can say that there is every reason to believe that you will feel better with a commitment to work on your recovery. Suicidal thoughts do not last forever, but suicidal actions do.

Assessing the severity of trauma symptoms at your starting point will not only help you know what you need, it will enable you to mark your progress as you recover. Marking progress is important. It provides us with opportunities to cultivate gratitude which is key to our recovery process. Celebrations, even small ones, give us strength to continue hopefully on our journey.

Your Thought Life

The first area to reflect on is your thought life. Parental trauma impacts our thinking by putting us in a survival mode. Our minds can gear up to fight a battle, run away, or simply go blank. The patterns in the table *Thought Life* that follows are typical for estranged parents. These don't mean that you are sick or mentally ill, but they are indications of trauma.

Thought Life Which of the following has become your experience since the estrangement began? Check all that fit.
☐ I am having trouble concentrating at work or on important tasks at home. ☐ I find myself ruminating on the events leading up to the estrangement. ☐ I can't stop fantasizing about taking a trip, or running away. ☐ I am having negative thoughts about myself or others. ☐ I am in a mental haze. ☐ I find myself not making the best decisions. ☐ I am easily startled by loud noises or sudden movements. ☐ I am overwhelmed with thoughts about past conversations, or imagined future ones. ☐ I am confused about what steps to take in a number of areas of my life. ☐ I have questions about parental estrangement, and I don't know where to get information. ☐ I don't know if I have been clear enough with my adult child that I want to heal our relationship. ☐ I have trouble thinking about the future in any positive way. ☐ I am having thoughts about injuring or killing myself. ☐ I am having unwelcome memories or flashbacks to painful moments in the past.

☐ Other thoughts that bother you: _____

Your Emotional Life

The second area for reflection is your emotional state. What have you felt most strongly in the wake of the estrangement? Our emotions demand to be recognized, and the more precisely we can identify them, the more likely they will calm down. However, many times it is difficult to name what we feel, and it is easier for us to point to a word on a list than to come up with it on our own.

In the table *Emotions*, lists of feelings can be found under four headings. The first three headings are Sad, Angry, and Scared. These are the most common descriptions of how estranged parents are feeling. These are often referred to as negative emotions, though every emotion has an appropriate function. Some words under those headings may resonate more precisely than others with our particular inner state. Take a moment and scan down those first three columns.

The fourth column has a heading that reflects a very different set of emotions. Sometimes a relational cutoff provides a sense of relief, mixed in with the other emotions of sadness, anger, and fear. A parent can feel relief when there has been an extended, painful conflict. Relief can also be experienced when there is some form of physical or emotional abuse, legal issue, or financial misconduct on the part of an adult child. This doesn't negate the love that a parent feels for their child. One of the things that recovering parents learn is that it is actually healthy to experience multiple, seemingly contradictory feelings at the same time.

Emotions

Which of the following words best describe how you are feeling since the estrangement began? Circle the five words that resonate the most.

Sad	Angry	Scared	Relief
Ashamed	Abused	Afraid	Accepting
Condemned	Angry	Anxious	Agreeable
Crushed	Anguished	Apprehensive	Alleviated
Demoralized	Betrayed	Concerned	Assured
Depressed	Controlled	Defensive	Calm
Deserted	Deceived	Desperate	Clear
Devastated	Dominated	Doubtful	Completed
Discarded	Exasperated	Fearful	Composed
Discouraged	Exploited	Frantic	Decided
Disheartened	Frustrated	Guarded	Finished
Disillusioned	Furious	Guilty	Freed
Distraught	Humiliated	Horrified	Liberated
Empty	Incensed	Insecure	Mellow
Exhausted	Irritated	Intimidated	Neutral
Hopeless	Offended	Nervous	Open
Injured	Outraged	Overwhelmed	Peaceful
Isolated	Patronized	Panicky	Quiet
Mournful	Perturbed	Scared	Ready
Neglected	Pissed	Shaken	Relieved
Regretful	Provoked	Shocked	Resolute
Rejected	Rebellious	Skeptical	Resolved
Resigned	Resentful	Stunned	Safe
Sad	Sabotaged	Suspicious	Serene
Sorrowful	Seething	Tense	Settled
Unappreciated	Spiteful	Threatened	Steady
Unwanted	Stifled	Tormented	Tranquil
Worthless	Throttled	Unsure	Unburdened
Wounded	Used	Vulnerable	Untethered

Your Physical-Medical Symptoms

A number of years ago, I took a course in neuro-biology. During one of the lectures the instructor was describing the functions of different parts of the brain, and where different kinds of information were stored. Noticing that trauma was not mentioned, I put up my hand and asked, "But where is trauma stored?"

And without missing a beat, she responded, "In the body."

I found that fascinating. Without getting into the considerable body of evidence that supports this assertion, I can say without hesitation, and after speaking with scores of estranged parents, that parental trauma almost always affects some aspect of the physical body. Sometimes estranged parents don't make the connection between the onset or worsening of a medical condition and their estrangement experience. Completing the exercise in the table *Physical-Medical Symptoms* can help make that connection.

Physical-Medical Symptoms

Which of the following symptoms have begun or worsened since the estrangement began? Check all that fit.

- ☐ Cardiovascular problems like arrythmias, increased blood pressure, angina, heart attack.
- ☐ Pulmonary problems like pneumonia, bronchitis, shortness of breath.
- ☐ Nervous disorders like panic attacks, anxiety attacks, tremors, restless legs.
- ☐ Skin issues like rashes, hives, acne.
- ☐ Gastrointestinal issues like functional dyspepsia, diverticulitis, digestive issues, nausea.
- ☐ Sleep disorders like insomnia, hypersomnia.
- ☐ Autoimmune disorders, fibromyalgia, chronic fatigue syndrome, lupus.
- ☐ Skeletal-muscular issues like joint pain, back pain, arthritis.

> ☐ Head and neck issues like headache, grinding of teeth, TMJ, stiff neck.
> ☐ Other _____

Your Behavioral Patterns

One of the aspects of trauma many estranged parents struggle with are the changes in behavioral patterns they exhibit. Dealing with what we think and feel inside is important. But it can create real difficulties for us when those thoughts and feelings are translated into actual behaviors. In "Our Common Experiences," we say each week that "The intensity of our feelings sometimes boils over into behaviors that we are not proud of. We feel, and sometimes act, crazy. We use coping mechanisms that are not the best." Saying that our problematic behaviors are trauma-related doesn't mean that we are no longer responsible. The phrase "We understand parental trauma as a way of forgiving ourselves, not excusing ourselves" applies here. We still need to take responsibility, apologize, and ask forgiveness. But we also need to have compassion on ourselves. Review the impacts of parental estrangement in the table Behavioral Patterns.

> **Behavioral Patterns**
> Which of the following have become your experience since the estrangement began? Check all that fit.

> ☐ I am more irritable and curt in my interactions with others.
> ☐ I am more short-tempered. I sometimes explode.
> ☐ I am more critical of others.
> ☐ I drive more aggressively with less patience for others.
> ☐ I am getting into more arguments with friends and loved ones.
> ☐ I am more withdrawn from relationships and activities.
> ☐ I am more impulsive. Sometimes I make decisions I regret.
> ☐ I am more likely to engage in risky behaviors without enough regard for my safety.

- ☐ In conversations with others, I am more silent.
- ☐ I find myself using inappropriate humor that I wish I could take back.
- ☐ I am eating more or eating less.
- ☐ I am experiencing a change in my sexual desire.
- ☐ I am smoking or using tobacco more.
- ☐ I am using more alcohol or other mood-altering substances.
- ☐ I am practicing poor sleep habits, staying up late, having too much screen time, using too much social media at night.
- ☐ Other

Your Relational Patterns

Parental estrangement not only impacts the individual parent, it inflicts collateral damage on a range of relationships. These can include the following:

- Tension with spouses who may or may not be equally estranged from an adult child. In cases of a subsequent marriage, tensions may be focused on the preoccupation of a spouse with the parental trauma, creating an emotional unavailability and a relational distance. "You're here, but you're not here."
- Other children who may feel caught in the middle, especially if one of them is able to maintain a relationship with a sibling who is estranged from their parent(s).
- Parents and adult children will be tempted to bring family members into the situation which will risk splitting the family into factions.
- Given the cultural expectations of previous generations, grandparents may not be able to comprehend what is happening. They may be wounded by the lack of contact from grandchildren resulting in a tension with the estranged parent. "Why can't you fix this?"

- When a family business is involved, estrangement can impact a range of business relationships, and create awkward situations with associates and clients.

Use the categories in the table *Relational Impacts* to reflect on these patterns.

Relational Impacts

Rate the negative impacts on your relationship with the following persons on a scale of 1 to 5, with 5 being "major negative impact," and 1 being "little negative impact," and NA for "not applicable."

____ Your spouse	____ Family friends
____ Your other children	____ Non-estranged friends
____ Grandparents (both sides)	____ Faith community members
____ Aunts and uncles (both sides)	____ Business/work associates
____ Your adult child's in-laws (if partnered)	____ Other _____

They say that a journey of a thousand miles begins with a single step. A more accurate statement is that it begins with acknowledging where you are. Without that information, you don't know in which direction to take that first step. For some estranged parents, their trauma symptoms are few with relatively mild impacts. Those parents will not relate well to heart-rending, emotion-laden stories that others tell about their estrangement experience. A step in that direction will simply frustrate them. Reading an informational article or two may be all they need.

Most, however, are facing the most devastating experience of their lives. Their trauma symptoms need to be taken seriously. Untreated trauma not only results in a life of unmitigated suffering, it can put you at risk to accelerating aging, and take years off your life.[23] Parental estrangement should not be an early death sentence. You are worth the investment in your own self-care. You are worth saving.

Questions for Reflection and Discussion
What surprises, if any, did you discover in doing this exercise?

After reviewing your assessment, what words or phrases best describe your starting point?

Which statement more accurately describes how you are feeling:
  I know what I am dealing with. I am ready to begin the work of recovery.
  I feel somewhat overwhelmed by what lies before me. I need encouragement.
  I don't believe my situation is any more difficult than other challenges I have faced in my life.

Now that you know your starting point, what do you need to do next?

What resources do you need to help you move forward?

What would you like to see different in your life one year from today?

---

[23] https://www.healthline.com/health-news/ptsd-linked-to-faster-aging-earlier-death-050815

If you are using this book in a group discussion, what did you gain from hearing others speak? From speaking?

Chapter 5
Understanding One Another
Types of Estrangement

Most of us have been in a situation where we shared some experience from our lives with a group and heard crickets in response. When that happens, our talking not only fails to help us feel better. We walk away feeling even more isolated. We all want to have the experience where someone gets us, where they respond to us in a way that completes a circuit and causes us to say, "Exactly!" That experience is called feeling understood.

Feeling understood is an essential aspect of our emotional and physical health. In research published in the *Journal of Research in Personality*, it was found that feeling understood had a direct effect on increasing life satisfaction while reducing physical symptoms.[24] Feeling understood is an essential aspect of the PEAK recovery process as well. The better we understand one another, the deeper will be the recovery. We will feel more satisfied with our lives, and see a reduction in our trauma symptoms.

In this book, I speak broadly about parental estrangement and its resulting trauma. After interacting with hundreds of estranged parents over the last few years, I have come to realize that not all parental estrangement is the same. For example, a soldier returning from a combat situation who cuts himself off from his parents is not quite the same as a daughter who marries someone from a different culture, and subsequently estranges her mother. I have noticed that when these two

---

[24] Lun J, Kesebir S, Oishi S. "On Feeling Understood and Feeling Well: The Role of Interdependence" *Journal of Research in Personality*. 2008 Dec;42(6):1623-1628.

parents are in a conversation, they tend to miss one another. This is partly because they are trying to fit what they are hearing into their own experience. We can do a better job of supporting one another if we sharpen our understanding of the different types of parental estrangement. When we respond to other estranged parents, we want them to say, "Exactly!" And we want that experience for ourselves.

There are four basic types of parental estrangements. While there is some overlap among these types, I observe that one type tends to be dominant for most estrangements, with other factors being secondary.

Leveraged Estrangement

In the first type of estrangement, a third party is applying pressure on the adult child in the direction of estrangement. One example of this is known as parental alienation. In an article published in *Social Work Today*, author Amy J. L. Baker, PhD writes:

"Among the many areas of concern for social workers working with divorced or separated couples with children are two related problems: parental alienation, or the efforts on the part of one parent to turn a child against the other parent, and parental alienation syndrome, or a child's unwarranted rejection of one parent in response to the attitudes and actions of the other parent."[25]

Alternatively, the person applying pressure in the direction of estrangement can be the adult child's spouse or romantic partner, but it can also be a therapist, spiritual advisor, business associate or friend. In every case the third party is influential, and in a relatively permanent relationship with the adult child that is unlikely to change. Given the intensity of the pressure exerted on the adult child, I call this a *leveraged estrangement*. One person who works with estranged parents observes that a third party is involved in the estrangement over 90% of the time.

---

[25] Parental Alienation Syndrome — The Parent/Child Disconnect, Amy J. L. Baker, PhD, Social Work Today Vol. 8 No. 6 P. 26

Leveraged estrangements tend to be the most complex because of the additional parties involved who are often working behind the scenes. This usually increases the sense of powerlessness for estranged parents. The perception that an intruder has spoiled a functional or at least salvageable relationship also tends to intensify feelings of anger and resentment. Parents dealing with leveraged estrangement need to be given multiple opportunities to vent without being rushed too quickly toward forgiveness. This will help them feel understood.

If you are a parent dealing with leveraged estrangement, you may have to work harder at understanding parents who are struggling with other types of estrangement and whose feelings may be less intense. Acknowledging that they also need support will help them feel understood as well.

Hard-Wired Estrangement

In the second type of estrangement, there are factors that tend to be genetically, developmentally, or systemically woven into the personality of the parent or the adult child. These can be difficult to change. For example, an adult child with a psychotic condition may cut off the relationship with a parent as a result of their mental illness. Medication can help with these types of issues assuming the adult child will accept treatment and stay compliant. When they are unwilling to comply, a parent can be dealing with an adult child who cycles in and out of estrangement for years.

Three adult daughters. Youngest is 26 diagnosed bipolar 1 and has cut ties with me. Claims she needs to find healing through alternative medicine and needs space from me. I am heartbroken.
N.C. from Bend, OR

Then there are issues of temperament. Temperament is an aspect of personality concerned with emotional dispositions and reactions as well as their speed and intensity; the term is often used to refer to the prevailing mood or mood pattern of a person. Wide differences in temperament can make it difficult for two persons to relate to one another. A mechanically intelligent, gregarious father may find it difficult to relate to a quiet, conceptually intelligent son. They may engage in endless debates trying to change the other. Unfortunately, temperament is relatively fixed. Two persons with different temperaments can learn to accommodate one another. However, it takes work even by two people in the same family. When they are both unwilling to invest in that work, estrangement becomes more likely.

While core values may not to be genetically fixed, they can be wound so deep developmentally that they also can be difficult to change or negotiate. An adult child who feels damaged by a divorce may adopt a value system that makes a parent's behavior unforgivable. Patterned behaviors using cutoff to manage anxiety can be unconsciously transmitted from previous generations. These are baked into the family system rather than into the individual involved. Parents and their estranged children can be playing out an issue from their grandparents without even knowing that they are doing it.

I refer to these as *hard-wired estrangements*. Like leveraged estrangement, hard-wired estrangements are relatively permanent, except that it is not a third party that is fixed, but a condition within the adult child, the parent, the relationship, or the family system. We can install different apps on our Android smartphone. But we can't change an Android into an iPhone.

This is a description, not an explanation. There are many adult children who are dealing with a mental illness that do not estrange their parents. The same can be said for differences in temperament, values, and generational patterns. However, when hard-wired estrangements do occur, parents often grieve in a particular way, especially as they realize these internal factors are difficult to change. Faced with hard-wired factors, estranged parents may be more sad and less angry. One father's bi-polar daughter estranged him eight years ago and disappeared. Parents dealing with other types of estrangement may tell their story with a degree of fury. As he tells his story, he is heartbroken.

When other parents observe and reflect back this intense sadness or heartbreak of things that neither they nor their adult child can easily change, it will help the parent of a hard-wired estrangement feel better understood. They may not outwardly express the intense anger or resentment of parents dealing with other kinds of estrangements, but we must be careful not to underestimate the depth of their feelings.

Therapeutic-Developmental Estrangement

In the third type of estrangement, there are also factors that tend to be internal to the adult child or the parent, but these are either more temporary or treatable. For example, a young adult may exhibit poor decision-making simply because his or her brain has not fully developed. One of those poor decisions may be to cut off the relationship with a parent. This can change with maturity. In contrast to psychoses and personality disorders, mental health issues such as depression and anxiety disorders are generally more treatable. Given the right motivation, many addictions can be successfully treated as well. Sometimes an estranged, addicted child will reconnect after hitting bottom. In cases where a parent's communication patterns contribute to the estrangement, new skills can be learned that may lead to a reconnection.

I call these *therapeutic-developmental estrangements*. In these estrangements the factors are also internal to the parent or adult child, but unlike hard-wired estrangements they are more likely to change. Changes may occur because the adult child gets help dealing with treatable issues in their life (therapeutic), because they further mature (developmental), because they hit a crisis point that motivates them to reconnect, or because the parent addresses issues in their own behavioral patterns that make a healthy reconciliation possible.

However, there are no guarantees. Personal growth in a parent may not result in reconciliation. What one hopes is a temporary stage that an adult child will outgrow can sometimes harden into a long-term pattern of estrangement. If an adult child traces their mental health issues back to the relationship with their parent, they can begin to view estrangement as an essential step in their return to health. In those cases, a parent's worry over the mental health of their adult child can quickly morph into the horror of being blamed and exiled from the relationship. These are some of the most devastated of estranged parents. When an authority figure is involved like a therapist or spiritual advisor, an estranged parent can experience all the anger and resentment of a leveraged estrangement combined with the guilt and shame that are typical characteristics of this therapeutic-developmental type of estrangement.

Given the assignment of blame, parents dealing with therapeutic-developmental estrangements are often feeling a strong sense of betrayal. The professional resource they believed would help them reconnect or better connect with their adult child has actually deepened the estrangement. Hearing and reflecting back these feelings of betrayal is an important component of helping these estranged parents feel understood. Given the different kinds of estrangements that parents bring into a group, parents are going to have different experiences of professional caregivers ranging from life-saving to life-threatening. It will be important to avoid debates about the value of these resources, and better to understand the different experiences that people have had without the need to pass judgement.

Situational Estrangement

The fourth and final type of estrangement involves circumstances that almost certainly will change. The most common is a young adult living on a distant university campus. The child suddenly stops communicating with their parent. Occasionally we see the same thing happen with a military assignment, though the cutoff is more likely to be the result of some kind of psychological issue. More frequent is conflict over an event that leads to estrangement. Planning a wedding or making funeral arrangements are usual suspects. A pandemic which forces a degree of isolation can also become an occasion for estrangement. Dr. Keli Rugenstein observes adult children using a pandemic as cover for testing their tolerance for a break in the relationship that may eventually become permanent.

I call these *situational estrangements*. On the face of it, situational estrangements tend to be the least traumatic of all the other types. Parents of non-communicative university students tend to see the experience as an extension of adolescent entitlement rather than a long-term estrangement. While they certainly feel hurt and somewhat anxious, they may also feel frustrated and annoyed. They may start dealing with questions related to funding. If my child won't communicate with me, do I continue paying for their tuition, books, cell phones, spring break, gifts, etc.? Parents who stopped receiving visits from their adult children during the pandemic were able to attribute it to the quarantine. However, when the pandemic eased and restrictions were ended, they experienced a total cutoff. What began as an extended absence becomes a traumatizing, long term estrangement.

Parents dealing with situational estrangement tend to be the least anxious and traumatized compared with other types of estrangement. They need to be supported in biding their time until the situation changes. They need other parents to understand how their situation is distinct without hearing dark predictions about how bad it might get or how many years it might last. In turn, parents dealing with situational estrangements need to understand how other parents might be suffering with a greater degree of intensity.

A Description not an Explanation

What we have then are four different types of estrangements as represented in the table *Types of Estrangement*, along with a single sentence description of that type. It is important to understand that this is a description, not an explanation. There are left-handed and right-handed people in the world. That's a description of how they interact with the world, not an explanation of why they prefer to use one hand over the other. We can make other observations about their experience in the world like the fact that left-handed batters do better against right-handed pitchers, and that they are better at art. But these aren't explanations.

So, for example, when we say that an adult child made a decision to estrange their parents after seeing a therapist, we can't also say that the

Types of Estrangement

	Internal Factors	External Factors	
More Permanent	**Hard-Wired** A difficult to solve issue within you or your child is a large factor in the estrangement.	**Leveraged** A significant person outside your relationship is a large factor in the estrangement.	**More Permanent**
More Temporary	**Therapeutic-Developmental** A potentially solvable issue within you or your child is a large factor in the estrangement.	**Situational** A circumstance that will eventually change is a large factor in the estrangement.	**More Temporary**
	Internal Factors	External Factors	

therapist is the explanation for the estrangement. However, we can say that when a therapist becomes involved, like any third party, the estrangement becomes more complex. We can also observe that the feelings of powerlessness of the estranged parent are going to be intensified when the perception is "it's now two against one."

Human behavior is complex, and can rarely be reduced to one or two factors. In addition, external influences always have an internal predisposition that they exploit. It is rare that dissatisfaction with a parent has been planted by a romantic partner in an adult child for the very first time. Nonetheless, I observe that in most cases of parental estrangement there is some combination of dominant factors that coalesce into one of these four types with secondary influences from the other three.

Understanding Others and Feeling Understood

Here's the bottom line. In any group of estranged parents, you are likely to meet some who are outright furious, some who are inconsolably sad, some who are confused and annoyed, and some who are utterly devastated. Some may be tempted to look at others and wonder why they are so upset. Some may be tempted to look at others and wonder why they are so calm. We may be tempted to judge others whose experiences do not line up with ours. We must resist that temptation. It is important to use our inspired imaginations to understand someone else's experience when it is somewhat different from ours. By doing so, we can help others feel understood which is healing to both body and soul.

We can also try to accept that not every estranged parent may be able to relate to our story. Some will understand better than others. In those moments, we can remind ourselves of what we have in common. Whatever our type of estrangement, or the severity of our pain, most of us are facing what will be the hardest emotional experience of our lives with repercussions in our bodies, our relationships, and our beliefs. No one is going to get through the experience of parental estrangement completely unscathed. No one is going to fit our experience precisely. Sometimes we have to allow the fact that others *want* to understand to be enough.

Understanding your estrangement type might not only help you feel understood, it may also provide insight into your particular recovery path. Abraham Maslow wrote that if we only have a hammer, we tend to treat everything as a nail.[26] In PEAK, we want to offer one another an entire toolbox of recovery tools ranging from spending time in forests to spending time in forgiveness. Find the ones that work for you as we begin this journey together.

In the movie, *World's Greatest Dad,* the father played by Robin Williams says, "I used to think that the worst thing in life is to end up all alone. It's not. The worst thing in life is ending up with people who make you feel all alone."[27] Let's do everything within our power to spend time making people feel less alone. And let's give other people a fair shot at helping us feel the same.

Questions for Reflection and Discussion
Tell about a time in your life when you felt truly understood regarding something important? How did that affect you?

What part(s) of your estrangement experience do you feel are most understood so far? What part(s) do you feel are least understood?

Of the four types of estrangement described in this chapter (Leveraged, Hard-Wired, Therapeutic-Developmental, Situational), which is the best fit? Which is the second best fit? Which one do you not relate to at all?

Can you think of estranged parents who might have a different type of estrangement from yours? What can you do to better understand their experience?

---

[26]Abraham Harold Maslow, *The Psychology of Science: A Reconnaissance* (Harper & Row, 1966).
[27] Goldthwait, R. (2009). *World's Greatest Dad.* Darko Entertainment

Based on your best estimate of your estrangement type, what particular needs do you have for your recovery?

What part of your estrangement story feels different from everyone else's? Is that OK? If not, what do you need from others to make it OK?

If you are using this book in a group discussion, what did you gain from hearing others speak? From speaking?

PEAK: Parents of Estranged Adult Kids
A Resource for Recovery

Chapter 6
Two Stories

I find that the movie *Mamma Mia! Here We Go Again* offers an interesting perspective on the relationship between parents and their adult children. For those unfamiliar with the story line, here is a summary.

Upon graduating from college, a young woman adventures through Europe. She lands on a Greek island where she has sex with three different young men over a period of a few days. When she discovers she is pregnant, she has no idea which of the three is the father. (DNA testing would have settled this, but ruined the movie.) She tells none of them. They sail off unaware and totally uninvolved in the life of the daughter (Sophie). Sophie's mother hides the truth of her birth, which is only discovered when Sophie reads the diary of her mother, who dies shortly afterward.

Here is what happens next.

Sophie feels totally betrayed by her mother who, as revealed in her diary, was exceedingly promiscuous. She is scandalized by the thought that she has no idea which of three men is her father, but is clear that all of them are cads who took advantage of her emotionally vulnerable mother. She writes all three men a letter telling them how much she detests them, asking them never to contact her. In addition, she trashes every memory of her mother: gifts, letters, and photographs.

Wait a minute! That's not what happens! Sophie adores her mother and makes the prime directive of her life fulfilling her mother's dreams. As for her three potential fathers, she reaches out to them at some expense to herself. She embraces them all, including her "witch" of a rich grandmother who only shows up when she can be the center of attention. The movie is fun and entertaining, but it also represents a parent's ultimate fantasy—that their adult children will not only be able to forgive whatever mistakes were made by their parents, but embrace them and even their dreams in a way that makes all those years of parenting count for something.

Which Story Is True?

The painful one, in which her mother and father are defective, and worthy of rejection? Or the celebratory one, with flawed, but beautiful mother and father, worthy of embracing? Well, they are both true depending upon how you want to tell the story. The facts are the same, but the assigned motivations are not. As a result, the two stories are totally different. In our journey together as estranged parents, we see these two stories all the time. One is the story that estranged parents tell themselves about the situation. The other is the story that estranged children tell themselves about the situation. They are often factually identical, (though not always), but emotionally polar opposites.

Here is an example. An estranged mother is so desperate to see her granddaughter, that she occasionally drives to the school she attends at close of day, just so she can see her face. Unfortunately, another parent sees her who happens to be friends with her estranged son. The friend gets on his cell phone with the estranged son, who immediately calls the police, and says that his child is being stalked by her grandmother. The police arrive and ask her to leave.

The facts are beyond dispute, but the stories are quite different. In one storyline, we have a heart-broken woman who takes the benign step of positioning herself, without any intended interaction, to see her granddaughter's face. In the other storyline, we have a woman who is brazenly stalking a child after being told repeatedly by the father that he wants his child to have nothing to do with her. One is a love story. One is a horror story. Same facts. Two different stories.

What We Think Should Work, but Doesn't

That's what it feels like to be an estranged parent. There are certain parental reflexes you have developed over decades that feel as natural as tying your shoes. To your absolute bewilderment, you discover that these simply don't work anymore. What you think is a love story, is seen as a horror story.

Based upon hundreds of communications with estranged parents, here is what estranged parents think should work—but often doesn't.

What we think should work: Saying "I love you."
This is at the top of the list. Entire movies have been filmed where an adult child is trying to get their self-contained, unexpressive father to say those words. But these words have been central to our motivations for so many years, and feel so deep and primal, we believe saying them again must have some positive benefit.

But what actually happens is…

Our adult child says (a) they already know that, (b) they don't believe us, or (c) the fact that we keep saying it to them is a violation of their boundary and proof that we are more self-centered than loving. The words are integrated into the storyline of a parent who is insincere and manipulative.

What we think should work: Saying "I'm sorry."
Here we are following the wisdom of many spiritual and healing traditions. We take responsibility for ways we know we have failed, or even for ways we must have failed for estrangement to be the solution. Though our children are flawed human beings as well, we may not even ask for any acknowledgement of that reality. We own our mistakes.

But what actually happens is…

Our adult child (a) doesn't believe we are really sorry, (b) can't forgive us, (c) says they forgive us, but remain estranged, or (d) the fact that we keep sending them the message when they have asked us to stop is seen as a boundary violation.

What we think should work: Sending gifts.
One way that we believe we can demonstrate that love is more than words is by sending gifts: birthday gifts, holiday gifts, anniversary gifts, or outright cash. We believe that will soften the sharp edges of the relationship.

But what actually happens is…

Our adult child either (a) returns them unopened, (b) refuses to acknowledge them, (c) accuses us of trying to manipulate them or our grandchildren with money, or (d) the fact that we keep sending gifts when told not to is seen as a boundary violation.

What we think should work: Showing up.
We believe that just showing up, whether invited or not, is a clear demonstration of how much we love them. After all, "showing up" at school functions, graduations, and special occasions is how we demonstrated our love for them over the course of decades. And it works in the movies.

But what actually happens is…

Our adult child experiences our showing up as an intrusion into their space, which creates an awkward situation that makes them uncomfortable. Instead of love, they may frame our showing up as stalking, invasion, and, in some cases, feel the need to call the police.

What we think should work: Asking "What went wrong?"
We believe that opening ourselves to feedback about how we have contributed to the estrangement is an act of love. If we understand what we did wrong, it naturally follows that we should be able to fix it.

But what actually happens is…

Our adult child either (a) won't tell us, (b) won't tell us because they say we don't listen, (c) tells us something that is totally counterfactual, (d) tells us, but makes it clear that it can't be fixed, or (e) the fact that we keep asking when they have told us to stop is seen as a boundary violation.

What we think should work: Asking "What about your grandparents?"

We spend a significant amount of energy caring for our aging parents. We point out that this is what adult children do, even though our parents weren't perfect, and there were problems in our relationship, too. In addition, the relationship with grandparents who have done nothing wrong seems unfair and unwarranted.

But what actually happens is…

Our adult children may interpret our care for aging parents as a sign of weakness on our part, an indication that we are not able to stand up for ourselves against our parents…as they are standing up against us. This suggests that we were not only flawed as parents, but weak as adult children as well.

What we think should work: "Honor your father and your mother."

If we raised our children in a faith tradition that is meaningful to us, citing a religious authority as a source of guidance is simply a continuation of that pattern. We look to the many verses in the Bible which encourage forgiveness and reconciliation as instructive.

But what actually happens is…

Our adult children indicate that (a) they do not believe in God, (b) point out examples of our moral failures, (c) cite verses in response that address our failures, or (d) indicate that their first commandment is not to honor their parents, but to honor themselves.

These responses are not from hypothetical dialogue spun out of a writer's imagination. They are paraphrased transcriptions from actual conversations with scores of estranged parents. It is difficult to overstate the negative impact these have on estranged parents. I'll mention three.

Three Negative Impacts

First, when what has worked before with our adult children suddenly stops working, it leaves us feeling dazed and confused. It is almost impossible at the beginning not to internalize our experience as feelings of incompetency, defectiveness, and powerlessness. Remember, confusion and powerlessness are two of the three components of complex trauma.

A related source of confusion is what is known as the estranged parent Catch-22. This is the damned if you do, damned if you don't experience. If you don't send a birthday gift to an estranged grandchild, it is proof that you don't care. If you send a birthday gift to an estranged grandchild, you are putting him or her in the middle, also proof that you don't care.

A second negative impact is that we may prematurely give up on perfectly good relational tools that continue to work in other relationships. If you can say "I love you," if you can say "I'm sorry," if you can send a gift on someone's birthday or a card when they are suffering, if you can show up at celebrations, but also at grievings, you can be one of the most precious things the world has to offer: a friend. But, these miracle-working qualities may no longer work with your adult child. Don't stop being the best version of you in the other areas of your life!

> **I am estranged from my son who is grown with his own family. His dad and I divorced when he was in college. That's the point where he became estranged.**
> M.K. from Billings, MT

The third negative impact is when we become trapped by going back to these same failed approaches over and over again. At a weak moment, when our impulsivity gets the better of us, we may fall to the temptation of trying one of these approaches again. Besides not working, it threatens to distract us from doing the one thing that is most important: making a decision to focus on our own recovery.

By the way, the list of what we think should work in the above paragraphs is a pretty good summary of the well-intentioned advice we will receive from non-estranged parents and well-meaning, but untrained counselors. How many times I have spoken with an estranged parent being advised by others, "Don't take 'no' for an answer! Go sit on their doorstep! Take the high road! Say you are sorry! Write a letter making amends." And the parent will simply breathe out a sigh of exhaustion, and say, "They just don't understand."

In addition, it is important to note that our adult children may not always be wrong. We may need to do a better job honoring boundaries, giving them space, listening to their feedback, etc. However, we must be clear on this point. No change on our part alone will lead to a healthy reconciliation. Our best path is to invest in our own recovery.

Creating a Redemptive Story

All this may sound negative and defeatist, but there is an important, positive lesson here. The facts of your life are not the story of your life. The facts are a given, but the story is yours to create. PEAK is not simply about helping parents cope with the pain of the estrangement from their adult child. It is about supporting them in the creation of a redemptive story.

A redemptive story is one that progresses from negative beginnings to positive endings. There are basically six stages.

Stage #1. A *blind spot* that that conceals a hidden weakness is maintained by a temporary stability.

Stage #2. A *crisis* that breaks the person down and introduces a degree of chaos.
Stage #3. A *revelation* of the weakness as the blind spot is removed.
Stage #4. A *battle* to overcome the weakness and grow beyond it.
Stage #5. A period of development where the new character grows stronger by *testing*.
Stage #6. A *final trial* where the person fights against something that symbolizes their old self.

Joanna has two daughters. When she gave up her career after they were born, Joanna poured her life into raising them. She read to them when they were young, was active in their classroom activities, and strongly encouraged them to excel in a variety of curricular and extra-curricular activities. But Joanna had a problem. She had little of her own personal identity. And except for occasional church attendance and nominal membership, she had established no spiritual foundation in her life. However, her busyness with her daughters kept her too preoccupied to notice her own emptiness. [Stage #1 – The Blind Spot]

Her oldest daughter began dating a musician of whom Joanna disapproved. Three months later, she ran off, got married, and moved to a different state. She cut off contact with her mother the day they eloped. That was three years ago. The younger daughter started a promising career as a forensic accountant in Germany. With both daughters gone, and one estranged, Joanna went into a slow downward spiral. She began drinking more than her usual glass of wine with supper. She had clear signs of depression. She found herself picking fights with her husband. She came close to having an affair. [Stage #2 – The Crisis]

I just want you to know that attending a PEAK recovery group was life-changing for me.
K.D. from Pasadena, CA

Joanna spent a lot of time complaining about the unfairness in her life, some to other people, but much of it in her own head. Then, by some coincidence, she happened upon an estranged parent recovery group. She realized for the first time that she was not simply the victim of her two daughters' choices. She had failed to develop a personal identity with any more substance than her children's latest successes. It was hard on her pride to admit this, because it meant she had to stop blaming her daughters for her misery. [Stage #3 – The Revelation]

She began taking positive steps in her own personal development. She found a group that met weekly to practice meditation and contemplation. She also started journaling. She began working on big questions: Who am I? What is my life assignment? Some days were better than others. She struggled to forgive herself for living so long with such a shallow perspective on life. She wished she could start over with her daughters. But, little by little, Joanna was growing. [Stage #4 – The Battle]

However, tensions were growing with her husband. He didn't share in Joanna's growth. He felt threatened by her involvement in different groups. He still loved the woman he married, and Joanna was not that same person. He asked her to return to who she used to be in order to save their marriage. Joanna held her ground. She couldn't go back to the emptiness, but she did agree to see a marriage counselor which kept them together. [Stage #5 – The Testing]

On the next Mother's Day, Joanna was asked to give a presentation in her faith community about being an estranged mother. As she looked out at many of the other women seated with their children, and some not, she had an image in her mind of sitting in a row with her daughters on either side. She had some feelings of failure, some feelings of envy. But she remembered what she had gained in her recovery process, a solid identity, a purpose in her life, and knowledge that she was in possession of a love that could never be taken away. And she looked at the mothers sitting alone.

She took a breath, looked up, and said, "Hello. My name is Joanna, and I am the mother of an estranged adult child." [Stage #6 -The Final Trial]

The elements of Joanna's story, the stressful investment in raising her children, the unfairness of their responses, the empty-nest crisis, the problem with her drinking, the tension with her husband, all could be spun into a very sad and bitter story. Instead, Joanna created a different story from those same facts, a redemptive one.

Overcoming Our Resistances

There is a natural resistance in most of us to developing a redemptive story out of the pain of parental estrangement. The initial suggestion hits a wall of resentment. Nonetheless, many studies have shown that those who are able to create redemptive personal stories are more productive, form strong identities, have better mental health, and are more resilient in the face of life's challenges and low points.[28] In addition, the research suggests that people prefer to be with others who tell redemptive stories about their life experience. They are simply more fun to be with. An estranged parent's recovery process is incomplete until they can create a redemptive story from the facts, none of which they now have control over.

A redemptive story is only one of many that can be constructed around the same set of facts. When estranged parents and their adult children have a shared history, but two different stories in which they are emotionally invested, the risk of estrangement increases. A reconnection that does not deal with the widely divergent stories of what happened can never be considered a healthy reconciliation. The proverbial elephant in the room takes up too much space.

Keli Rugenstein, Ph.D., addresses the issue of reconciliation through the development of what she refers to as a cocreated narrative. Her process is a subject addressed in her newest book,[29] but it basically requires parents and adult children to acknowledge and validate the

---

[28] Kate C. McLean, Brianna C. Delker, William L. Dunlop, Rowan Salton, Moin Syed; "Redemptive Stories and Those Who Tell Them are Preferred in the U.S." *Collabra: Psychology* 1 January 2020; 6 (1): 39.

[29] Keli Rugenstein, Ph.D., *Relationsnip: Is there life after your adult child rejects you?* (BookBaby, 2022).

experience of one another, even if they don't agree with their conclusions. The goal is to create a single story focused on the relationship, with a set-up, crisis, and resolution. This generally requires a major investment of time and energy, not to mention the services of a skilled family therapist. It is for this reason that Rugenstein believes healthy reconciliations between estranged parents and their adult children are relatively rare.

Steps Toward Recovery

What actions can we take to move toward the creation of a redemptive story?

- Accept that the estrangement is not about the facts, but a difference in the stories created around the facts. It will not be resolved by more information.
- When you find yourself engaged in imagined conversations with your adult child where you "set them straight," gently bring yourself back to the present moment.
- If a recitation of the facts helps you remember how you got to where you are with a healthy degree of self-compassion, write them down, and share them with someone who will listen non-judgmentally.
- Decide if you want to create a redemptive story out of your estrangement experience. Find a resource who can help you do that. That resource might include a skilled therapist, spiritual director, or a wise friend. Alternatively, just begin journaling that story on your own.

Every spiritual path has a redemptive story at its heart. Buddha faced a crisis when confronted with the suffering of those around him, and nearly starved to death. Moses killed a man, and lived with the fear of discovery. Jesus was crucified on a cross, after his disciples betrayed, denied, or abandoned him. The power of a spiritual life lies in the capacity to understand our own spiritual evolution as it is forged out of elements we cannot control. We did not get to choose how our story began, but we do get to choose how it will be finished.

Questions for Reflection and Discussion
Over the history of your relationship with your child, beginning with their birth, what are some of the indisputable facts that come to mind?

How have you experienced the two different stories aspect of parental estrangement?

What steps have you tried to take that have been misinterpreted or totally backfired?

How have you experienced the estranged parent Catch-22?

What weakness in your life has parental estrangement revealed to you?

Is it possible for you to think about a redemptive story, or is it too early in your recovery process?

How did this chapter leave you feeling?

If you are using this book in a group discussion, what did you gain from hearing others speak? From speaking?

Chapter 7
Ghosting and Shunning

Beginning around 2011 a new concept emerged in the context of online exchanges: *ghosting*. Ghosting is breaking off a relationship by ceasing all communication and contact with a person without any apparent warning or justification, as well as avoiding or ignoring and refusing to respond to the person's attempts to reach out or communicate.

There is now a lot of Internet chatter on the effects of ghosting, which appears to be on the rise. Some mental health professionals consider ghosting to be a passive-aggressive form of emotional abuse, a type of silent treatment or stonewalling behavior, and emotional cruelty.[30] But we don't really have to wait for additional research on the effects of ghosting; it has already been studied but under a different name: *shunning*.

What Is Shunning?

As we have seen in previous readings, it is almost always adult children who end the communication with estranged parents rather than the other way around. This is a form of shunning.

When most people hear the word *shunning*, they think of certain agrarian or ethnic religious practices. Alternatively, they think of practices featured in historic literary works such as *The Scarlet Letter* where adulterers are required to wear a red A on their foreheads and suffer the scorn of their community. In the Old Testament, the penalty levied against Cain for killing his brother was not capital punishment

---

[30] https://en.wikipedia.org/wiki/Ghosting_(relationships)

but a mark on his forehead that would lead to his shunning. It is a testament to the power of shunning that Cain's response was, "My punishment is greater than I can bear."[31] While Cain was permitted to live physically, psychologically he had been given a social death penalty.

That's how most people think of it, as a kind of Old Testament practice. Shunning is considered either rare or an artifact of the past, something that happens somewhere else. It is interesting to note that the frequency of the use of the word has dropped consistently since the early 1800s until the last several decades when it has begun to be used more frequently.[32] The word *ghosting* has become so common that it is beginning to be included in dictionaries. In spite of perception, "Shunning is a common practice that many people have suffered or perpetuated, yet it is surprising how little attention has been paid to this ubiquitous form of aggression."[33]

To *shun* is defined as "to persistently avoid, ignore, or reject (someone or something) through antipathy or caution."[34] Shunning usually occurs in response to a failure, real or perceived, on the part of the person being shunned. Breaking contact with a parent with whom an adult child is angry because of their choice to remarry is an act of shunning. Deliberately and habitually refusing to take phone calls, respond to text messages, answer emails, recognize birthdays, or show up on holidays is an act of shunning. While most estranged adults would initially not use that word, it is actually a precise and concise way of describing what they are experiencing.

While the root of the word "estrange" means literally "to treat as a stranger," shunning cuts deeper than that. Shunning doesn't treat a person as a stranger; it treats them as non-existent. It is experienced as indifference to whether a parent lives or dies. This is an important

---

[31] Genesis 4:13
[32] https://books.google.com/ngrams/
[33] https://www.psychologytoday.com/us/blog/beyond-bullying/201309/the-silence-shunning-conversation-kipling-william
[34] Google dictionary

distinction. Parents get birthday cards from their insurance or real estate agent, but not from their estranged children. A person will generally check on a neighbor who appears to be in trouble or has gone missing. Even total strangers will assist a person in an emergency. But the indifference of parental estrangement is silent in the face of the inevitable losses and deterioration of old age.

During the recent 2020 pandemic, when one out of every ten elderly persons who contracted COVID-19 died, most parents were not contacted at all by their estranged children to check on how they were doing, a task that fell to near or total strangers. News of the death of a parent or grandparent brings expressions of sympathy from nearly everyone who hears, even bank tellers and postal workers who ask how you are doing. But time after time, estranged parents report that their children do not respond to this kind of news at all, let alone attend funeral services for their grandparents. Even a stranger is a person. To shun is to render someone a non-person.

Just recently had my youngest adult son cut me off without telling me why. Trying to navigate this without anger.
V.T. from Belmont, NC

The Pain of Shunning

Shunning is a form of rejection that gives rise to some of the most painful of human emotions. The same part of the brain that registers the physical pain when you strike your thumb with a hammer also registers the emotional pain of being shunned. While shunning doesn't leave bruises or blackened eyes, the pain is often deeper and lasts longer than a physical injury.[35] Estranged parents often wonder why the rejection by their adult child is so painful. The pain they suffer may

---

[35] https://www.amenclinics.com/blog/ostracism-causes-lingering-pain-in-the-brain-2/

be worse than that caused by any other experience in their lives including childbirth.

An article by psychologist Guy Winch, PhD, explains why emotional pain can be so much worse than physical pain. Emotional pain is reexperienced by memories in a way that physical pain is not. Physical pain (like exercise) can help distract us from emotional pain but not vice versa. Emotional pain can make physical pain even harder to bear. Physical pain garners more empathy from others than emotional pain. Think of a broken arm in a cast. Finally, emotional pain is triggered by holidays and anniversaries in a way that physical pain is not.[36]

All these factors work in combination to make the pain of parental estrangement extremely difficult to bear.

Shunning in families may begin with an angry spouse in a divorce, but then expand to include children if they feel impelled to take sides. Estranged parents may be shunned by one adult child, several adult children, or even the entire family. Shunning may include a total severing of communication or reduction of contact to a few tense, obligatory conversations. Either way, the impact can be both immediate and long term, obvious and subtle.

Reactions to Shunning

The modern language of ghosting provides a vivid image of the effects of shunning. A ghost is invisible. People go on with their lives as if they don't exist. Ghosts also have no agency in the world, no power to impact others for good. Their existence makes absolutely no difference to anyone or anything. All they have left are memories of when they were actually visible. Ghosted people, including estranged parents, spend time wondering if anyone ever remembers them, misses them,

---

[36] https://www.psychologytoday.com/us/blog/the-squeaky-wheel/201407/5-ways-emotional-pain-is-worse-physical-pain

or longs to see them. They consider different ways of *ghostbusting* the relationship, showing up or taking some action that will force others to see them. These attempts almost always fail.

In research projects where the reactions of adults interacting in a game are observed, feelings of control, belonging, self-esteem, and meaningful existence are reduced within minutes of being excluded from the game.[37] In just a few minutes of being ignored, an estranged parent can begin to feel badly about themselves and even question whether their life means anything.

In a desperate move to avoid shunning, parents may attempt to change their behavior to gain acceptance: complying, obeying orders, being submissive, mimicking laughter, or criticizing others, anything to stop the pain of being shunned. However, the assault to their own dignity can have multiple, long-term consequences including the obvious loss of self-esteem and depression, but also physiological symptoms such as ulcers, suppression of the immune system, anxiety, psychosis, a loss of feeling valued, or having any meaningful existence, which results in increased risk for suicidal thinking, suicide attempts, and death.[38]

At first, estranged parents who suffer from shunning may not realize what is happening to them. They may have a vague sense that something is wrong but may not be able to name it. They may go through a period of denial where they try to convince themselves that what they are experiencing is normal. Since no parent is without his or her own failures, they may live in the guilt of feeling that they deserve to be shunned. They may go through years of bargaining, hoping to finally be accepted back into the family. They may make no connection between psychological or medical problems they are experiencing and the shunning they have endured.

---

[37] https://www.psychologytoday.com/us/blog/beyond-bullying/201309/the-silence-shunning-conversation-kipling-william
[38] Ibid.

Later they may decline into a state of resigned bitterness and anger where they push everyone else away at a time when they need others the most. By engaging in such self-exiling behavior, they simply reenact and expand the sick abandonment they experienced in their families.

Whose Fault Is It?

Being shunned or ghosted can happen to any parent. It can happen to parents with criminal records who clearly understand there may be justification for the estrangement. It can also happen to people who by any reasonable measure have been model parents. For most of us human beings, we fall somewhere on the spectrum of human fallibility. Research indicates that the majority of parents do not know the reason(s) for their shunning.

In a subsequent chapter, I will describe in more detail what I mean by a no-fault philosophy toward parental estrangement. For now, I will simply suggest that a recovery process from parental trauma does not depend upon establishing who is at fault. In fact, blaming is counterproductive in the healing process since it either wastes energy by focusing on another person over whom you have no control or by lamenting your own past failures in a way that thwarts future possibilities. If you are stuck on your failures, it might help to ask yourself a few questions:

- How do you benefit by focusing on your failures?
- How do those you are in relationship with (who love you and you love) benefit by focusing on your failures?
- How do the people you are called to serve in your community and world benefit by focusing on your failures?
- How do your adult children benefit by focusing on your failures?
- If you are a person of faith, how does focusing on your failures benefit your relationship with God?

- How does focusing on your failures help you achieve important goals for the future?
- How do you personally benefit by focusing on your failures?

There is only one category of people who benefit by your focusing on your failures: those who have an emotional need for you to hurt. Sometimes it is the parent themselves who need to hold onto their pain as a way of avoiding change. Here's the truth—you are the only one responsible for where you focus your attention, and you are the only one who has the power to take whatever steps are required and move forward.

Hitting Bottom

While attempting to fix blame is not helpful, understanding how being shunned (or ghosted) is affecting you as an estranged parent is extremely important. Every person is different, and the way that the impacts of shunning express themselves in each life will be different as well. However, they all fall under the heading of trauma. It then is no surprise that researchers have observed a high prevalence of PTSD among persons who have been shunned. To get a clearer idea of the potency of shunning, researchers have observed that even being a bystander to shunning can have dire psychological consequences.

In addition, the intensity of the impact will vary as well. For some estranged parents, the intensity of the impacts may be quite low while for others so significant that it is almost debilitating. It is one thing when parental estrangement causes insomnia once or twice a month; it is a totally different degree of intensity when it is occurring every night of the week. Symptoms of sleep psychosis, including visual and auditory distortions can begin after only 48 hours of sleeplessness. Some estranged parents may not fully realize how being shunned is affecting them until they are given permission to talk about it. They may feel that parents should be an inexhaustible supply of physical and emotional resources for their adult children. The impacts and intensity of shunning may not fully hit them until they realize that this "omnipotence" is an unrealistic expectation for themselves, and it is okay for them to hit bottom. For many of us, hitting bottom is what springs the prison door. Realizing that parental estrangement can lead to years of misery and an early death finally gives us permission to take the steps required to literally save our own lives.

How Healing Begins

Given all the impacts of shunning, parental estrangement is a serious condition. Left unaddressed, the psychological, social, and even medical impacts can be devastating. Coming to grips with this reality is the first step to healing. In order to take their own healing seriously, estranged parents must believe themselves worth saving regardless of the particular details of the estrangement or the nature of their human failures.

Sometimes estranged parents make the mistake of thinking they can simply let their adult children know how painful it is to be shunned. They hope, for example, that if they give their adult child the information in this chapter, a change will occur in their behavior. Unfortunately, this rarely helps. It is the equivalent of a ghost "haunting" a house, which typically results in feelings of alienation and disgust rather than peace and reconciliation.

The Ghost of Estrangement

I have learned to see my children
as a ghost must view the living,
separated not by distance,
but by a veil of disgust.
My appearance to them would be a haunting,
and their reaction would haunt me as well.
My touch is that of a loving gaze

toward a photo of long ago,
as upon a sleeping toddler.
I am possessed of that peculiar sadness
that the first sadness is passing away:
the beginning of serenity.
—Fe Anam Avis

The emotions leading to estrangement are powerful. When adult children are able to be honest, they may be so angry that they *want* their parent to suffer. As one researcher put it, letting people know how badly it hurts just doesn't get rid of it.[39] Only when estranged parents realize this do they stop waiting for their adult children to change so that they can take the first steps toward recovery.

In their recovery process, estranged adults begin to recognize shunning for what it is: a failed attempt of adult children to deal with their own issues of hurt, anger, or fear. The goal is not to blame estranged children or exonerate ourselves as parents, but to find insight and healing through our Spiritual Source. Every person will need to explore their own spiritual traditions with regard to those who have been marginalized because of some personal failure. While the Christian Church may often fail to live up to the perspectives of its founder, Jesus has quite a bit to say in defense of those who were shunned. In fact, he had such a reputation for un-shunning people that it tended to get him into real trouble.

A Story of Religious Shunning

While in the home of a prominent religious leader named Simon, Jesus is approached by a woman known to be a sinner.[40] Her designation as

---

[39] Janice Harper, "The Silence of Shunning: A Conversation with Kipling William," *Psychology Today* (posted Sept. 4, 2013).
[40] Luke 7:26-50

a sinner suggests that she has failed in some manner deemed reprehensible, publicly known, and worthy of relational exile. Simon, and every other respectable person in the community could make the decision to shun her without the slightest sting of conscience. Jesus turns the whole scene on its head when he takes the shunned woman's side with the words, "The one who is forgiven much, loves much." He says this after what must have been a painful, point-by-point depiction of how unloving Simon had been. Jesus implies that Simon is unloving because he does not know how much he has been forgiven, and Simon does not know how much he has been forgiven because Simon has not really joined the human race, where everyone is flawed. This incident is not an exception in the Gospel accounts. It is characteristic of Jesus to take the side of the shunned and the marginalized, provided that they learn the most basic of lessons: the importance of compassion and gratitude.

Of course, the world has not changed, and the woman walks back out into the street forgiven by God, but remains unforgiven by her community. If she is unable to get the unforgiving voice of Simon out of her head, if the voice of God's love is not strong enough to deliver her from the emotional distress of the community's rejection, then her religion is of no real benefit to her. In order to find peace, she must be able to differentiate the gracious and loving voice of God from all the other voices in her life.

Whatever their particular faith tradition, this is the situation in which many estranged parents find themselves: forgiven by God, unforgiven and shunned by their adult child. In the words written to one estranged father, "I suppose God will have mercy on you. But as for the rest of us? Good luck." Recovery from the intensity of this kind of rejection requires a process of spiritual differentiation. Spiritual differentiation is the capacity to find peace and direction from the Divine voice within us, especially when it is in contrast to other harsh voices clamoring for our attention.

Spiritual Differentiation

Middle Eastern shepherds can allow their flocks to intermingle as they graze without anxiety about how to separate them. The sheep know their shepherd's voice. At the end of the day, all the shepherds call their flocks, the sheep recognize and move toward the voice of their shepherd, and he returns them to their resting place for the night. This has been a metaphor over millennia for the process of spiritual differentiation.

In order for estranged parents to find peace, we must be able to hear our Shepherd's voice. For many of us, God is only known as One who is mediated through a religious institution. For others, God is emotionally undifferentiated from our father, our mother, our spouse or ex-spouse, our children…the list goes on and on. In that sense God does not exist apart from the echo chamber of all these other voices. When those other voices are cruel or judgmental, we are unable to find comfort in God, because God has no voice that is separate from theirs.

The work of spiritual differentiation begins with a commitment to developing a personal relationship with our Spiritual Source. This has many different expressions. For some it is expressed through the third step of a Twelve Step program: "Made a decision to turn our will and our lives over to the care of God as we understood Him." For some it is "receiving Jesus Christ as my Lord and Savior." For some it is "giving as much of myself as I know, to as much of God as I know." For others, it is participating in a renewal of baptism where vows taken at infancy become personal. Whatever the words that are used, the key elements of the process are that it is (a) personal, (b) intentional, and (c) trusting.

Sometimes church is described as the place where the rubber meets the sky. Shunning is the place where faith becomes a matter of living or dying. Shunning can be a terminal condition which threatens us with premature death. A personal relationship with our Spiritual Source promises that we can walk through the valley of the shadow of death, and fear no evil.

Steps Toward Recovery

What steps can you take in your recovery from the impacts of shunning and ghosting?

- If you are carrying guilt from mistakes of the past, decide that bearing this burden benefits no one. Offer it up to God, and let it go, once and for all. If you find it necessary, offer it up again tomorrow, once and for all! Eventually, the nickel will drop.
- Decide that you are worth saving, and not deserving of an early death from the impact of shunning. Do something symbolic. Pull the obituary page out of a newspaper. Safely set it on fire, and throw the ashes into a body of water.
- Accept that sharing your pain with your adult child will not change the situation. If you have not done so already, make the decision to stop. If YOU care about your pain, THAT will change the situation.
- If you have not gone through a process of spiritual differentiation where you have connected directly with your Spiritual Source in a personal way, take that step.
- Use this mantra, or something similar, every day for a week:
  My family's voice is not God's voice.
  My estranged child's voice is not God's voice.
  My faith community's voice is not God's voice.
  The voice of the unforgiving is not God's voice.
  The silence of those who shun, is not God's silence.
  The estrangement of those who withdraw is not God's estrangement.
  The judgement of my critics is not God's judgement.
  Only God's voice is God's voice.
  I hear only one voice.
  Only God is God.
  I have only one God.

The greatest risk for us as estranged parents is not what another will do, but whether we will self-exile or ghost ourselves. There lies within each of us a seed of goodness and beauty, full of potential, and waiting to emerge. Whether we name that the Image of God, our Divine nature, our Higher self, or the Holy Spirit, the greatest tragedy of life is if we abandon ourselves, and join others in pretending that we don't exist.

Questions for Reflection and Discussion
How and when did shunning or ghosting develop in the relationship with your adult child?

How much are you focused on your failures from the past and how those may have affected the relationship with your adult children? How much are you focused on their failures?

How has being shunned or ghosted affected you?

Do you think your estranged child understands how much pain you are in? How hard is it for you to let that go?

Does God, however you define God, have a separate voice in your life? Compared to other voices, internal and external, how strong is God's voice?

If you are using this book in a group discussion, what did you gain from hearing others speak? From speaking?

Chapter 8
After the Fire

It was a cold, January night in western New York. I parked my car along the side of the road and walked the rest of the distance across a thin layer of snow crunching beneath my boots. In the bright yellow light of the house burning down, I could make out the figure standing in front of me. Her name was Louise, and it was her house that was burning down.

"We built that house with our own hands," she said, pushing out the words. "Thirty years of life, gone."

Estranged parents often wonder what is happening to them. Not only are they bewildered by the decisions their child or children are making; they are equally confused by all the reactions they are having. Sixty-year-old estranged parents confess to me thoughts, feelings, and behaviors that are totally new to them.

"I actually threw a plate against the wall in the kitchen." one mother said. "It shattered into a hundred pieces. I've never done anything like that in my entire life. What's wrong with me?"

How many of us as estranged parents have felt that way! There's nothing wrong with her, or us, except that a chunk of our life is burning down. Our recovery requires an acknowledgement of this reality: parental estrangement is the relational equivalent of a house fire. All the long-term investments into the life of a child from the changing of diapers, to the financial expenditures for food and shelter, to the bandaging of skinned knees, to the attendance at middle school band concerts, all the effects of these seem to be vaporized by the estrangement. In contrast to a house fire, you still have the photographs and objects, but these reminders of the past have been transformed from sources of comfort to painful triggers. In the last chapter, we explored how shunning makes parental estrangement painful, but it is not the only source of pain. There is also the burning down of meaning. This chapter will look at how that loss of meaning impacts us.

Parenting as a Source of Meaning

Meaning is essential to our well-being. When there is clear purpose for our lives, human beings can endure a great amount of suffering. A soldier will absorb the brunt of an explosion as an act of love for his fellow combatant. A father or mother will work multiple jobs, and live on little sleep, in order to provide for their children. But when life loses the meaning provided by love, work, and the courage to overcome, it becomes difficult to even survive. Holocaust survivor and psychotherapist Viktor Frankl wrote: "Life is never made unbearable by circumstances, but only by lack of meaning and purpose."[41] The erosion of meaning is one of the most damaging impacts of parental estrangement. It can make life feel unbearable.

I cannot get past my grief. I pray every day and can't seem to stop being self-critical. I did the best that I could.
M.H. from Charleston, WV

Parents bring children into the world, and by doing so, bear responsibility for meeting their physical and developmental needs. They are joined in this effort by other elements of the community such as extended families, friends, schools, faith communities, and neighborhood organizations. Over a thirty- year period of time, they strive to nurture their children from absolute helplessness into adults who are able to function independently in society.

One of the major benefits of this investment is that it offers parents a sense of purpose or meaning. In fact, it is not simply a source of

---

[41] Viktor Frankl, *Man's Search for Meaning* (Beacon Press, 1st edition, 2006).

meaning; for most parents, it is the most important source of meaning. In a 2018 study conducted by the Pew Research Center, researchers asked 4,729 U.S. adults to indicate the most important source of meaning in their lives.[42] Their results are listed in the table *Most Important Sources of Meaning*.[43]

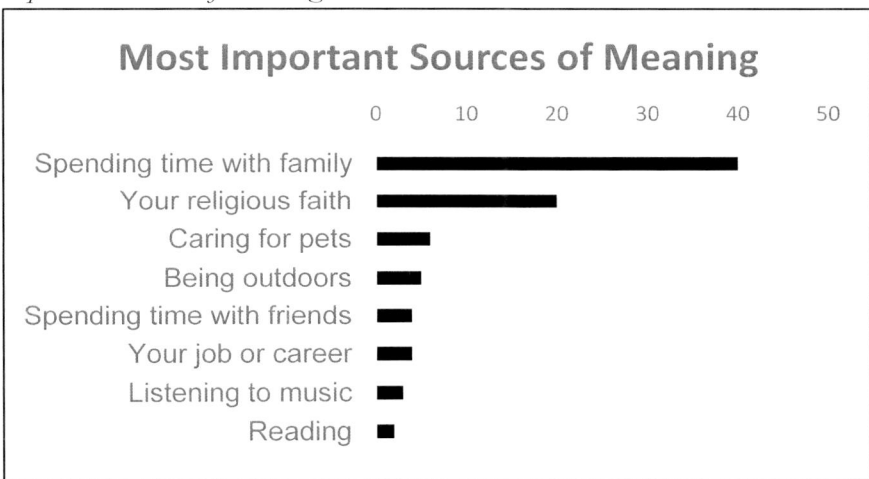

Note that spending time with family is listed as the most important source of meaning for Americans. It is named twice as often as religious faith, six times more frequently than caring for pets, eight times more frequently than spending time outdoors, and ten times more frequently than spending time with friends. But there is more. When the same respondents were asked an open-ended question about the particular aspects of family they were thinking about, 34% of them said children or grandchildren. Only 20% said a spouse or partner. In other words, spending time with family is not only the most important

---

[42] Pew Research Center, Nov. 20, 2018, "Where Americans Find Meaning in Life."

[43] The graph in the previous edition of this book contained different results because it used information from a similar study conducted in New Zealand. However, the priority of family as a source of meaning is the same in both studies.

contributor to meaning in most Americans' lives, it is spending time with children and grandchildren in particular that is most significant.

The priority of spending time with family, especially grandchildren, remains at the top of the list for older adults.[44] In most cases, the amount of time spent with family is substantial. Over a third of adult children are in touch with their parents daily.[45] Forty-two percent of grandparents see their grandchildren weekly; twenty-two percent see them daily.[46] On average, grandparents 65 – 74 years old spend four hours a week caring for their grandchildren.[47] That doesn't count the hours spent in other activities with their grandchildren. Parental estrangement strikes a triple-blow. It not only eliminates the largest source of meaning from our lives. It also leaves large blocks of time empty that would otherwise be spent in those relationships. In addition, it creates a gap in experience between ourselves and other parents who are engaged on a daily or weekly basis in ways that we are not.

Recovery and Finding New Sources of Meaning

Recovery for estranged parents requires a significant shift, both in how we find meaning and where we spend our time. The second source of meaning in the figure above, cultivating religious faith, is one of the most promising. Many estranged parents bear witness to a significant spiritual rebirth or renewal as part of their recovery. We live in a time of great opportunity for spiritual exploration. Not only do we have the

---

[44] https://www.pewresearch.org/social-trends/2009/06/29/growing-old-in-america-expectations-vs-reality/
[45] https://www.pewresearch.org/social-trends/2015/05/21/6-keeping-in-touch-across-generations/
[46] https://www.today.com/parents/modern-grandparents-busier-hands-happy-1d80128716
[47] https://www.urban.org/sites/default/files/publication/42866/311203-Many-Older-Americans-Engage-in-Caregiving-Activities.PDF

range of traditional religious institutions to explore, the Internet is making available a greater variety of possibilities for spiritual growth than ever seen in the history of the world.

Many people find that contact with nature, either through owning pets or being outdoors is another rich source of meaning. Numerous studies reveal that owning a pet not only offers companionship, but can also help alleviate depression, facilitate psychotherapy, lower blood pressure, and prevent premature death from heart attacks.[48] Spending time in nature, what the Japanese have named "forest bathing," has been proven to have similar benefits. Spending time in forests, or simply looking at trees, reduces stress, lowers blood pressure, and improves mood.[49] A dog that you love will never estrange you. Neither will a forest. Nor will God. There is probably a connection.

Developing solid friendships is such an important part of recovery from parental trauma that I have dedicated an entire chapter to it. On average, older adults spend over 10 hours alone each day. Loneliness has the same health risks as smoking a pack of cigarettes a day. Meaningful friendships can help, but most Americans have never had any training on how to develop or maintain a friendship. They tend to believe, erroneously, that people are born "friendship-ready."

Estrangement not only impacts the meaning of how we spend our time in the present. We also have to deal with how it impacts the meaning of our past.

The Development of Older Adults

During the formative years of parenting this large dose of meaning is required to sustain the significant and often sacrificial commitment to the task of raising children. It also reinforces the primary drive of

---

[48] Fitzgerald FT. The therapeutic value of pets. West J Med. 1986 Jan;144(1):103-5. PMID: 3953064; PMCID: PMC1306544.
[49] https://www.dec.ny.gov/lands/90720.html

persons in the middle years, the motivation to "generate": children, careers, businesses, houses, prestige, resumes, and so forth. This works well in this stage. The need of parents to generate matches the needs of children to "consume" as they grow.

However, adults continue to develop long after they have finished the primary tasks of parenting, even into old age. A psychologist named Eric Erikson noted that as adults enter their sixties, they begin to reflect on their lives.[50] As they look back, some feel content and fulfilled. They believe that they have led a significant life and contributed substantially to the world. However, some feel a sense of despair. They see more of their failures than successes. This makes it difficult to approach death with serenity. This is the stage when individuals would ask, "What was the point of life?"

During this stage, the thought that any major endeavor of life was pointless or meaningless triggers emotions that are extremely painful. One major investment for many people is the time and energy they have spent in a job or career. The play *Death of a Salesman*[51] dramatizes the struggle of a man to come to grips with the limitations and failures of his vocation. During this later stage of life, the individual desires to feel a sense of achievement in their work and that he or she has made a meaningful contribution to the world.

Using the physical analogy, we spent our lives building a house. For much of our lives we were too close to see what it really looks like. In our later years, we finally stop building. We step back to get a view of what we have built. Is it something we can be proud of? Is it something we can comfortably live in during our final years? Or using the analogy at the beginning of this chapter, has the fire burned that down as well? From the standpoint of a meaningful past, are we psychologically homeless?

---

[50] Erik Erikson, *Childhood and Society* (Norton & Company, Incorporated, W.W.,1993).
[51] Arthur Miller, *Death of a Salesman,* 1949

The Parental Investment

Few human endeavors require a greater investment than that of parenting a child into adulthood. From a financial standpoint alone, the investment is significant, about $250,000 to age seventeen. Parents also invest thousands of hours in time and emotional energy to educate, support, and advocate for their children. The great majority of parents are not tracking these investments, nor is it helpful to use "I put a roof over your head," to leverage a later obligation to stay in relationship with parents for whom they have no affection.

But neither is it fair to exclude from the category of love the sustained and multiple efforts required to provide material security. There is no question that simply providing food, shelter, and clothing is an impoverished form of love if the emotional, educational, and spiritual dimensions are absent. However, the converse is true as well. A rich emotional connection while keeping a child ragged, hungry, and homeless, is also traumatizing. Fulfilling our basic responsibilities is also love, not simply the things we do over and above them.

Ideally, as parents are entering their sixties and into a stage of life where they are reflecting on the meaning of their lives, their adult children are simultaneously reaching a point where they can become a significant source of affirmation focused on the value of all the investments a mother or father made in their development. In the words of Proverbs 31:28: "Her children rise up and call her happy." This contributes to a sense of fulfillment, peace of mind, and well-being. It is part of what enables the parent to face death with serenity.

Society gives a nod to the importance of this stage of life, at least informally, through the institution of special occasions like Mother's Day, Father's Day, Grandparent's Day and parental birthdays. Nonetheless, most adult children are unaware of the emotional significance of this stage of life for a parent, which rivals that of adolescence in its importance. In the case of parental estrangement, holidays and celebrations actually become occasions of increased pain as they pass by without acknowledgement. In spite of the long-term emotional consequences of such omissions, trying to change the behavior of adult children by telling them how much hurt they are causing is not a productive approach. It is experienced as nagging and drives estranged adult children further away.

The Sounds of Meaninglessness

In the case of those estranged parents, adult children are either unable or unwilling to make this contribution to the parent's developmental need. Whether this is due to real or perceived failures on the part of the parent or issues within the lives of the adult child is irrelevant. The failure of the estranged parent to find meaning in their investment in the life of their adult child threatens their ability to view their life as something that mattered.

Estranged parents may think or say things like:

- All that effort I put into helping him through school, and now he won't even talk to me.
- I put a roof over their heads and food on the table. It apparently means nothing.
- I was there for them in their toughest times, and it didn't matter.
- I feel so worthless. What's wrong with me?

Suggesting that parents are persons who have developmental needs that should be met by their adult children will be an alien thought to many. I realize it is a radical idea. Some adult children are simply too wounded, hurt, or angry to make that contribution. But the fact that many adult children find it impossible, given their history, does not negate its importance. Some parents are not able to provide for the basic developmental needs of their preschool children, but that doesn't diminish their importance.

No one deserves to be left feeling their life was meaningless. The trauma of this unmet developmental need in older adults can run deep. While society as a whole is unaware of the emotional consequences of parental estrangement, and the powerful signal it sends that their life did not matter, it is every bit as consequential as deprivations at other stages of life. Most people are aware of the damage done to the psyche of a teenager who is bullied and shunned by peers at the very stage of life when peer relationships are critical. Most are also aware of the trauma experienced by couples who want children but discover they are unable to conceive or bear them at the very stage of life when "generating" is critical. The pain experienced by estranged parents who are deprived of contact with their adult children (or grandchildren) and who interpret that absence as a deprivation of meaning in their lives is equally traumatic. It is the fire that feels like it is burning down the past.

Exclusion and a Deprivation of Meaning

Exclusion has a profound effect on how we as human beings perceive whether life is meaningful. In one study, 121 persons were invited to play Cyberball. While ostensibly a ball-tossing computer game, it is actually designed for research on social exclusion. After a few minutes of tossing the ball back and forth, the computer begins to exclude the player. Remarkably, this exclusion not only affect how the person feels about the game, but about life in general. Only forty-five minutes later, the excluded person was more likely to indicate on a survey that *life,* overall, was less meaningful.

Clearly, exclusion has a powerful, negative affect on a sense of meaning in our lives. In the same study of others who were socially excluded, four impacts of social exclusion were observed that led to feeling life was meaningless:

Loss of purpose – perceived that their current activities did not lead to any worthwhile future outcomes.

Loss of efficacy – felt that they had no control of important future outcomes or made a significant difference.

Loss of value – were less able to view their actions as having positive value or as being morally justified.

Loss of positive self-worth – were less able to perceive themselves as persons with desirable traits.[52]

There are remedies to all of these, many of them addressed in this book. However, this requires that estranged parents invest in the work required by searching for new sources of meaning, and strengthening previous ones. Unfortunately, the research to date suggests that social exclusion does not motivate persons who are shunned to engage the work of this quest. Not all estranged parents are going to engage in the work of recovery. Their pain will become an excuse to stay stuck.

Not an Excuse

I have gone to some length in this chapter describing the devastating blow that parental estrangement delivers to a sense of meaning. I want you, as an estranged parent, to understand some of the reasons that you feel so devastated. However, I do so at some risk. You may think I am giving you an excuse to remain in your devastation. That would be a huge mistake. I am not giving you a reason to excuse yourself; I am giving you a reason to understand, and even forgive yourself. There is a reason someone throws a dish against the wall who has never done so previously. That person doesn't need an excuse, they need self-compassion.

Holocaust survivor, Viktor Frankl said that there are three sources of meaning: love, work, and courage. More love and more work may have little impact on how you feel about the meaning of your life. More courage might. You are still alive. Knowing that you have faced one of the most difficult experiences of your lifetime, honestly saying that you

---

[52] Stillman TF, Baumeister RF, Lambert NM, Crescioni AW, Dewall CN, Fincham FD. "Alone and Without Purpose: Life Loses Meaning Following Social Exclusion." *Journal of Experimental Social Psychology*. 2009 Jul;45(4):686-694.

did not buckle under the temptation to descend into cynicism or wallow in self-pity, that you rose up every time you fell down, that you reached out rather than caving in, and that you made the world a better place by becoming the best version of you possible, that is all the meaning any person needs to get up every morning.

Steps Toward Recovery

In order to avoid falling into the trap of excuses, what does this chapter suggest are important steps to our recovery?

First, as with shunning, it is important to realize that the pain you are experiencing is the result of a significant emotional trauma from which you need to *recover*. You have been through the psychological equivalent of a car crash. Left untreated, the scars can become permanent resulting in despair, disdain, or cynicism.

Second, shifting responsibility to your estranged adult children is not an effective avenue toward recovery. Reminding them of everything you have done for them will not work. Neither will engaging in a process of assigning blame; this only serves to delay your taking responsibility for your own recovery.

Third, the fact that your adult children do not acknowledge your contribution to their lives does not negate the fact that you have. The adult children of estranged parents can be highly functioning adults in significant roles and making valuable contributions to society. Someone has said that when you see a turtle sitting on top of a fence post, you know it didn't get there by itself.

Fourth, you may not be able to do this alone. You will likely need other people who can help you realize the significance of your life. It will be important for you to share your thoughts with them, but also to open your heart and mind to their positive input.

Fifth, it is important to realize that children are only one source of meaning as you reflect on your past. Other sources of meaning include careers, volunteer activities, service projects, the maintenance of other significant nonfamily relationships, and participation in a faith community. Sometimes we can find meaning in our past by listing all the lessons we have learned, even those learned through mistakes we have made. Have you been a good friend to someone? Have you helped someone grow to become a more capable person through coaching, mentoring, or just setting a positive example?

One of the activities that can be beneficial for recovering a sense of meaning is a structured life review. A life review is a comprehensive reflection on the entirety of one's life. I will be saying more about this in Chapter 24.

Recovery Takes Time

Finally, this recovery process will take time. If you stay with it, you will gradually begin to feel more positive about your life.

Slowly, the pain of estrangement will release its grip. However, it is important to be clear: time alone will not heal this wound. You must take seriously your own responsibility in the recovery process.

A number of years ago, I sustained an ankle fracture severe enough to require surgery with the implant of a plate and screws on one side and a pin on the other. The next Sunday, a nurse chased me down after church (which was not hard given the fact that I was on crutches).

"I have one thing to say to you," she said sternly, looking me straight in the eyes. "Don't think time will take care of this. Do your physical therapy. I don't want to hear you tell me how hard it is. Do your therapy and you'll be fine."

That was how she showed her love.

I did my physical therapy. It was hard. I am fine. I run three miles on that ankle every day without pain.

Think of me as a kind of spiritual nurse. This is how I am showing you love.

Don't think the passage of time will take care of this. Do the work outlined in this book. I don't want you to tell me how hard it is. Do the work and you'll be fine.

Some say you never get over parental estrangement. If by that they mean that you are sentenced to a lifetime of the debilitating effects of parental estrangement—emotional, physical, medical, and relational—I vigorously reject the statement. If by that they mean that you will always have access to a sense of loss and a bit of sadness that accompanies it, sure. As I wrote in the preface, "a little sadness is the tear of wax running down the candle of love that lets us know that the wick is still lit." You will never be able to eliminate all the sadness in your heart without snuffing out all the love as well.

What can you reasonably expect?

- The recovery begins when you risk moving out of isolation. You will discover that parental estrangement is not rare. By gradually releasing the burden of unexpressed grief, you join others in the journey toward gentleness, humor, love, and respect.
- The process allows you to begin to see yourself as the biological instrument of your children's existence. Their true parent is a Spiritual Source that some of us choose to call God. Our Spiritual Source is the wellspring of healing and vital living, both for us as parents and for our adult children.
- This is the action and work that heals: You use the concepts of this book; you use your conversations; you talk with others. You share your experience, strength, and hope with each other.
- You learn to restructure your thinking one day at a time. When you release your adult children from responsibility for your actions, you become free to make decisions as actors, not as reactors. You progress from hurting, to healing, to helping. You return to a sense of wholeness.
- We all make mistakes that affect other people including our adult children. It is always important to be willing to examine ourselves. However, parental estrangement affects even the best

of parents. Through this work you will be reminded that parental estrangement is not a reliable measure of your love, your mental health, or your competency.
- By doing this work over the next several weeks you will begin to see parental estrangement for what it is—a mystery that we can only partially explain, a choice by adult children who we cannot change, a problem that can totally deplete us and leave the situation no better. You will learn to keep your focus on yourself in the here and now. You will take responsibility for your own life and supply your own needs for relationships.[53]

Questions for Reflection and Discussion
In your experience, how is parental estrangement like a house fire?

List the top five sources of meaning in your life that make your life worthwhile:

Source of meaning #1:

Source of meaning #2:

Source of meaning #3:

Source of meaning #4:

Source of meaning #5:

What do you do if one of those sources of meaning is weakened?

Which steps suggested under "Steps Toward Recovery" do you need to focus on?

---

[53] From Appendix A: Key Affirmations of PEAK, "The Way Forward," patterned after the promises of Adult Children of Alcoholics.

Review the list under the sentence heading above: "What can you reasonably expect?" Is that enough to keep going?

If you are using this book in a group discussion, what did you gain from hearing others speak? From speaking?

PEAK: Parents of Estranged Adult Kids
A Resource for Recovery

Chapter 9
The Pain of Ambiguous Loss

As older adults, estranged parents are no stranger to life's losses. On average they have started and left a dozen different jobs, moved in and out of communities about the same number of times, and roughly half will have gone through a divorce. They have also experienced losses to death. By the time the average parent reaches age 55, they will have lost grandparents, one or both of their own parents, perhaps an older sibling, and often one of their friends. However, if you are an estranged parent, it is likely that you have never experienced anything in your entire life approaching the sense of loss that comes with being cut off from the relationship with your adult child. Is that an exaggeration?

A person goes missing. Friends and family members have no idea where the person is or what has happened to them. Here's the question: "Which is harder on the family, hearing from the police that they have no further information or hearing from the police that the family member has died?"

Missing Persons and Prolonged Grief Disorder

Researchers Steve Powell, Willi Butollo, and Maria Hagl found the families with unconfirmed losses had higher levels of traumatic grief as well as severe depression. The study, published in the journal *European Psychologist,* found that "the unconfirmed loss of a family member produces more distress, compared with enduring a confirmed loss. The authors conclude that the particularly high levels of severe depression, including suicidal thinking, in this group was especially worrying."[54] These are the symptoms of what is referred to as prolonged grief disorder.

A parent's experience of estrangement from their adult children is similar to that of families where a member goes missing: a) Communication is cut off. b) Estranged parents are often uncertain what has happened. In some cases, they do not know where their child lives or if they are even alive. c) There are feelings of loss that trigger a grief process. d) It is uncertain whether the relationship will be restored or if they will even see them again. It is an ambiguous loss. The parents I have spoken with who have both lost a child to death, and an adult child to parental estrangement share that these elements of a prolonged grief experience make it the more difficult one to bear. For some parents who are estranged from more than one child, and their grandchildren, the loss is similar to a horrific accident during a family outing that takes them all away in a moment of time.

> *I feel I have lost my identity. How do you cope with the 'living death' of a child?*
> P.L. from Concord, NH

Where does one turn to get help in dealing with this kind of grief? Members of grief support groups typically struggle to understand how estrangement is a loss comparable to the death of their loved one. Nevertheless, the components of prolonged grief experience are similar to other grief processes with variations particular to parental estrangement. Even though the stages are rarely linear, it is not difficult to track the grief of estrangement along a trajectory of recovery.

The first component of a prolonged grief experience is *shock*. Shock is defined as the initial reaction to a sudden upsetting or surprising event or experience. The great majority of parents give birth to and raise children thinking that the relationship will endure for their lifetimes. Certainly, every relationship has its ups and downs, but at that moment when a parent first realizes that their child has cut off the

---

[54] https://www.psychologytoday.com/us/blog/slightly-blighty/201706/coping-not-knowing-what-happened-missing-loved-one

relationship with them, perhaps forever, an emotional blow is delivered that has few parallels in life experience. A chemical reaction within the human brain helps us remember shocking events with some precision, the assassination of John F. Kennedy, the Challenger disaster, and 9/11. Most parents can probably describe their initial estrangement experience in detail, including when it happened, where they were, and what they were doing.

The second component of a prolonged grief experience is *denial*. Denial occurs when a person is faced with a fact that is too uncomfortable to accept and rejects it instead, insisting that it is not true in spite of overwhelming evidence.[55] Denial in a prolonged grief experience can be deepened by the fact that there is always hope for a reconnection.

For estranged parents, denial can express itself in two ways. First there is denial of cause. When adult children are asked if they have shared with their parents the reason for the estrangement, 67 percent said they had. In their response to the same question, 67 percent of estranged parents denied that they had.[56] It is likely many parents are in denial about the estrangement from their adult children that keeps them from actually "hearing" those reasons. Or it may be difficult for them to accept that the reasons they are being given rise to a level that estrangement is a reasonable response.

Then there is the denial of severity. Estranged parents tend to hold out hope for reconciliation when the evidence suggests that the break in the relationship is likely long-term. Unfortunately, many professional caregivers such as therapists and clergy unintentionally support a degree of denial. As discussed in Chapter 10, the prognosis for a healthy reconciliation is relatively poor, especially when the estrangement occurs after 25. Surveys of estranged parents indicate that they tend to hold out hope for reconciliation while surveys of their

---

[55] https://en.wikipedia.org/wiki/Denial
[56] https://www.verywellfamily.com/when-adult-children-divorce-their-parents-1695810

adult children indicate that they do not. Denial is not an indicator of a deficiency in estranged parents. It is a way of pacing the grief process so that they do not have to deal with difficult emotions until they are ready.

The next component is *anger*. The anger of a prolonged grief experience can be intensified compared to that of a death because there is an element of rejection in estrangement not present when a person dies. The anger of an estranged parent might be expressed directly through face-to-face conversations, phone calls, letters, text messages, emails, or on social media. It might also be expressed indirectly to third parties in contact with the estranged child: friends, family members, church members, or work associates. Finally, anger might not be expressed at all. It can remain confined to the interior life of thoughts and feelings.

The anger is generally focused on behaviors of the adult child, but can also be focused on major influences in his or her life, particularly their spouses, in-laws, and divorced parents. Anger is important in the grief process because the emotional combustion generates the energy required to move forward. Anger becomes a problem when it descends into a blaming process that keeps an estranged parent stuck and prevents them from taking responsibility for their own well-being. It also becomes a problem when it is directed at other parents who have positive relationships with their adult children.

One of the most significant components in a prolonged grief experience is *bargaining*. Bargaining is based on feelings of desperation and the thought that "I will do anything to keep this relationship." This bargaining may be directed toward God, but more often results in a season of pleading by an estranged parent that may seem to work for a time or may be rejected at the outset. I am not talking about editing one's thoughts for the sake of the relationship. It is one thing to not interfere in the way your child parents your grandchildren. It is another to witness a grandchild being abused and then being warned that any action taken will be at the cost of the relationship.

It is during the bargaining that guilt feelings may become acute. Since no parent is perfect, it is typical during this period for the parent to become aware of their shortcomings, and to offer apologies as a part of the bargaining process. Sometimes this succeeds. When it does not, a parent may end up being repeatedly reminded of those failures to a point that is detrimental to their well-being. In "Our Common Experiences," we regularly recite "When we try to make amends to our estranged children our efforts are either ignored or the admissions used against us."

Nonetheless, bargaining is a particularly important aspect of the grief work for an estranged parent; it encourages them to grow in their self-awareness and to be more realistic about their strengths and shadows. Bargaining also helps parents explore multiple possibilities for reconciliation so that by the time they come to acceptance they can do so without feeling that they simply quit. Bargaining becomes a problem if it negatively impacts the self-esteem of the parent either through the abandonment of their own needs or excessively apologizing for failures that are never really forgiven.

The next component in a prolonged grief experience is *depression*. This depression is not a sign of mental illness though it may have many of the same characteristics: withdrawal, sadness, and lack of energy or interest in things that once were sources of vitality. For estranged parents, feelings of depression are intensified by the fact that most parents they know have relationships with their adult children and grandchildren. Not only have they lost the relationship with their adult child, they have lost the ability to relate to their peers in an area of life that is very special to them. Depression also serves an important role in the grief process. It deters us from engaging in an endless bargaining process by sapping the energy required to sustain it. It also sets the stage for taking positive steps that will restore us to a vital, purposeful life when we find ourselves saying, "I don't want to live this way for the rest of my life."

The final component is *acceptance*. Acceptance is not affirmation. Most therapists would probably say that estrangement is not a good solution in most cases either for the parent or the adult child. Acceptance is not affirmation; it is adjustment to reality. A person who loses a leg or an arm in an accident would never be asked to affirm their impairment as something positive. However, their acceptance of that reality enables them to climb mountains, run races, and adapt in other ways that inspire us all. Acceptance of parental estrangement enables us to make practical adjustments to the losses of estrangement. This can include developing relationships with other family members and friends, exploring the possibilities of surrogate children and grandchildren, and investing in hobbies or service opportunities. Acceptance also opens estranged parents to consider legal and financial issues that will need to be addressed like powers of attorney, estate management, and final arrangements.

This can feel like giving up hope. In reality, we are beginning to shift our focus from the hope that we will immediately be reconciled to our adult child to a focus on the hope that we can reinvent ourselves to become vital and purposeful. This shift in hope is important. Otherwise, hope becomes a two-edged sword, inspiring at times positive optimism and a desire to keep fighting on, but if or when hopefulness becomes dashed, perhaps even deeper despair follows. If acceptance is not realized, the turmoil of contrasting emotions, endlessly oscillating between hope and despair, renders this kind of grieving particularly stressful, and may prevent "closure" or finding mental peace.[57]

As mentioned earlier in this chapter, the process of working through grief is rarely this linear. Rather than thinking about *stages* of grief, it might be more accurate to think of *aspects* of grief that people experience in different ways and at different points of time. Even after someone has accepted the loss, they may cycle back through familiar questions: Is this really permanent? How could I have messed this up so badly? Maybe there is something more I can do? This is a natural

---

[57] https://www.psychologytoday.com/us/blog/slightly-blighty/201706/coping-not-knowing-what-happened-missing-loved-one

part of the process. However, it can also be helpful to understand that there is a natural sequence to the grief process. For example, it will be impossible to deal with any other aspect of grief as long as a person is denying emotionally that a loss has occurred.

Even though prolonged grief experience is a deeply emotional condition, I sometimes find it helpful to think about it using a formula that can explain the pain.

$$Estrangement\ Pain\ =\ \frac{Loss \times Rejection}{Support}$$

Estrangement multiplies the loss by feelings of rejection. Support, on the other hand, tends to reduce the pain somewhat. The death of a child generally elicits an outpouring of support which is soothing. A parent's estrangement by an adult child generally results in isolation and a reduction in support. As feelings of rejection increase, and support approaches zero, estrangement pain grows exponentially. Estranged parents may not realize the impact of these different factors. They don't need an equation to tell them that the pain is intense, and sometimes feels unbearable. They are living it.

Ways to Ease the Pain

But the formula doesn't just explain the pain. The good news is there are some things we can do to significantly ease that pain. The first is that we can increase our level of support. As we increase our support, the pain is often reduced. Many of us have found relief by moving out of isolation and sharing our experience with others who will not judge, minimize, or try to fix us. This is one of the primary purposes of PEAK. For many people, simply reading this book, and finding validation of their experiences is enough to make their suffering bearable.

The second thing we can do is find ways to reduce the feelings of rejection. Of course, we cannot change our adult child's decision, but we can diminish the rejection attached to it. When I was a pastor, the Ku Klux Klan placed a cross on the State House lawn. They had every right to do so, and there was no legal option for having it removed. Instead, the area churches decided to fill the entire State House lawn with identical crosses, so that the one symbol of hate was diminished to insignificance. We can reduce the significance of our rejection feelings by flooding our mental and spiritual space with affirmations of all kinds, those that come from sacred scriptures and inspired writings, but also affirmations from others. Sometimes we just need to call up a friend with an affirmation request: "I need you to deposit some affirmation in my emotional bank account today. Tell me two things you think are good about me."

And don't forget to affirm yourself! Here is what I have learned. Developing a commitment to your own life is a gift no one else can give you. You must give it to yourself. A thousand voices can affirm the preciousness of your life, but the silence of your one voice will mute them all. Of all the beautiful vows we take in life, we must make this one first, or all the rest will mean nothing. People die prematurely, literally or metaphorically, when they cannot keep this promise themselves. I will always be your cheerleader, but the "I do" to yourself must be yours alone.

We do everything possible to help one another and ourselves ease the pain of parental estrangement, and in the early stages that must be our sole focus. But we will also need to find ways to live with that sadness without allowing it to cripple us, and to summon the courage to engage the heroic journey that the world needs us to complete. It takes courage and perseverance simply to read this book, not always the easiest thing to do. And yet, you are doing it. We have been on a journey exploring why parental estrangement is so difficult. Previously, I used a formula to illustrate the pain of a prolonged grief experience. In the graphic, I illustrate how the three forces, shunning, meaning deprivation, and prolonged grief experience contribute to broken-heartedness, both figuratively and literally. For many estranged parents, having a visual way to understand their pain is helpful in and of itself. Broken heart syndrome, also known as stress cardiomyopathy or takotsubo syndrome, occurs when a person experiences sudden acute stress that rapidly weakens the heart muscle.

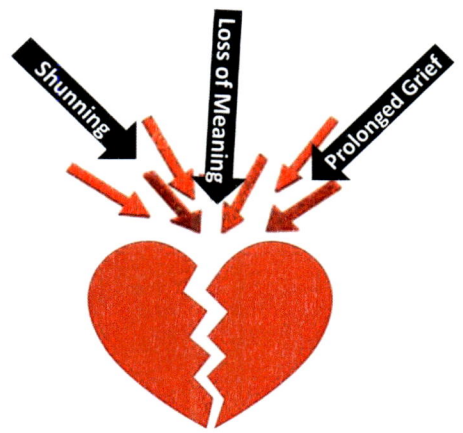

This chapter ends Part I - The Estrangement Experience. The purpose of this section has been to help you, the parent, gain a better understanding of what parental estrangement is, how it is affecting you, and why you are experiencing such intense pain. Before moving on to Part II - The Journey Toward Recovery, I would like to close this chapter with a few steps in dealing with a prolonged grief experience.

Steps Toward Recovery

In addition to the steps mentioned above, finding additional support among other estranged parents and increasing the amount of affirmation in your life, consider these as well:

- Instead of trying to keep all sad thoughts at bay all the time, occasionally allow yourself to fully engage them for an hour or two. Listen to sad music, write in a journal, pull out a photo or two, and, perhaps, cry some tears. Then pack things away, say a prayer of blessing and release, and move on with your day until the next time.
- Put some emotional fuel in your tank by reading some inspirational stories about people who have lost limbs but have

managed to make significant achievements in spite of their loss. Send the person a thank you note.
- Engage the spiritual resources of your faith. Explore how your particular faith tradition deals with grief, and see how that might apply to you.
- Be creative. Use music, art, dance, poetry, writing as ways to process your grief. Then share it with another estranged parent who might find it helpful.

The chapters that follow in Part II present some alternative ways of thinking about parental estrangement. Simply reading these chapters will be of some help, but the real benefit can only be realized by adopting the different ways of thinking that these pages describe. This may require a change of mind and a commitment to realign your behavior. I will be elaborating these practical steps at the end of each chapter.

Questions for Reflection and Discussion
What were some of the most difficult losses in your life? How is the pain of parental estrangement similar or different?

Which of the following aspects of prolonged grief disorder are you dealing with now?
    Shock
    Denial
    Anger
    Bargaining
    Guilt
    Depression
    Acceptance

In your own words, what is the difference between acceptance and affirmation?

Rank the following factors from most painful to least. Say a few words about why the one at the top of your list is so painful.
> Shunning
> Deprivation of meaning
> Prolonged grief experience

How open do you feel right now to changing some of your thinking about parenting?

If you are using this book in a group discussion, what did you gain from hearing others speak? From speaking?

PEAK: Parents of Estranged Adult Kids
A Resource for Recovery

Part II
The Journey Toward Recovery

Chapter 10
Recovery and the Unwelcome News

In the song "Live Like You Were Dying," singer Tim McGraw tells the story of a man in his forties who receives news from his physician that he has a terminal illness. (McGraw, T. 2004). He sits in shock for a couple days looking at x-rays, and reviewing options. But then something remarkable happens. He begins to really live. He skydives, climbs mountains, and rides in a rodeo. He has a spiritual renewal, conducts a life review, forgives those who have wronged him, and becomes a better friend. He leaves the world with one hope for those left behind, that they will have the chance to live like they were dying.

Since the song has sold over two million copies, and been played millions of times more, we must assume that it has struck a chord in the contemporary psyche. Deep in our souls, do we not intuit that the challenges of life are meant to make us more vital, loving persons? In the long run, we are all dying. The song lays before each of us two insistent questions: "Are we really living? Do we have to wait for a terminal illness to begin living?"

The events of the song all hinge on one person's action: the physician's delivery of unwelcome news to a man who has no idea how serious his situation is. As difficult as it always must be, it is the doctor's honesty that springs him from the trap of his taken-for-granted, uninspired living. This is the unexpected twist in the song. It is the worst news a person could ever receive that leads to the best days he will ever live. Hard as it is for us to believe when we are in the depths of parental trauma, this is true for estranged parents as well. Please take a deep breath. This chapter is about to deliver some unwelcome news.

The Difficult to Deliver News for Estranged Parents

"In the first few days after my daughter broke off all communication with me, I felt like I was going to die." I have now heard these or similar words repeated many times by estranged parents. I believe they are literally true. There is ample evidence that the kind of trauma experienced in parental estrangement, untreated, can take years away from a person's life.

Fortunately, this parent could go on to say, "I really appreciate you and everything that PEAK brought into my life for recovery. I have grown so much since I started the recovery group for estranged parents. Life is so much better. More peace, more joy and just a better quality then it was before estrangement. I had no idea even how to survive this thing called estrangement. When I found PEAK, it was the first glimmer of hope. I thank God." This is what recovery sounds like.

However, before an estranged parent can recover, they must grapple with some unwelcome news, equally difficult to deliver. Once a relationship has been totally severed, the prognosis for reconciliation with an estranged child is poor. As with an actual medical diagnosis, we can never be 100% certain of the future. There is always the chance of a miracle. But hoping for a miracle does not serve us well if it simply enables us to keep living the same lackluster way we always have. Hope for reconciliation can become its own kind of life-eating cancer if it results in decades of postponed living while we wait in agony for someone else's change of heart.

In a major research project conducted by the Center for Family Research at the University of Cambridge, and Stand Alone, an organization serving estranged parents, both adult children and estranged parents were asked to respond to the statement, "We could *never* have a functional relationship in the future." Roughly 75% of adult children clearly agreed with this statement. Only 5% clearly disagreed, but even their relatively positive response is guarded. They are focused on a future *functional* relationship, not necessarily the warm or close one that their parents may have in mind.[58] Based on this kind of research, and her own professional experience with estranged parents, Dr. Keli Rugenstein estimates the rate of reconciliation between parents and their estranged adult children over the age of 25 where there has been a total cutoff is likely 10% or less. This is as low as the survival rate for the most serious forms of cancer, mesothelioma (7.2%), pancreatic cancer (7.3%) and brain cancer (12.8%), all of which doctors would instantly disclose to their patients. Yet we are not disclosing this information to estranged parents.

Perhaps the most heartbreaking statistic of this study is found in the response of estranged parents to this same statement. In stark contrast to the 75% of estranged children who clearly agree that they could *never* have a functional relationship in the future, only 15% of estranged parents clearly agreed. In other words, estranged parents are overwhelmingly optimistic about a reconciliation that, based on the attitudes of their children, will likely never take place. How is it that parents are so unrealistic about the prospects for reconciliation?

Why Parents Are Misjudging the Severity of their Estrangement

I think there are several answers.

First, many believe reconciliation will 'just happen' especially if their previous pattern has been to reunify after conflict "as if nothing had happened" - a really typical communication pattern in estrangements. Not only do parents tend to be conflict avoidant, they avoid talking about their conflict avoidance!

Second, the stories of reconciliation that pop up on the internet after parents have gone searching for resources are anecdotal, and not representative of the entire population of estranged parents. After several years of working with estranged parents, I also could provide a

---

[58] https://www.standalone.org.uk/wp-content/uploads/2015/12/HiddenVoices.FinalReport.pdf

few isolated stories of reconciliation. However, these would be exceptions among hundreds of long-term estrangements, and I would never use them as sources of inspiration. The fact of the matter is that estrangement is a stubborn, long-term reality for the great majority of estranged parents.

Third, articles and books addressing estranged parents which suggest that reconciliation can be achieved by following their guidance tend to focus on one particular type of estrangement descripted in Chapter 5 which is relatively uncommon: therapeutic-developmental. They never disclose the low probability of success overall, particularity with leveraged estrangements which are the most common of all. Parents who take these approaches to heart end up with disappointing outcomes, internalize the failure as a personal defect, and end up in a worse state than before they began. Alternatively, they join the thousands of angry, bitter parents in online groups, hardened by the realization that their adult children may never return.

> *Our daughter is 51 years old and has cut herself off from us for nine years through silence, a cold shoulder, and curt remarks when she does speak to us at all.*
> D.R. from Atlanta, GA

Fourth, whenever human beings are presented with particularly painful news, they tend to go into denial as a form of emotional protection. For a time, denial refuses to acknowledge reality or ignores the consequences of that reality. Estranged parents often activate an emotional filter that will only admit information favoring the possibility of reconciliation, blocking the rest. However, for most of us, denial ultimately gives way to reality. It is one thing to be in denial about the death of a loved one for several days after first hearing the news. It is another to be denying that a loved one is gone years after their death. Yet, it is not unusual for parents who have been estranged for over a year to still be in denial of the severity of the break with their adult child, and expectant of an imminent reconciliation.

However, I believe the fifth and final answer is decisive. Those who serve estranged parents in professional roles, clergy, lay ministers, therapists, physicians, etc., are not providing parents with accurate information that most estrangements are likely to be long-term, and possibly permanent. They are failing to disclose this information because (a) they are not aware of the research, (b) they are ignoring the research for fear that disclosing it will impact their relationship with the parent, (c) they are trying to avoid the discomfort of sharing bad news, or (d) they are anxious about dealing with the parent's reaction.

Of course, those in the medical profession have no such luxury. The doctor in Tim McGraw's song, who, by his honesty, precipitated a crisis "when a moment came that stopped me on a dime," can't simply decide to avoid the topic. He, and others, are bound by the AMA Code of Medical Ethics, "Physicians should sensitively and respectfully disclose all relevant medical information to patients... Withholding medical information from patients without their knowledge or consent is ethically unacceptable."[59] It would be unethical for a physician to diagnose a patient suffering from a condition with a poor prognosis for recovery, and withhold that information from the patient.

It would also be unethical for me, as a person serving estranged parents not to disclose this research. I take no joy in having to do so. I am fortunate to have readers who trust me enough to be honest about their initial reactions to these disclosures. "I hate this book." "After reading this chapter, I wanted to throw the book across the room." "I felt gut-punched." For most, these reactions are a temporary, but necessary stage they must go through. Afterwards, they can move forward in their recovery process with fresh energy and realistic hope.

---

[59] Virtual Mentor. 2012;14(7):555-556. doi: 10.1001/virtualmentor.2012.14.7.coet1-1207.

Why Disclosing Information Is Important

Why is a finding of parental estrangement with a poor prognosis for reconciliation important for an estranged parent to hear?

1. A finding of estrangement, with an assessment of its severity, along with its poor prognosis for reconciliation is the parent's information, not anyone else's. The parent is entitled to that information.
2. Based upon this information, there will be additional decisions that the parent needs to make. They may not include skydiving and Rocky Mountain climbing, but the investment in life-affirming activities, spiritual renewal, forgiveness, and friendship may be tragically postponed if all the parent's psychic energy is siphoned off into a fruitless pursuit of an unlikely reconciliation.
3. It spares other support services like PEAK from the ethical dilemma of having to lie or deceive the parent to avoid contradicting a trusted resource like a therapist, clergyperson, or physician who is withholding information.
4. If research from the medical field is any guide, most parents pass through the stage of denial, and, eventually, want to be informed about the likely developmental trajectory of something as serious as parental estrangement. Again, we are dealing with a disorder than can shorten someone's life, not a paper cut.
5. At some point, parents are going to find out the uncomfortable truth about the poor prospects for reconciliation from their own personal experience anyway. On top of the fact that years may be wasted in that process, is the additional fact that parents are likely to blame themselves, or, equally tragic, lose all faith in trusted therapeutic relationships that have withheld the truth from them.

When an adult child says, you are dead to me, you are lost to me, you are gone for me, I will make sure your grandchildren never know you, believe them. It is for this reason that PEAK focuses on the recovery of estranged parents, not on their reconciliation. Each week, we hear the group leader speak these words: "By working the PEAK program, we begin to emerge from the emotional, relational, and medical impacts of parental estrangement, regardless of the choices made by our adult children. The focus of our hope shifts from the behavior of our adult children, which we cannot control, to a choice fully within our power: the decision to recover."

The Good News about Trauma

It is not all bad news: there is good news to disclose as well. *While the prognosis for reconciliation between a parent and their estranged child is relatively poor, the prospects for recovering from the many impacts of parental trauma are extremely good.* This is one of the most important sentences is this entire book. Given the right resources, and the necessary motivation, an estranged parent can grow beyond the mental, emotional, physical, and relational suffering that accompanies a complex trauma, and into a life with meaning, purpose, and zest.

Studies have found that between 77% and 100% of patients who attend regular, customized trauma therapy sessions will see a reduction in their symptoms.[60] A 2014 study of another approach to trauma found that 80% to 90% of people saw results within the first 3 sessions.[61] Actually, there are a variety of therapeutic approaches, but research suggests that all of them can be equally effective.[62] When taken as a whole, 90% of estranged parents can expect to see significant improvement in their parental trauma symptoms. Contrast this with the less than 10% who can expect to see reconciliation as an outcome of their investment of time, energy, and money.

---

[60] https://sbtreatment.com/program/therapies/trauma-therapy/
[61] https://psychcentral.com/health/best-types-of-therapy-for-trauma#emdr
[62] https://www.health.harvard.edu/blog/psychotherapy-leads-in-treating-post-traumatic-stress-disorder-2019091217611

Recovery groups like PEAK have been shown to be effective in helping parents recover. Research by the organization Stand Alone confirms what we observe as well where 93% of participants find support groups helpful. In addition, estranged parents who accept the long-term implications of estrangement and focus on recovery instead of reconciliation see benefits in their lives. When parents were asked if there were any ways in which estrangement has had a positive effect on their lives, 80% said that it had. A typical sentiment is reflected in this person's comment:

> I am here! Alive. Every day is an opportunity to live a happy fulfilled life and that is what I strive for every day. To be the best person I can be. To not let my experiences affect me in a negative way but to turn them into a positive and driving force is what I work towards. It is hard and sometimes I feel like giving up, like I am going to collapse. But I must keep going. I feel happier, less stress, more at peace.[63]

Finally, we have found that the best preparation for a healthy, sustainable reconciliation, when that occurs, is doing the work of recovery. Without it, reconnecting parents and adult children are likely to carry back into the relationship the same issues that contributed to the estrangement in the first place. In addition, they will bring the untreated trauma impacts into the renewed relationship as well, which will threaten to sabotage what may be a once-in-a-lifetime opportunity for healing.

Steps to Recovery

From both research and personal experience, there is every reason to believe that estranged parents can recover from parental trauma. However, time does not heal all wounds. If we accidently cut ourselves

---

[63] https://www.standalone.org.uk/wp-content/uploads/2015/12/HiddenVoices.FinalReport.pdf

with a kitchen knife while making dinner, the wound will automatically heal itself with the passage of time. The same cannot be said of parental trauma. We must set our intention and take action. Here is what is required of us:

- We must actively embrace the fact that, in most cases, our children do not have a vision for reconciliation that will recreate the close, warm relationship we hold in our memories. As we will discuss further in a later chapter, this is a kind of death that must be grieved.
- We must energetically engage in a recovery process with the positive expectation that our trauma symptoms will lessen over time.
- We must be willing to accept the principle that we are not victims of our thoughts, that we are spiritual beings who have the capacity to change our thoughts, and that by choosing different thoughts our lives can change.
- We must be willing to explore some of our deepest beliefs about our identity, our parenting and our purpose, and, where necessary, update our thinking. In a later chapter, we call this a "thought-swap."
- We must be willing to think holistically about our recovery. Our bodies need exercise, sunlight, trees, movement, massage, breathing and other kinds of self-care every bit as much as our minds and hearts need companionship, reassurance, compassion, and guidance.
- We must be open to the possibility that the losses of parental estrangement, however painful, may lead to our own growth and serenity in ways we cannot now imagine.

You have now received the unwelcome news I sought to prepare you for earlier in the chapter. For some of you, it will come like a cancer diagnosis. I am truly sorry to have had to share this with you. I wish there were an easier way. Take some time to process it. There is no need to rush.

Some of you may feel your situation is an exception, and it may very well be. Others may hold on for a miracle. Now that I have been honest, I will walk with you whatever you decide. A few may be angry at me. Write and tell me that. Anger has its rightful place in our recovery process. All I ask is that you get with someone you trust, "talk about your options, and talk about sweet time."

Questions for Reflection and Discussion
Some difficult news about parental estrangement was delivered in this chapter. Is this the first time you heard it? If so, why do you think it is not more common knowledge? If you have heard it before, where did you hear it?

Being as honest as you can, how did this unwelcome news make you feel?

Why do you think it is important (or not), for estranged parents to have the information in this chapter? Why do you think it is important (or not), for you to have the information in this chapter?

"While the prognosis for reconciliation between a parent and their estranged child is relatively poor, the prospects for recovering from the many impacts of parental trauma are extremely good." Does this statement leave you more hopeful or more discouraged?

How hopeful are you that your trauma symptoms can be lessened over time, and you will begin to feel better?

Do you believe that you can choose your thoughts, and therefore change them? Are there any thoughts you need to change right now?

The life expectancy in the United States is now 77 years. List five words you want to describe your remaining years.

If you are using this book in a group discussion, what did you gain from hearing others speak? From speaking?

Chapter 11
Parental Estrangement and a Spiritual Perspective

Melanie is a divorced, 59-year-old woman whose 35-year-old son ended the relationship with her a year ago. When I first talked with her on the phone, she was having difficulty speaking without breaking down. She seemed at her wits' end trying to understand why this had happened to the two of them. She and her son had always been close, but over a period of about six months, he had become increasingly angry at her for what she thought were little things. He had developed a group of friends who were in and out of trouble. She came home from work one day, and noticed that her house had been broken into, and some money had been stolen. It became clear that her son was responsible. When she confronted him, he became extremely angry, and threatened to damage her car. Finally, he made a total break, and told her he didn't want to see her again.

It seemed clear on the phone that she was depressed, and her anxiety level was through the roof. She indicated she was having trouble sleeping at night. Migraine headaches that had bothered her once or twice a year were now occurring on a weekly basis. She was struggling to keep up at work. I told Melanie that we didn't have a support group for her yet, but I would let her know when a new one was starting.

When I called her three months later, Melanie sounded like a different person, calm and confident. She said that she had gone through a spiritual experience that had changed everything. She had attended church services most of her life, and considered herself a religious person. But several weeks ago, she had joined a group that took prayer much more seriously than she ever had before. She felt safe enough in the group to share everything that was happening with her son.

"I am taking God at his word. I am a child of God, loved and cherished. My son belongs to God. He is in God's hands, not mine." These were new thoughts to her.

In the last few years, I have seen this more than once. An estranged parent who previously had been nominally religious was moved by their parental trauma into a deeper spiritual practice. The effect was transformative. While issues still remain, most of the trauma symptoms have been significantly reduced or eliminated. A vitalizing spirituality had accomplished what might have required years of therapy or medication.

Regaining a Spiritual Perspective

In his book *Modern Man in Search of a Soul*, Karl Jung wrote:

> I have treated many hundreds of patients. Among those in the second half of life - that is to say, over 35 - there has not been one whose problem in the last resort was not that of finding a religious outlook on life. It is safe to say that every one of them fell ill because he had lost that which the living religions of every age have given their followers, and none of them has really been healed who did not regain his religious outlook.[64]

By definition, parental estrangement generally occurs in the lives of folks 55 and older. If Jung is correct, and I believe he is, parental trauma is a spiritual problem at its root. No recovery process will be effective if it does not include this dimension of life. While I have not engaged in a formal research effort, it is clear to me that parents who

---

[64] Carl Jung, *Modern Man in Search of a* Soul, Chapter 11 "Psychotherapists or the Clergy" (1933)

find a deepened spiritual perspective recover faster and more completely from their trauma symptoms than those with none.

A growing body of research is demonstrating the connection between a robust spiritual practice and recovery from trauma. A National Center for PTSD notes that

"Aspects of spirituality are associated with positive outcomes, even when trauma survivors develop psychiatric difficulties such as PTSD or depression. Research also indicates that healthy spirituality is often associated with lower levels of symptoms and clinical problems in some trauma populations. For example, anger, rage, and a desire for revenge following trauma may be tempered by forgiveness, spiritual beliefs, or spiritual practices."[65]

A Spiritual Perspective on Parenting

Without embracing a particular set of doctrines, PEAK adopts a spiritual perspective on parenting. Nowhere is this more clearly articulated than in the statement: "The process allows us to begin to see ourselves as the biological instrument of our children's existence. Their true parent is a Spiritual Source whom some of us choose to call God. Our Spiritual Source is the beginning of healing and vital living, both for us as parents and for our adult children."[66] The ability to view our parental role in this binocular way, with one eye on the biological and one eye on the spiritual is key to our recovery.

The fact that I make references to a Judeo-Christian tradition is not an attempt to be exclusive. Persons from other traditions, Judaism, Islam, Buddhism, Hinduism, etc. will need to do their own work of integration which I encourage. From my particular faith perspective, the designation "child of God" permeates our tradition. At twelve

---

[65] https://www.ptsd.va.gov/professional/treat/care/spirituality_trauma.asp
[66] While this specific language is borrowed from Adult Children of Alcoholics, the concept of humans as spiritual children of God is common to many belief systems, particularly the Christian tradition.

years old, Jesus speaks to his mother, the biological instrument of his existence, as if he had another parent, a spiritual one. "Did you not know that I must be in my Father's house?"[67] Followers of this tradition affirm that they, also, are "children of God, who were born, not of blood nor of the will of the flesh nor of the will of man, but of God."[68] As with Jesus, there is a clear distinction made between our biological parentage, and our spiritual Parent. The Lord's Prayer, which many Christians pray weekly, begins with the words, "Our Father." The implication is clear. God is our Father. We are all God's children. At this deepest of all levels, our adult children are not our children at all. They are actually our spiritual brothers and sisters.

Beyond Compartments

This is not new information. So why does it sound so strange to our ears? And why has it been so little help to us up to this point? I believe the answer is clear: we have effectively compartmentalized it. The notion of God as the true Parent of our adult children sits as a concept in a hermetically sealed container located in the upper reaches of our cerebral cortex. It doesn't intersect or modify any of our other beliefs. It doesn't resonate emotionally. It doesn't influence our behavior. It doesn't affect our relationships. It's like a comet that makes its appearance in the solar system of our thoughts every now and then, is interesting to observe, but quickly speeds out of sight with no real significance to our real life.

What might it look like if we allowed the concept of God as our adult child's true Parent to break out of its compartment, and into our consciousness? First, we have to get specific about what it means to say our child's true Parent is a Spiritual Source.

---

[67] Luke 2:29
[68] John 1:13

Biologically, we gave birth to our children. We named them and gave them legal status. We sheltered, clothed, fed, and educated them. We helped them develop into adults. This could be described in great biographical detail with documents, photographs, and keepsakes. When we claim them as our children, we are generally thinking in this biological and biographical sense.

Spiritually, our children came to life from another dimension. This other dimension has various names: Kingdom of God, Heaven, the Universe, Nirvana, and Brahman. In this book, I will simply refer to it as the Spiritual Reality. That Spiritual Reality has assigned them a purpose with a four-part assignment: (1) work to do, (2) lessons to learn, (3) someone to love, and (4) experiences to share. Our task is to support them in discovering their assignment, and in taking it in hand.

This Moment Awaits Your Arrival

In order to release our adult children into their assignment, we must first embrace our own.

Instead of seeing our past as shaping our destiny, a spiritual perspective sees destiny as shaping our past. In other words, the Spiritual Reality has brought us to this very place in life, because it is this very place in life where our assignment needs to be fulfilled. From a spiritual perspective, a person isn't sitting in an AA meeting because they are an alcoholic. They are sitting in an AA meeting because this is where they can fulfill their assignment. As a parent, you are not reading this book, (and I am not writing it), because you are estranged from your child, or I am estranged from mine. From a spiritual perspective, you are an estranged parent reading this book so that you can fulfill your assignment. This moment has been waiting for you to arrive, because your assignment is of critical importance, not only to you, but to someone else. From a spiritual perspective, we are not here because of our successes or our failures. We are here because the world needs us to fulfill our assignment in this place, and at this moment in time.

The words of Jesus apply here. "…and what shall I say? 'Father, save Me from this hour'? But for this purpose, I have come to this hour."[69] In other words, this moment has been waiting for him. Spiritually, I think we can say that about every moment in each of our lives. Every moment has been waiting for us to arrive and fulfill our assignment: work to do, someone to love, lessons to learn, experiences to share. As estranged parents we cannot fully recover until we begin to discover our assignment, and fulfill it as if the world is waiting on tiptoe for us to arrive.

Staying in Our Lane

It is not enough to simply give intellectual assent to these principles as theoretical concepts. We must conform our actions to their expression. As parents, our job is to provide the sacred space for our adult child to discover and fulfill their assignment. Whether they are conscious of it or not, this assignment has been given them by their Spiritual Source. We know we have crossed a line and stepped into God's lane when words like "direct, control, prevent, insist, and protect" describe our actions relative to our adult child. For example,

- We try to direct how our adult child contributes to the world, their career, their volunteer activities, their political efforts, their money, or their organizational affiliations.
- We try to control our adult child's affections, their fascinations, their romantic interests, life partners, or friends.
- We try to prevent our adult child from making mistakes, learning their own lessons, and growing in their own way. We insist on their learning our lessons.
- We try to protect our adult child from painful experiences, or risks they feel are necessary to vital living.

---

[69] John 12:27

When we attempt to interfere with our child's assignment, we are not only usurping God's role in their lives, we are taking the first step into profound suffering. If we want to have the authority to alter their assignment, we must be ready to accept the responsibility for everything that occurs downstream with all the anxiety, guilt, and regret that comes with it. The appearance of these feelings on our emotional dashboard is a signal that we have strayed out of our lane and into God's.

Assistance from the Other Side

Adopting this spiritual perspective is not easy, but we are not left alone in these efforts to release our children to their true Parent. We are given spiritual assistance. A number of years ago, I had a dream that my son, Michael, was going to die an early death. It was so vivid that I called his mother, and asked her to keep a close eye on him. Days passed, and he was fine. About fifteen years later, I was talking to my wife about a feeling I couldn't shake.

"I wonder how I'll feel if Michael dies tomorrow."

Just after noon the next day, I received a phone call. The voice on the other end of the line said,

"Mr. Avis, I'm so sorry to have to inform you that your son, Michael, has passed away."

Michael was my only unestranged child. At the biological level, Michael's life was cut short, and his death was tragic. But in my heart, I believe that Michael's assignment was completed, and our Spiritual Parent had been preparing me for this moment for years. It is how I have escaped a deep and prolonged period of depression that many parents experience upon the death of a child. Why was I given this gift? It is certainly not because I am exceptional. My particular spiritual assignment demands that I be resilient for the purposes I have been given. This moment has been waiting for me, just as it is waiting for all of us. I must stay focused on my assignment.

I pause here to acknowledge that sometimes trauma has the opposite effect; persons move away from their spiritual practice rather than deeper into it. This is because they have a misconception of God as one who should protect them from all experiences of suffering and unfairness in life. This includes unfortunate encounters with institutional religion which becomes an excuse for avoiding their own spiritual development. They do not understand themselves as spiritual beings having a human experience in a necessary stage of their spiritual evolution. They become bitter rather than better. This attitude causes great suffering for them, and must eventually give way to an awakening. However, that will only occur at a time and place that friends and loved ones cannot control.

Viewing Parental Estrangement through a Spiritual Lens

There is another aspect of our spiritual parentage to consider. When parents insist on a relationship with an adult child who has opted out, a spiritual perspective provides them with a different way of viewing the situation beyond focusing on individual contributions to the estrangement. From a spiritual perspective, parents start from the assumption that both they and their adult children are working out a purpose assigned to them before they were born. From this perspective, the experience on both sides becomes part of a sacred journey. Like every other sacred journey, it needs to be surrounded by ritual, release, guidance, and blessing.

Over the course of our PEAK study, scales were lifted, paths were explored, decisions were made, and peace was tasted, more than once.
L.W. from Rochester, NY

From a spiritual perspective, parents are challenged to focus on their own journey, working out the purpose they were assigned prior to their birth. They must discover "their people," those relationships in which they need to invest, the people they are called to love that go beyond their biological family members. They must discover what they are called to do in the world beyond being a parent, what gifts and motivations have been planted in their souls, and where those intersect with the needs of the world. They also must discover the deeper lessons they are to learn, even from the estrangement, about themselves, about the universe, and about their place in it. Finally, they must welcome the various experiences of life which expand the heart. Sometimes we are the wounded, and sometimes we do the wounding. Both can cultivate compassion.

The ability of parents to adopt a spiritual perspective on estrangement is, of course, hampered by the very human frailties inevitably discovered in the close quarters of daily living, including frailties rendered invisible to those living outside the walls of family intimacy. How can an estranged parent be assured that their ever more distant child is inspired by divine destiny and not simply following the vagaries of their own broken, self-centered thinking? The answer, of course, is that they can't.

What if They Are Making a Mistake?

What a parent can know is that there are only two possibilities.

The first possibility is that an estranged child is doing precisely what they need to do. Whatever their motive, whatever their flaws, their decision to estrange themselves is leading them along the path laid out for them before they were born. Estranged parents must have the humility to acknowledge, as with Joseph in the Old Testament, that even what others intend for evil, God can intend for good.[70] If an estranged child is doing precisely what they need to do, it is wise for parents to release them with their blessing.

The second possibility is that an estranged child is making a mistake, and that it is God's intention that the child learn from that mistake. In

---

[70] Genesis 50:20

that case, the mistake and its lessons become part of that child's spiritual curriculum, "something to learn." One thing is certain, an estranged parent cannot help with this learning process. Again, it is wise for parents to release them with their blessing.

In both cases, the spiritual path for estranged parents is the same, as is the serenity that is the fruit of letting go.

Facing Resistances

However, the journey toward a spiritual perspective on estrangement is usually a long one for parents. At first, the biological and biographical point of view holds them with such tenacity that a spiritual perspective seems as substantial as a mist rising from a lake in the moonlight. Questions about causes, faults, fairness, and ways to fix things dominate the thinking. There are intellectual obstacles and debates about the existence or goodness of God. The mind seems occupied by an implacable squatter armed with the replay of past conversations or the rehearsal of future ones.

In addition, parents will find a significant degree of resistance in their children to this spiritual understanding of the estrangement. In their children's narrative, the reasons for the estrangement are clear. Some deficit in the parent or unforgivable mistake of the past lies at the heart of the matter. They will be tempted to dismiss efforts of their estranged parents to find a spiritual perspective as rationalizing their failures. It will be important for parents to accept their children's perspective nondefensively. The picture of themselves as imperfect parents is not wrong, it is simply incomplete. Parents must be able to hold their own in this matter by maintaining a spiritual perspective on their lives even if their estranged children do not. It is impossible for an estranged parent to recover without this ability to differentiate.

Seeing in Two Ways

Research is mounting in support of Jung's observation cited at the beginning of this chapter. The science of neurobiology, armed with the tools of functional MRI's, is discovering that the human brain is hard-wired for spirituality, and the cultivation of this capacity is detectable at both the physical and the psychological level. A vital spirituality is essential for restoring our mental, emotional, and physical health from all the traumas our assignment requires of us. But, in order to access this spiritual reality, we must be able to "see" in two different ways, and give each a place in our thinking.

In the Salvador Dali painting "Lincoln in Dalivision," the artist creates an experience of two totally different images.[71] Which one appears to the human eye is determined by the observer's distance from the canvas. Viewed within a few feet, his wife Gala's figure is framed by the cruciform windows through which the viewer is led to a crucifixion. The figure of Jesus on the cross, appears in the clouds. The top of Christ's head glows representing the rising morning sun.

Move back about sixty-five feet from the painting and a different image appears, the visage of Abraham Lincoln. All the elements of the previous perception—Gala, Jesus, crucifixion, morning sun, and window looking out to the sea—disappear. For Dali, such an achievement was more than a clever, visual trick; it reflected his belief in a spiritual reality on top of the sensory reality, one difficult to perceive if we are dominated by the superficial impressions of the five senses alone.

And so, we stand, not in front of a painting by Salvador Dali, but before the scene of our own lives. We can stand three feet away, and see only the biological and biographical elements of our parental role. As estranged parents, it is easy to become convinced that there is nothing to see but failure, ours, theirs, or the collateral damage of a broken world, immersed in our pain, our anger, our guilt, our despair.

---

[71] See https://salvadordaliprints.org/lincoln-in-dalivision/

Alternatively, we can back far enough away that a new scene appears, a liberating one, one that is able to discern the outlines of greater purposes at work and an invitation to love, to work, to learn, and to experience.

Steps Toward Recovery

What does it mean to adopt the spiritual perspective of PEAK?
- Acknowledge that the recovery from parental estrangement can only be achieved with help from a Spiritual Source that many of us call God.
- Adopt the view that a Spiritual Source is the true Parent of your child.
- Engage in the discovery of your spiritual assignment, commit to carry it out as best you can discern it.
- Release your adult child to their own spiritual assignment, even if it is unconscious to them, and takes their lives in a different direction from yours.
- Recognize where you have strayed out of your lane by attempting to direct, control, prevent, insist, or protect your adult child. Seek God's forgiveness, and forgive yourself.
- Seek, recognize, and give thanks for spiritual help coming your way through dreams, insights, intuitions, synchronicities, teachers, and other spiritual guides.
- Gradually release your resistances to adopting a spiritual perspective, while holding your ground against others who resist it as well, including your adult children.

One final word about pride. We must yield up the notion that allowing our parental trauma to motivate us toward a spiritual perspective invalidates it. In my spiritual tradition, it is the brokenness of people that brought them to God for healing. No one was ever rejected for wanting to be healed. Brain research indicates that the site for depression in the brain is precisely the same location for spirituality. In other words, depression is often more a sign of spirituality malnutrition than it is an illness. In the words of researcher Lisa Miller,

> This sort of depression is a 'call of the soul,' a spiritual invitation to live more fully, love more deeply, and in open dialogue with the sacred universe…whether it occurs at a ripe life stage such as adolescence or midlife, in response to struggle or trauma—beckons into a lifetime of awakening.[72]

Questions for Reflection and Discussion

How would you describe your experiences with a religious/spiritual perspective? When have they been negative? When have they been positive? When have they been non-existent?

From a spiritual perspective, your adult child is your brother or sister. If true, how would this change the way you think of your relationship to them?

As best you can discern, what is your spiritual assignment?

    What work are you to do?

    Who are you to love?

    What lessons are you intended to learn?

    What experiences are important to your growth?

---

[72] Lisa Miller, The Awakened Brain, page 174

"This moment has been waiting for you to show up." Why does this moment need you to show up?

What attitudes or behaviors might need to change if you think of God as your adult child's true Parent with their own life assignment?

One way of seeing your adult child is as the biological and biographic product of their childhood. The other way of seeing your adult child is as a spiritual being having a human experience. How difficult is it for you to see both as true?

Is the pursuit of a spiritual awakening valid if it is an effort to find relief from trauma?

If you are using this book in a group discussion, what did you gain from hearing others speak? From speaking?

Chapter 12
The Sharing Drug

In 2015 the journal *Social Cognitive and Affective Neuroscience* published the results of a study by a team of scientists from the University of Munster. Researchers asked pairs of female friends to view a series of pictures.[73] One friend looked at the pictures within a magnetic resonance imaging (MRI) scanner while the other performed the experiment simultaneously in an adjacent room. Before each picture popped on the screen, participants were told whether or not their friend was seeing the same picture in the next room.

After viewing each picture, the participants rated how positive or negative they felt.

The participants reported feeling significantly more positive when they were told their friend was viewing the same emotional picture. This so-called "sharing effect" was true for both positive and negative pictures. This means that happy pictures made participants feel even happier when they felt they had shared that experience with a friend. And participants felt less sad seeing a sad picture when they thought their friend was viewing it too.

When researchers told participants in the scanner that their friend was viewing the same emotional picture, they saw increased activity in two parts of the brain's reward circuitry—the ventral striatum and medial orbitofrontal cortex—compared to when the participants were told their friend was not viewing the same picture. This is the same circuitry that is activated by other pleasurable experiences: a good meal, winning the lottery, or falling in love. It activates the brain's own internal pharmacy to produce chemicals similar to antidepressants and

---

[73] https://academic.oup.com/scan/article/10/6/801/1732379

anxiety-reducing drugs, but without the risk of addiction or side effects. In other words, sharing with people who have had similar experiences releases a "sharing drug" that reduces pain and enhances our sense of well-being.

The Cause is the Cure

In Chapter 3 we learned that trauma is the experience of an unexpected, deeply distressing event in which you feel alone, confused, and powerless. I wrote that if some evil genius were to come up with a plan to profoundly traumatize older adults without doing anything illegal, it would look a lot like parental estrangement. The resulting parental trauma produces symptoms similar to what we see in persons returning from combat zones. In some cases, those symptoms are largely alleviated with the passage of time, especially when the source of the trauma can be left in the past. But parental trauma is a complex trauma with recurring experiences. Again, time alone rarely heals those wounds. Healing requires an intentional recovery process.

In this part of the book, we have turned our attention to recovery. I began by observing that while the prognosis for a healthy reconciliation is not great, the prospect of recovering from trauma is extremely positive. I then wrote about the importance of a spiritual perspective in our recovery process. We are ready to take the next steps forward in our recovery process.

Great comfort is to be found in sharing with people in anguish over parent-child estrangement. After two years of being "shunned" by our daughter, I have gotten some insights and understandings.
B.F. from Huntington, IN

It sounds appealing to think that there might be a pill of some kind that will do the trick. I thought so as well. I spent a considerable amount of time with my physician going over all the chemical options for treating my insomnia, anxiety, and other trauma symptoms. I learned that many medications have no more success at helping a person recover than taking a sugar pill. Almost all have significant side effects, including an increased risk of dementia, a disease which took the life of my mother at age 90, my favorite uncle at 77, and my kid sister at 65. Certainly, the benefits of medications sometimes outweigh the risks, especially when they are used for a fixed period of time in combination with other approaches. Given the choice between taking a medication or sharing my story in a recovery group, I am going to choose the latter every time.

Sometimes estranged parents self-medicate using methods that are not helpful in the long term. Self-medications can include alcohol, prescription opiates, or street drugs. In addition to self-medications, there are problematic distractive behaviors such as gambling, compulsive spending, or excessive use of social media. Of course, the benefits of all these behaviors are short lived, and self-medication will serve to make matters worse in the long run, increasing health problems, damaging relationships, and providing a poor coping mechanism that cannot be safely sustained. Finding safe, effective ways of dealing with the pain of parental estrangement is a critical component of the recovery process.

Sometimes the cause holds the seeds of the cure. If feeling alone in an unexpected, deeply distressing event is one of the major factors in parental trauma, it makes sense that reversing those alone feelings needs to be part of our process.

We return to the sharing drug. While it was only documented in 2015 using the brain scans of modern technology, the experience of healing through open, honest conversation goes back millennia.[74] The sharing drug has been demonstrated to be effective with no side effects. It helps provide relief from the symptoms of parental trauma as persons are able to share honestly and openly with one another the

---

[74] An example from the Bible written around AD 65 says "Therefore, confess your sins to one another and pray for one another, that you may be healed." (James 5:16 ESV)

impacts of estrangement on their lives. Ideally this occurs in a small group characterized by:

- Commonality—Group members all share the common experience of parental estrangement. There are no "expert" parents in the room.
- Anonymity—The identity of parents is protected so that they can feel assured that their participation in the group will not be disclosed to the larger community, particularly family members or adult children.
- Confidentiality - Parents need to feel assured that information they share will not be disclosed beyond the group.
- Empathy—Members of the group need to listen empathetically without judgment or criticism of one another.
- Scope—The group understands its purpose as being present to one another without straying into problem-solving, giving feedback, or offering advice.
- Recovery focus—Members are working toward recovery by taking responsibility for their own decisions and behaviors.
- Resourced – The group utilizes a recovery resource(s) that can help members progress in their healing process.

Any group possessing these seven characteristics can be helpful in administering the sharing drug. One option is to start a PEAK recovery group in your community (Parents of Estranged Adult Kids). Resources can be found at www.parentsofestrangedadultkids.com.

Second on my list of pain reducers is physical exercise. Physical exercise releases the same chemicals into your brain as those that are manufactured by sharing experiences with others (the sharing drug). Engaging in even a moderate amount of physical activity has significant benefits including:

- Improved mood
- Reduced stress as well as an improved ability to cope with stress
- Improved self-esteem

- Pride in physical accomplishments
- Increased satisfaction with oneself
- Improved body image
- Increased feelings of energy
- Improved confidence in your physical abilities
- Decreased symptoms associated with depression

Third on my list: get out of the house. Sunlight helps boost the same chemical benefits in your brain as sharing and exercise, and that can give you more energy and help keep you calm, positive, and focused. Not getting enough natural sunlight has been linked to obesity, diabetes, substance abuse, depression, and other diseases. Sunlight aside, a series of experiments from the University of Rochester found spending time outside in green, natural environments can boost your vitality—a feeling of physical and mental energy—by nearly 40 percent. Spending time indoors has the opposite effect.[75] For problems that require creativity, spend some time working in a coffee shop. Research by Ravi Mehta has demonstrated a "coffee shop effect" where low levels of ambient noise helped participants be more creative in thinking outside the box.[76]

Fourth on my list: psychotherapy. In some cases, it can be valuable to augment the group experience with the services of a professional counselor. A therapist friend who has read this book has cautioned me that not every therapist is going to be qualified to deal with this issue. In selecting a counselor, it is important to choose someone who a) has experience dealing with parental estrangement, b) accepts parental trauma as a primary issue to be addressed rather than simply the result of another underlying problem, and c) recognizes that recovery is an appropriate goal when reconciliation is not possible in the short term.

---

[75] http://time.com/4306455/stress-relief-nature/?iid=sr-link4
[76] https://www.theatlantic.com/health/archive/2012/06/study-of-the-day-why-crowded-coffee-shops-fire-up-your-creativity/258742/

Finally, medications can be useful when other measures do not provide adequate relief for the pain of parental estrangement. As stated earlier, I recommend that medications be seen as a temporary solution required to provide the energy and emotional space to do the work outlined later in this book. There are exceptions that should be discussed with a qualified physician.

Inevitably there will be readers who hope to recover without taking any of these steps, particularly those that require sharing feelings and experiences with others. My goal is to help you recover from the effects of parental estrangement and rediscover a path to a productive and meaningful life. Some people may be able to do that on their own simply by reading this book and taking the steps outlined in it. Hopefully there is enough information here about parental estrangement that even a cursory reading will reduce the feelings of isolation.

There are other ways of sharing besides joining a group. A small step that may feel more possible is to find one other estranged parent, give them a copy of the book, and ask them to read it with you. Then meet occasionally to discuss your reactions. Remember, the benefits of the sharing drug kick in simply from knowing that one other person is experiencing what you are, and reading this book with them may be all that you need.

Sometimes estranged parents are hesitant to talk about their experiences with others because they feel that to do so is a betrayal of an implicit contract that members will not speak to those outside the group about problems within the family. "Don't talk, don't trust, don't feel" are the rules by which many families function.[77] However, it is important for us as estranged parents to realize that by not speaking our truth or owning our reality is the ultimate act of betrayal to yourself.[78] It is also important to realize that the purpose of sharing our experience is not to focus blame on our adult children by exposing

---

[77] Adult Children of Alcoholics, page xx
[78] Adult Children of Alcoholics, page xxiii

their faults. This simply keeps us stuck as victims. The purpose is to begin taking responsibility for our own recovery process. This purpose, along with confidentiality, should be core values for any group where sharing by estranged parents takes place.

Another obstacle to sharing with others is the feeling that we should be able to handle the impacts of parental alienation on our own, and that seeking help only deepens our sense of failure. As with many other issues in life, the healing begins when we admit we have a problem that we can no longer manage—and ask for help. As noted earlier, parental trauma is at a level of intensity equal to that of a car accident, a divorce, or being the victim of a crime, problems for which we would not hesitate to ask for professional help from doctors, lawyers, or police officers. Our hesitancy to seek out help for parental estrangement is the consequence of our own prejudices, not a testament to our strength. In a phrase attributed to psychotherapist Carl Jung, "What we resist, persists." Few things are more tragic than years of life lost to the guilt, confusion, and anguish of parental estrangement, especially when they may be the last years of one's earthly sojourn.

Parents can't function as parents forever (they will die eventually if nothing else) but sometimes the expectation of both parents and adult children is that they should. Therapist Michelle Snyder puts it this way:

> I think that one of the reasons estranged adults don't talk about it is because they haven't shifted their thinking that, developmentally, parents eventually reach an age where they shouldn't have to absorb whatever the child wants to throw at them. To the extent that parents understand that it is their role to always "take it" (like I mostly appropriately feel towards my adolescent children), they might be disinclined to talk about it since they consider it to be their role, painful as that role might be.[79]

---

[79] From a personal conversation.

Steps Toward Recovery

Forrest Gump said that life is like a box of chocolates. Here is what I would add: the world is like a medicine cabinet. There are a variety of medications that can help us recover from parental estrangement that are not in pill form. They provide us an opportunity that a medication bottle does not: the opportunity to grow. If it is possible to speak of any positive purpose of parental estrangement, it is that it opens a portal to our spiritual evolution that we would otherwise have missed. But this requires that we make a series of choices.

- We must avoid the path of least resistance. Every day, do something a little more difficult, a little less convenient, or a little scarier as a part of your recovery from parental trauma.
- We must set an intention to recover from our parental trauma, even if our adult child continues to choose estrangement. Write it down, and say it out loud: "Everyone deserves to recover from parental trauma, and I intend to be one who does."
- We must give up any loyalty to personal or family pride that becomes a betrayal of our own recovery process and keeps us isolated in our trauma.
- We must exercise faith that the steps we take will lead to improvement. We must recognize and renounce any tendency on our part to hang onto our pain as a way of avoiding responsibility for our growth.
- We must pray for opportunities to connect with other estranged parents, and be open to the serendipitous events that are the answers to those prayers.

In the movie *The Edge*, Anthony Hopkins plays the role of Charles Morse, one of three business men who are stranded when their small airplane crash lands in the Alaskan wilderness.[80] Morse, an avid reader with an extensive memory, helps the three survive by telling stories of

---

[80] Tamahori, L. (1997). *The Edge.* 20th Century Studios

how others have survived similar challenges. His mantra is "What one man can do, another can do."

I have now seen many estranged parents find a pathway to reclaiming their lives. And what one man, one woman can do, another can do.

Questions for Reflection and Discussion
Can you think of a positive experience made more positive or a sad experience made less sad because you shared it with a friend? Describe it.

What unhelpful self-medications have you found yourself trying as a way of dealing with the pain of parental trauma?

How would members in the family you grew up in react to hearing that you were talking with others about a problem in the family, like an estrangement between members? How much influence does that still hold over your life?

As you think about sharing your estrangement story, reflect on these questions:
Describe the relationship with your child prior to the estrangement.

How did the estrangement happen? When did you know that something had gone wrong?

Going back to the work in Chapter 3, what might be a succinct summary of the current effects of parental estrangement on your life?

What is the level of communication with your adult child now?

Which of the steps listed in the chapter for dealing with the pain of parental estrangement make sense for you at this point in your journey?

What obstacles do you need to overcome to take the steps you have indicated?

If you are using this book in a group discussion, what did you gain from hearing others speak? From speaking?

Chapter 13
Doing the Work

A research project led by Dr. Luc Pelletier from the Brain and Mind Research Institute of the University of Ottawa, explored this question: "What is the impact of therapy on people who are largely focused on relieving the pain of guilt, anxiety, and low self-esteem versus those who are interested in gaining a deeper understanding of themselves in order to become more confident and better people?"[81] The answer is that those who wanted more than pain relief had remarkably better outcomes from therapy. They were more likely to end up feeling more positive, more satisfied with life, with higher self-esteem, less depression, and were much more likely to persist with what they had learned. They were also more likely to feel positive about their therapist.

While recovery from parental trauma and psychotherapy are different, they hold this in common: the full potential of a human soul is not realized by simply avoiding pain. In the previous chapter, I introduced the almost magical power of the "sharing drug" to reduce the pain of parental estrangement. But there is a hidden pitfall here. Sharing the story of our pain can only take us so far. If we never move beyond the pain de jour to take other steps in our recovery process, we are cheating ourselves out of the zestful living that is the ultimate goal of PEAK for every estranged parent we encounter. We may feel better temporarily, but we may also remain somewhat depressed, dissatisfied,

---

[81] Pelletier LG, Tuson KM, Haddad NK. Client Motivation for Therapy Scale: a measure of intrinsic motivation, extrinsic motivation, and amotivation for therapy. J Pers Assess. 1997 Apr;68(2):414-35. doi: 10.1207/s15327752jpa6802_11. PMID: 9107015.

and feeling badly about ourselves. We end up stuck in the rut of our gut.

It may be helpful to keep a single question in front of ourselves: "What am I working on in my recovery process today?" If the answer is "Nothing," or "I don't know," it means one of two things: (1) we are taking a necessary rest from the recovery process for a period of time, or (2) we are stuck.

In general, recovery steps should be specific, actionable, and recovery-focused. For example, "This week I am working on getting 15 minutes of sunlight each day." While excessive sunlight can be harmful, research shows that for folks living most of their lives indoors, getting 15 minutes of sunlight each day can increase our supply of vitamin D, improve our sleep, assist in weight loss, improve our eyesight, and help keep us calm, positive, and focused. This is only one example of hundreds of different recovery steps an estranged parent might take. Just notice that it is specific, actionable, and recovery-focused.

The particular recovery steps will vary from one parent to another depending upon their trauma symptoms, type of estrangement, and stage of recovery. However, they tend to fall into broad categories such as the ones that follow this paragraph. Many of these are described at greater length in other chapters. The goal of this chapter is simply to emphasize that the recovery process is one that requires us to take small, realistic steps as we move toward the vision of leading meaningful lives filled with purpose and zest.

☐ **Reduction of isolation**

Recovery begins as we choose to move out of isolation and join others in the journey toward gentleness, humor, love, and respect. Beyond participating in a PEAK group, recovery steps can include corresponding with other estranged parents one-on-one, meeting face-to-face with another estranged parent, joining another recovery group that fits your situation like ALANON or Adult Children of Alcoholics, returning to other groups or relationships you retreated from at the beginning of the estrangement, or exploring new relationships that might be mutually beneficial.

- ☐ **Understanding parental trauma**
  Understanding parental trauma is an important component of the recovery process. Beyond reading this book, recovery steps can include reading additional print materials, viewing videos, listening to audio files, or participating in workshops. However, in an age of misinformation it is important for parents to be discerning about what they read. I recommend that a parent ask three basic questions.

  a. Is what I'm reading research-based?
  b. Does it address the trauma of parental estrangement and its impact upon the parent?
  c. Does it adopt a no-fault philosophy with regard to parental estrangement rather than placing blame on parents or adult children?

  It is important in our recovery process that we become intentional about how our learning is going to shape our thinking processes. We choose to open ourselves to new ways of thinking. We cannot continue to think in the same ways that contributed to the parental trauma in the first place. When we are taking recovery steps in this category, it is a good sign when we can say, "Here is the new way of thinking that I am working on right now."

- ☐ **Self-empowerment**
  After we gain some basic understanding of parental trauma and the need to change our thinking, we must work to focus on taking responsibility for ourselves. Since it is usually our adult child that makes the decision to cut off the relationship, it is easy to get focused on what we can't change rather than what we can change: ourselves. Self-empowerment means making conscious decisions to take charge of the direction your life is going.

Recovery steps in the category of self-empowerment are almost limitless. They include developing a positive attitude, setting goals, spending time with positive people, being assertive about what you need, changing the way you tell "the story of your life," and taking a few risks. An example of a self-empowerment recovery step would be "I am going to do something that scares me a little every day."

☐ **Pain reduction**
When we accept the responsibility for our own self-care, we are ready to make choices that will help reduce the pain. We have already addressed some of these in the previous chapter. Again, sharing your estrangement experience with others is often an effective way to reduce pain, but it is not the only one. A multi-faceted approach generally works best. This becomes even more important on occasions which we can realistically anticipate will be more painful for us such as holidays, birthdays, anniversaries, and family gatherings. For example, a parent might indicate that they are working on a schedule for Christmas Day that includes strategies of (a) connection—talking to another estranged parent for support, (b) distraction—planning to go to a movie, (c) exercise—going for a hike in a natural environment, and (d) attending religious services. This is an example of doing the work.

☐ **Grieving toward acceptance**
Given the fact that we are dealing with an ambiguous loss, we realize that we must work toward acceptance rather than closure. We choose to explore experiences of denial, anger, guilt, and depression. We allow the failure of bargaining to do its work: bring us to the conclusion that we have done all that we realistically can to restore the relationship.

"What we resist, persists," Carl Jung reminds us, and nowhere is this wisdom truer than in dealing with grief. Ignoring grief will not make it go away. Deciding to learn more about grief can be a helpful recovery step. Find a book, video, or audio on the topic that others you trust recommend to you. While most of the stages of grief are not linear, it can be helpful to focus energy on one stage rather than all of them at the same time. A helpful recovery step, for example, is to focus on guilt. Journal all the ways that the estrangement brings up guilty feelings. Don't leave anything out. Write it all. Again, this is simply an example of a recovery step that is specific, actionable, and recovery-focused. You can repeat this with any other stage of grief.

- ☐ **Rebuilding identity**

    Since so much of our lives was invested in parenting, we may have developed a blind spot in our real identity which goes much deeper. As pain begins to loosen its grip on our lives, we must choose to shore up our understanding of who we are.

    Recovery steps in this area are going to tap into our spiritual beliefs and practices, perhaps to a degree that we have never experienced. Who does God say we are? What gives us worth? What kinds of spiritual practices affirm this core identity—or not? Is our faith community giving us what we need to strengthen this identity, or do we need something more?

    "I will write a mantra or statement about who I am in the eyes of God. I will say this every morning when I begin my day, and every night before I go to sleep. After a month of engaging in this spiritual practice. I will journal how my feelings about myself have changed."

    Again, this is an example of a recovery step dealing with the issue of identity. It is specific, actionable, and recovery focused.

- ☐ **Reestablishing purpose**

    We come into this world with a spiritual assignment: work to do, lessons to learn, people to love, and experiences to share. In this stage of our recovery, we become actively engaged in discovering all those aspects of our assignment, and fulfilling them.

    It is important in this area not to become overwhelmed by the scale of it, nor by setting goals that are unrealistic. Quitting your job to look for a new one may be more than you can handle right now. Taking some steps to explore your gifts, motivations, and personality type might be more manageable. "I will take a class on the Enneagram to learn more about myself," is the kind of step that can serve many different purposes in your recovery process. It can build self-esteem, grow your self-awareness, guide you vocationally, and help you build on strengths.

Again, this is only an example. Your God-given creativity can help you identify recovery steps that are just right for you.

☐ Reaffirming the past

By definition, parental trauma affects older adults who look back on their parenting years and wonder what it all meant. The reality is that our lives were about parenting, but also much more than parenting. In this stage of our recovery we choose to do a comprehensive life review that goes far beyond our parenting role.

This is addressed in depth in a later chapter and Appendix B. The point to be made here is the importance of actually doing the work of that life review process, not simply reading through the questions. This work is also best accomplished by breaking it down into smaller, manageable tasks.

For example, one recovery step might be "This week I will journal my answers to the first five questions in the section Who and What Have You Loved. Then, I will share what I write with someone I trust."

☐ Relational audit

How might we do a better job with our relationships? How might we be better friends, neighbors, co-workers, spouses, partners, parents? In this stage we match self-awareness with self-compassion and self-forgiveness. We get honest with ourselves without getting hard on ourselves—or others.

The tendency to get overwhelmed by the relational audit is second only to the work of the previous item, Reaffirming the past.

Nonetheless, it is important to do this work and not simply skim over it as a good idea. I find it helps to start with a relationship from the past other than an estranged child. Reflect on your relationship with a parent or a good friend.

Here is an example of a recovery step: "Over the next month, I will make a list of all the ways I was a good son or daughter to my parent. Then I will make a list of ways I could have been better. I will do this all with an attitude of self-compassion. If I feel it will be helpful, I will share it with a trusted friend, professional, or leader in my faith community."

- ☐ **Securing the future**

    Now we are ready to look to our future. We choose to be realistic and fiercely self-protective. We engage whatever professional resources are necessary to deal with legal, financial, and care issues.

    This is another large, but essential part of our recovery work. Again, it is important to chunk it down. A good first step might be interviewing others to develop a list of names of those professional resources they would recommend. Other recovery steps would follow until these items are fully addressed.

- ☐ **Serving the world**

    Part of our recovery requires that we use our new-found vitality to serve others. We take special note of opportunities to educate folks about parental estrangement, and reach out to other estranged parents.

    Estranged parents who have been in recovery for a while may fail to realize how much they have grown—and how valuable they could be to others dealing with the issue of parental estrangement. Again, start small. An example would be "In the next month, I will write an article for my faith community, local newspaper, or service organization."

    There are approximately five million estranged parent/adult child relationships in the United States. That means there are at least five million ways to serve other estranged parents. All it takes is imagination, motivation, and a concrete action step.

The above list is intended to be neither exhaustive nor exhausting. There are many possible concrete steps that can contribute to recovery. These only become exhausting when they are tackled on a scale that is unrealistic. In general, you should avoid changing more than one area of your life at a time. Pick one recovery step to focus on. No one who succeeds at running a marathon starts by running 26.2 miles the first day. It is impossible for most of us to tackle a 300-pound linebacker. But all of us could tackle six 50 pounders one at a time.

You Can Fight for Your Life

Parental estrangement is a serious, life-eroding, potentially life-shortening trauma. I have a good friend who was diagnosed with stage 3 ovarian cancer six months ago. She has made no secret of the fact that she intends to recover and live another ten to fifteen years. She has not only done her chemo. She has made a dozen other changes to her life to not only increase her chances of survival, but to make every day count.

I do not believe it is an exaggeration to say that the experience of parental estrangement is in the same league as a cancer diagnosis. In fact, the kind of chronic stress that is generated by parental trauma has been linked to cancer, diabetes, heart disease, and a host of other medical problems. What makes parental estrangement especially threatening is that it happens at a time of life when other losses are beginning to accumulate, job loss through retirement, relocation, and the deaths of parents, siblings, and friends. In addition, the onset of estrangement occurs at the very life stage where health is beginning to decline.

As an estranged parent, you may find this so overwhelming that you feel tempted to simply give up. I plead with you to hear a different message: YOU ARE WORTH SAVING. YOU CAN FIGHT FOR YOUR LIFE.

To fight for your life, you must know that it is a fight. A PEAK parent just sent me a book with a quote from the *The Lord of the Ring: The Two Towers*.

Theoden: I will not risk open war.

Aragorn: Open war is upon you, whether you would risk it or not.

This is not a battle you thought you would ever have to fight, nor one you sought. But by lot or by destiny, it has come to you, and you must exert yourself in ways never required of you before.

You must also know that you are not fighting your adult children. Instead, you are fighting the temptation to believe you are defective, your past is meaningless, and your future is unsalvageable.

You must realize *what* you are fighting for. You are fighting for your own recovery from the emotional, physical, spiritual, relational, and (sometimes) financial impacts of parental estrangement, even if reconciliation from your adult children is significantly delayed.

You must understand that you will not win this battle alone. You are going to need a team, a team that you will have to assemble. For many of us that team will include the support of other estranged parents, a therapist with experience in helping estranged parents, professionals such as massage therapists, yoga instructors, or acupuncturists who can help discharge stress from our bodies, spiritual companions who can send us positive energy through meditation and prayer, and our friends in the natural world: forests, lakes, flowers, and creatures of every description. (Research has shown that spending time in nature is healing.)

You must be open to the unseen forces that are waiting to help you. By whatever other name you call them, God, Spirit, Angels, Ancestors will come to your aid if you ask for help and are willing to fit into the plan that heaven has for your life.

Go ahead and release those suppressed emotions. Be hurt, angry, even outraged. But don't direct it at your children. Let the energy of those emotions propel you in the direction of your own recovery.

My best friend was killed in Vietnam in 1970. At his funeral, I vowed that I would live the life that he never got to live. Over the years, that has sometimes required that I fight for my life, just as he fought for my way of life, along with thousands of others.

You can fight for your life.

Steps Toward Recovery

Near the end of other chapters, I suggest practical steps for recovery. Since this chapter was focused on multiple areas with examples in each area, I will not list more here.

Instead, I would suggest that you think of another time in your life when you had to recover from a significant injury, illness, surgery, loss, or life set-back. Then, do some journaling in response to these or other similar questions. What was the challenge? What steps did you have to take to recover? How did you feel during the recovery process? How long did it take?

Now give yourself a pat on the back. The best predictor of future behavior is past behavior. If you succeeded before, you can do it again.

Questions for Reflection and Discussion

To what extent are you seeking to relieve the pain of parental estrangement versus exploring how to become a person with purpose and zest for living? (Hint: there is no wrong answer.)

If your Fairy Godmother could wave a magic wand, and all the pain of parental estrangement were to go away, what would you do next?

What are you working on today in your recovery process? If the answer is "nothing," is that because (a) you don't know what to do, (b) you know what to do but are not ready to do it, or (3) you need a rest from working on your recovery?

Of the bolded categories in this chapter with a checkbox,

    a. Which ones can you check off as "already worked on"?

    b. Which ones do you feel most motivated to work on next?

    c. Which ones aren't that important to you right now?

Respond to this statement: "I have received everything I need from sharing my struggles with others who understand. I don't need to do anything else."

If you are using this book in a group discussion, what did you gain from hearing others speak? From speaking?

PEAK: Parents of Estranged Adult Kids
A Resource for Recovery

Chapter 14
A No-Fault/No-Cause Perspective on Recovery

In their efforts to recover, estranged parents must swim upstream against a cultural narrative that goes something like this: A parent, rendered dysfunctional by their mental illness, personality disorder, addiction, abuse, issues from their own childhood, or sheer self-centeredness, creates an environment that becomes increasingly intolerable for the adult child. In an effort to save the relationship, the adult child attempts to talk with the parent many times. It never goes well. The parent makes excuses, challenges the facts presented, or offers non-apology apologies. Having exhausted every possibility for a healthy relationship, the adult child decides it is hopeless. The only option for the healthy adult child is to disengage, because it's too emotionally dangerous otherwise. The estranged parent acts shocked and bewildered by what has happened, but is simply refusing to acknowledge the fundamental reality of the situation. They have hurt their adult child in many different ways, created a toxic environment, refused to take responsibility for it, and estrangement is the only choice the adult child has left.

In doing the research for my writing on this subject, I have read scores of articles found in journals and major media outlets. The narrative in the first paragraph is a composite of scenarios I constructed from six of them. While they attempt a tone of objectivity in addressing this growing problem in society, the stories they choose as examples clearly and consistently lay the blame for estrangement at the feet of the parent. Even if they attempt to strike a positive tone with a story of reconciliation, it is typically one where the parent has gained insight into their errant behavior and mended their ways.

Whether estranged parents are conscious of it or not, this narrative is pervasive. It is not difficult to imagine its psychic undertow, and isolating force exerted on a parent trying to recover from parental trauma. In a PEAK recovery group, we acknowledge this impact every week when we read to one another from the list of "Our Common Experiences . . . We are isolated from other estranged parents who might serve as sources of insight, support, and guidance. We feel alone."

Do Parents Deserve to Be Estranged?

It is this cultural narrative that leads people to occasionally ask me, "How do you know that the estranged parents with whom you work don't deserve to be estranged by their adult children?" It always startles me a bit. It feels similar to questions like, "How do you know hungry people don't deserve to be hungry?" or "How do you know sick people don't deserve to be sick?" Nonetheless, my response is always the same. It is not for me to judge whether a parent deserves to be estranged. Here is what I do know: Every parent deserves to recover from the traumatic effects of being cut off from the relationship with their adult child. Period.

> *PEAK reached out to me, a complete stranger. I think this is the first time I was able to say anything like this without the fear of being judged as a bad mother.*
> *G.G. from Tulsa, OK*

The impacts of parental trauma are well known to those who have experienced it: depression, anxiety, guilt, despair, insomnia, headaches, GI disturbances, arrythmias, legal issues, and financial issues are a few, not to mention the collateral damage to relationships with spouses, siblings, and friends. Entire books could be written on these impacts. For now, suffice it to say that I am resolute on this point: no parent should be consigned to these maladies as a life sentence, whatever their real or perceived failures. In a car accident we don't wait to assess fault before treating a driver for serious injuries. Neither should we delay treating an estranged parent's trauma symptoms until we discover whether they are worthy of recovery. Everyone deserves to recover.

A No-Fault Perspective

This is the basis of what I call a "no-fault perspective" on parental trauma. In PEAK, we do not waste energy assigning blame for the estrangement. There are a number of reasons for this perspective. As already mentioned, parental trauma is not only mentally, emotionally, physically, and relationally devastating, the risk of suicide and increased mortality makes it potentially lethal. No parenting failure should be treated as a capital offense.

In addition, we don't know enough to sort out the real reasons for any particular estrangement to assign blame. In the same family, estrangement in one adult child leaves the relationship between a sibling and their parent intact. Factors that lead to estrangement in one family, seem to strengthen the parental bond in another. And the tendency of third parties like romantic partners, ex-spouses, friends, and even therapists to exacerbate or ameliorate potential estrangement issues is a total wildcard.

I am convinced of what the creators of no-fault divorce and no-fault auto insurance discovered decades ago: the additional damage caused by the process of establishing blame simply compounds the suffering. People feel pressure to distort the truth. Friends and family members are drawn into an otherwise private matter which expands the radius of the damage. Fear of judgement discourages people from growing in self-awareness, and the possibility of real reconciliation. But beyond all that, establishing fault as a prerequisite for compassion and healing violates our deepest spiritual values.

In the healing aspect of my particular spiritual tradition, Jesus never interviewed anyone to establish fault or blame before healing them.

Great crowds came to him, bringing with them the lame, the blind, the impaired, the mute, and many others, and they put them at his feet, and he healed them. I have come to believe that in those great crowds who were healed, there had to be those who swore a blue streak, lost their tempers, lied to get out of trouble, cheated on their spouses, and were jealous of what others possessed. Jesus never asked about these things. He just healed them.

The Spin Cycle of Blame and Shame

But the most important reason for a no-fault perspective on estrangement is not changing how other people think of us. It is how we think of ourselves. For estranged parents, the need to establish fault can be one of the biggest obstacles to our recovery process. My friend and colleague, Dr. Keli Rugenstein, is also an expert on parental estrangement. One of her many insights is this: "Parents tend to bounce back and forth between total guilt and total blame. One moment, they can lay the total blame on their estranged child, with all the frustration, helplessness, and even fury that accompanies it. The next moment, they can take on the entire responsibility as they remember some of their failings, with all the guilt, regret, and shame that comes with that."

Spinning is deceptive. It appears to be motion, but it doesn't take you anywhere. This spin cycle of blame and shame does nothing to advance our healing. Going back to our analogy of a car accident, it is like the victim of a head-on collision refusing to go to the hospital until a ruling is made by an officer establishing fault. Her broken bones are unset. Her lacerations are unstitched. Her bleeding is unstaunched. She may be dying, but finding fault, hers or another, is where her focus lies. She demands a verdict!

Ruminating on blame and shame is a dead-end. It distracts us from the one thing estranged parents need to do to survive: focus on our recovery. As we have seen, that focus will require that we take any number of actions: educate ourselves about trauma, join a PEAK recovery group, get more exercise, eat more nutritious food, write, meditate, pray, increase our time outside, do yoga or tai chi, spend time in nature, get a pet, spend time with someone else's pet, listen to music, find a skilled therapist, start a gratitude journal, read a daily devotional, breathe. I mention these again here only to draw a contrast between the focus of a recovery process, and the mental spin cycle of blame and shame.

In addition to a no-fault perspective, we also need a no-cause perspective. Similar to a focus on fault, we can become focused on the various possible causes of the estrangement, theorizing one possible cause after another, with little real information. Maybe our adult child is depressed. Maybe on the spectrum. Maybe they met someone. Maybe they're just busy. Maybe it's because they were adopted. Maybe it was the incident in high school. There is a time and place for reflecting on causes, but when it becomes the sole focus of our process, we are likely using it as a distraction from what we really need to be paying attention to: recovering from the trauma of our estrangement. Focusing on why is an alibi; it is an excuse to stay stuck.

I want to finish this chapter by making a simple point that seems to be missed in much of the writing in journals about parental estrangement, including the cultural narrative I led with. Adult children are human beings, and as human beings, suffer from the same vagaries of the human condition as their flawed parents. I point this out because the impression that we are often given is that adult children are the healthy, open, flexible, communicative ones trying to make headway with flawed, controlling, self-centered, tone-deaf, and headstrong aging parents. Such a view draws on some of the worst stereotypes of older adults, that they are stubborn, grumpy, useless, and isolated. It is a subtle form of ageism that is unhelpful at best, damaging at worst.[82]

---

[82] https://us.sagepub.com/sites/default/files/upm-assets/90251_book_item_90251.pdf

Our Shared Human Condition

At the risk of putting too fine a point on it, I have created the table *In a Typical Group of People* that follows. It is populated from lifespan data collected from a number of sources.

In a Typical Group of People

Parents over the course of a lifetime	Their children over the course of a lifetime
Will change jobs 12 times[83]	Will change jobs 12 times
Will move 11 times[84]	Will move 11 times
50% will end up divorced[85]	50% will end up divorced
50% will experience a mental illness[86]	50% will experience a mental illness
46% will have an affair[87]	46% will have an affair
33% will have a criminal record[88]	33% will have a criminal record
21% will have a drug addiction[89]	21% will have a drug addiction
5% will spend time in prison[90]	5% will spend time in prison

---

[83] https://www.zippia.com/advice/average-number-jobs-in-lifetime/
[84] https://fivethirtyeight.com/features/how-many-times-the-average-person-moves/
[85] https://www.psychologytoday.com/us/blog/living-single/201702/what-is-the-divorce-rate-really
[86] https://www.cdc.gov/mentalhealth/learn/
[87] https://psychcentral.com/blog/how-common-is-cheating-infidelity-really#statistics
[88] https://www.brennancenter.org/our-work/analysis-opinion/just-facts-many-americans-have-criminal-records-college-diplomas
[89] https://ontario.cmha.ca/addiction-and-substance-use-and-addiction/
[90] https://bjs.ojp.gov/content/pub/pdf/Llgsfp.pdf

Careful readers will recognize that I have cheated a bit in constructing this table. While older adults have lived the majority of their years, our adult children, mostly in their 30's and 40's, have not. It is impossible to provide accurate lifespan data for them, but do we really believe they are going to be that different?

However, unless we expect to see an unprecedented moral/ethical/spiritual miracle that radically purifies the behavior of coming generations, these will likely continue with small increases in some, small decreases in others. My point is simply this. While it may take the greater part of our lifetimes to emerge, all of us, parents and adult children alike, are flawed human beings, and in very similar ways. Parents can be controlling, self-focused, stubborn, and short-tempered. Adult children can be controlling, self-focused, stubborn, and short-tempered. We may be more bound together by our common human frailties than we are by our soaring aspirations.

On Listening

Let's take the issue of listening, a common complaint. There is no evidence that a 35-year-old-child is any better at listening than a 65-year-old parent. In fact, research shows that listening comprehension is essentially flat from age twenty to just over seventy.[91] However, emotional filters begin to kick in for both parents and adult children when we are agitated by what we are hearing. We begin to turn down the volume on our listening until we are practically deaf. A fault-based approach to the listening issue spends its energy in the spin cycle of blame and shame. A no-fault approach recognizes a shared deficit. None of us is as good a listener as we think we are.

An article from the *Harvard Business Review*, not particularly known for its focus on the family, is clear on this point: we don't know how to listen. "It can be stated, with practically no qualification, that people

---

[91] https://www.ncbi.nlm.nih.gov/pmc/articles/PMC4610268/

in general do not know how to listen. They have ears that hear very well, but seldom have they acquired the necessary aural skills which would allow those ears to be used effectively for what is called listening."[92]

If we as estranged parents can step back and think about this from a no-fault perspective, we might reflect on how poorly our educational system has prepared us to listen, particularly when compared with reading, writing, and speaking. Our curricula prioritized reading and writing. Most of us may have made an oral presentation or two. A few had a speech class. Almost none of us, outside of a clinical specialty, had any training that taught us how to listen. And yet, all the research on successful relationships reverses this order. Listening is at the top of the list, followed by speaking, then writing, and last of all, reading.

In my experience, it takes about ten hours to teach someone the critical elements of listening. I recommend this basic training for every estranged parent, not because it will necessarily fix the relationship with our adult child, but because it will aid our recovery from parental trauma. It will help us become better family members, friends, neighbors, employees, leaders, and spiritual companions. In addition, it will help us as we support other estranged parents.

In PEAK, we adopt a no-fault approach to our support for one another. Among other things, this means listening without judgement. We reinforce this perspective every week when we read this to one another: "We find that listening to one another is healing. As estranged parents, very few people have ever listened to us. We are so accustomed to protecting our family's reputation from the judgement of others, the invitation to care for ourselves feels new and liberating. We allow others to experience intense emotions without well-intentioned efforts to calm them down or take them out of their feelings."

---

[92] https://hbr.org/1957/09/listening-to-people

Steps to Recovery

What does movement from a fault-based/cause-based to a no-fault/no-cause perspective on your recovery from parental trauma look like? Here are some ways you know you are making progress:

- You are able to adopt a detached attitude toward individuals or groups who assign blame to parents or adult children as a group. This includes those who focus on alleged deficiencies in either group. Among other healthy responses is the ability to spot authors who engage in these kinds of fault-based perspectives out of their own emotional needs, and laugh!
- If you are unable to detach, and you find yourself emotionally agitated by the fault-based perspectives of individuals or groups, you are able to establish a boundary for yourself, and stop reading or listening to them.
- You become aware of your own spin cycle of shame and blame. When you are ruminating on (a) the flaws in your children, or (b) the flaws in yourself, you replace those thoughts with a compassionate mantra, meditation, or prayer.
- When you feel overwhelmed with guilt, you remind yourself that your adult child is also flawed, and will likely exhibit those same flaws in a different way, to a different degree, and at a different stage of life. You make the decision to have compassion on both them and yourself.
- When you find your thoughts are racing around various causes of the estrangement, you are able to say to yourself, "Asking why is an alibi." You can then return to a question about yourself: "How am I feeling?"
- When listening to another estranged parent, you are able to resist the temptation of judging them or giving advice.

None of this is meant to imply that a process of self-examination is not also critical to recovery. However, the purpose of that self-examination is never to establish blame for the estrangement, but to evolve spiritually into a better person. You have the rest of your life ahead of you, and you want to be prepared for the best life possible. If your child decides that reconciliation has become an option for them, you will be better prepared for that process as well. I will address this in Chapter 26: A Fearless Relational Audit.

Questions for Reflection and Discussion
How have you experienced the cultural narrative described at the beginning of this chapter that essentially views all parental estrangement as the parent's fault? How has this affected you?

Do you think you deserve to be estranged by your children? Why or why not?

If parental trauma is like a car accident, what are some of the ways you have been injured?

Do you deserve to recover from parental trauma?

Tell about a time you experienced the spin cycle of blame and shame? How often does this happen?

A no-fault, no-cause perspective leaves you with the question "How am I feeling?" How are you feeling right now?

What flaws do you believe you and your adult child may have in common?

What will be the hardest part for you to adopt a no-fault/no cause perspective?

If you are using this book in a group discussion, what did you gain from hearing others speak? From speaking?

PEAK: Parents of Estranged Adult Kids
A Resource for Recovery

Chapter 15
Powerlessness

We begin as parents with an infant in our arms, often by birth, sometimes through adoption. The child is powerless; by comparison, we are omnipotent. A child has absolutely no power to compel the parent to care for him or her. The child's entire survival is dependent upon their ability to hold the attention of the parent through the shape of their face, an evolutionary strategy that developed over millions of years.

Baby faces on animals such as puppies and kittens have a similar power over human behavior. When my brother retired; he and his wife bought an RV and planned to travel extensively. After the death of their last dog, they decided not to get another one. That all changed when his wife saw a photo of a puppy on her smartphone. When my brother reminded her of their decision not to get another dog and all the reasons they had discussed, she responded with, "But, she is SO cute." Needless to say, they are now the proud, sleep-deprived owners of a golden retriever puppy. The power of a babyface!

With time the child matures and develops the capacity to act with increasing independence. The parent's power is gradually diminished. In the case of an estranged parent, the tables have totally reversed. The parent is now powerless; the adult child holds all the cards. There is one key difference: there is no built-in evolutionary mechanism that makes the older adult attractive. No one looks at a photo of the typical old person and says, "I need to get me one of those." Once children are raised to self-sufficiency, no biological imperative to care for aging parents kicks in. It is for this reason that one of the Ten Commandments addresses the honoring of parents, but none of them is required to command the care of children. Cultural and religious standards must replace biological instincts.

In addition, a baby comes into the world with a clean slate. A parent on the other hand comes with a human track record of successes and failures, and reasons can always be found for alienation. Put bluntly, the human race will go extinct if it abandons its infants shortly after birth. But the race will survive no matter how adult children treat its aging, and relatively powerless, estranged parents. From an evolutionary standpoint, parental estrangement joins the list of other late-stage ailments like cancer, heart disease, and dementia. Evolution does not protect us from any of these because they occur past the age of reproduction.

Estranged parents understandably resist the notion that they are powerless. After all, they are full-fledged adults emerging from what is likely the most productive years of their lives. They possess a lifetime of skills they have developed to effectively address a range of problems. Surely there must be something they can say or do. There must be something they haven't thought of yet or some different way of saying it that will unlock the relationship. Since it happens in novels and movies, they think, why not in my life?

Estranged parents may be some of the most accomplished and powerful people in the world, but they are powerless when it comes to changing the heart and mind of the adult child who has cut off the relationship with them. There are three reasons for this powerlessness: the mystery of estrangement, a lack of control, and the finite parent.

Powerlessness and the Mystery of Estrangement

First, parents are powerless relative to the actual cause of the estrangement.

At the beginning of our recovery, we may approach the suffering of our estrangement by trying to understand its causes. We hope that by doing so we may discover the means by which we could gain some degree of control. By understanding what went wrong, we might find a way of reversing the error. Alternatively, we might discover that the causes of the estrangement have nothing to do with us, which at least might help alleviate our sense of guilt and feelings of failure. In either case, we feel that we have some degree of control over the situation by understanding what has caused it.

In truth, the actual causes of estrangement are almost impossible to discern. The following true stories illustrate what I mean. (Details have been changed to protect anonymity.)

A tale of two parents. As we listen to adult children describe their relationship with their parents, we are struck by how different they are. A sixty-year-old man who as a young child was physically and emotionally abused by his alcoholic father might appear to have good reason to cut off the relationship. Instead, he pursues the relationship with his father and works to maintain it. He speaks of his father's parenting as developing an inner mental toughness that has served him well in a variety of leadership roles ranging from the military to public service. Far from resulting in estrangement, he views his now deceased father with admiration and gratitude.

Contrast that account with this one. A single mother raises her only daughter alone. In addition to meeting her daughter's basic needs of food, shelter, clothing, and medical care, she regularly attends all school functions, invests in music lessons, and takes her on educational trips in the summers. She pays for her to attend an expensive private school. Upon graduation, her daughter goes to work at a hospital in her hometown where she meets a young man who practices a rather esoteric spirituality. Included in his beliefs is the necessity of breaking contact with one's biological parents. She falls under the spell of his beliefs. She not only stops seeing her mother, she stops returning phone calls or responding to letters begging her to get in touch. Nothing the mother can do or say changes things. Thirty years later, nothing has changed.

Here we have two different parents, one with clear and unmistakable deficiencies, another looking like a parenting instructor at the local YMCA. The first ends up with a close relationship with his son. The second goes through years of agonizing estrangement from her daughter. She consults her pastor, the pastor talks to the daughter, nothing changes.

Parents of every type of virtue and deficit. Between these two poles are parents possessed of every virtue and deficit: the soccer coaches and the addicted, the celebrity musicians and the poker players, the golden anniversary celebrants and the divorced, the cheaters and the betrayed, the PTA presidents and the military moms on assignment, the fathers who cared for three generations of their heirs and those who took off before their children were born. If you were to place all these different parents in a room and guess which ones were estranged from their adult children, you would probably be wrong 25 percent of the time.

This is the mystery of estrangement. Parents who you might expect would be candidates for estrangement have regular and significant contact with their children. Parents who have conformed as much as humanly possible to a parenting ideal haven't seen their adult child for years. To deepen the mystery, they often don't know why. When estranged parents are asked if they know why their adult child has cut off the relationship with them, 60 percent say they do not know the reason. The mystery is further complicated by the fact that of three adult children, all raised the same way, one may be estranged and the other two have a close relationship with both parents.

> My daughter is an adult 42-year-old. We have had problems since I divorced and remarried. We are now estranged. I have 2 boys who are very loving, thank God.
> W.R. from Aspen, CO

Adult children have issues in their lives that they trace back to us as parents, which may or may not be our responsibility. In his book *The Soul's Code,* James Hillman tells the story of twins separated from birth, both of whom grow to be obsessive compulsive nearly to the point of pathology. When the first was asked why, he blamed it on his mother who was also extremely compulsive, demanding that everything be in its place. When the second was asked why, he also blamed it on his mother whom he described as a slob; he saw his compulsive behavior as a reaction against her.[93] The problems in our adult children's lives may have little to do with us directly and may be more a matter of their genetic makeup than how we raised them.

Readers may wonder why I have not spent more time in this book listing all the causes for estrangement and possible ways of dealing with each of them. There are some books and resources that take that approach. I believe these can be useful for helping estranged parents feel more understood in their particular situation. On the other hand, I am not convinced that these are helpful in establishing a course of action.

Pick a number between one and one hundred. There are that many potential reasons for estrangement. They range from relatively benign issues like "just grew apart" or "personality differences" to actual criminal behavior like child abuse. In all but the most extreme and toxic parental behaviors, we will find children who embrace their parents and children who reject them.

The inability to establish a "cause" for parental estrangement is part of the powerlessness we have to accept. This enables us to stop hunting for the ultimate cause of the estrangement, which can become a distraction from what we really need to be doing—discovering what changes we need to be making in order to live a vital and purposeful life.

Powerlessness from Lack of Control

Understanding that the causes of estrangement are elusive is important, but the most significant source of our powerlessness is that

---

[93] James Hillman, *The Soul's Code* (New York: Grand Central Publishing, 1997), 67.

we cannot control another human being's behavior, particularly when it is deeply entrenched.

A number of years ago, my therapist coach had me stand beside her and lean into her.

"Lean harder," she said. I pushed; she pushed back to keep her balance.

The lesson: when you push against resistance, you create more of it. Pleading, cajoling, imploring, begging, criticizing, coaxing, flattering, berating, punishing, buying, and arguing are all attempts at controlling an adult child to return to a relationship. In spite of the advice of many counselors to keep trying, these generally don't work, and often make things worse. They simply create more resistance. Groups like Al-Anon have been pointing out for decades that families trying to control the behavior of a loved one who is addicted simply begin to take on characteristics of the addicted. Similarly, parents who try to control the behavior of an estranged adult child begin to exhibit characteristics that lead to or aggravate estrangement.

This begins to change when estranged parents begin to take responsibility for their own lives. It is important here to distinguish between taking responsibility for your own life and blaming yourself for the estrangement. Simply blaming yourself for the estrangement is unhelpful and may even be retraumatizing. Taking responsibility for your own life means that you are determined to recover and thrive regardless what your adult child does. You are done with excuses. You are powerless with regard to them, but you are not powerless when it comes to your own recovery.

Powerlessness and the Finite Parent

The final aspect of powerlessness relates to your own limited resources. Parents cannot provide an infinite supply of financial, physical, or emotional resources to meet the bottomless needs of anyone, including their adult children. This sounds patently obvious in principle but here is what it means in practice:

- Parents have a right to plan for their own reasonable financial security that will sustain them until their deaths. Divorced parents have a right to do the same.
- Parents should not be expected to deplete their financial reserves to meet the needs of their adult children, particularly if there is no assurance how or when those reserves will be replenished.
- Parents have a right to make decisions about their activities and physical environment that contribute to a lifestyle that is vital and sustainable.
- Parents should not be expected to live in an environment or engage in activities that put them at significant risk for debilitating injuries or medical problems.
- Parents have a right to make decisions for their lives that enhance their emotional well-being.

Emotionally, parents are permitted to have a reasonable expectation that their children will begin to move into a relationship of mutuality with their adult children. This means that the normal emotional needs of parents will be acknowledged including:

- The need for understanding the feelings generated by everyday living and the aging process in general.
- The need for forgiveness of flaws and failures.
- The need for acknowledgement of contributions to their children's lives.

The rights of parents will be more fully addressed in Chapter 22.

Sometimes the expectations adult children make of parents exceed their capacity to meet them. When that happens, parents become depleted. There is not enough money to meet their adult children's expectations and secure their future. They may end up having to choose between eating and buying medication. Parents may be expected to take on responsibilities that are physically too much for them or to live in geographical locations that are physically or emotionally detrimental. Adult children may expect that their parents continue to function as inexhaustible supplies of emotional care with infinite reservoirs of patience, understanding, and compassion, while withholding patience, understanding, and compassion from their parents.

In addition to the often catastrophic financial, physical, and medical impacts of this depletion are the devastating emotional consequences: loss of self-esteem, fear of self-expression and the resultant drag on creativity, chronic guilt feelings, depression, and even suicidal thoughts. While an estranged parent may feel that they have more to give and should be able to give in order to restore the relationship with their adult child, they simply can't without doing significant damage to themselves. It is like driving a car without ever looking at your gas gauge. When you are out of gas, everything stops.

Running on empty is simply another way of saying that you are powerless.

Estranged parents can only recover if they face their powerlessness. They may never understand the real, underlying causes of the estrangement, which are often multiple and complex. According to family systems theory, some of those causes may lie decades before in the patterned behavior of previous generations. Even if those causes became known through some rare ability to discern them at their root, parents can't resolve those issues on their own; no one has the ability to change another person. Estranged parents often envision some heroic effort on their part will save the relationship. The sad but important truth is that an estranged parent can exhaust their financial, physical, and emotional resources and still not achieve the relationship they long for.

Here is the potential contradiction in what I am saying. You can't change your estranged children. I can't change you, the reader, either. All that I have written in this chapter can support your decision to accept your powerlessness, but it will never convince you that you need to. In my experience, estranged parents have to go through a period of failed bargaining to get to that point. In fact, the purpose of the bargaining phase is to bring you to accept your own powerlessness. In the meantime, you may face another struggle: a sense of unfairness.

Estrangement and Unfairness

It is typical for estranged parents to look at other, equally flawed, non-estranged parents and feel a deep sense of unfairness. This unfairness can spill over into jealousy, resentment, anger, and self-pity. But the greatest problem is this: a focus on unfairness keeps us stuck and unable to progress in our recovery. An attitude of unfairness can drive out all the energy required for the positive steps we will need to take to begin to thrive.

Even after we initially let go of our attitude of unfairness, it can recur in our recovery process, especially at the stage of doing our fearless relational audit or making amends. We may harbor a deep-seated belief that our owning up to our mistakes should be matched by forgiveness from our adult children or even a similar confession on their part. When this does not happen, we succumb again to an attitude of unfairness.

Recovery requires that our attitude of unfairness gradually give way to acceptance. Even after we acknowledge our failures in the estranged relationship, we still may not understand all the reasons for it. We have to shift our thinking from "Why did this happen to me?" to "How can I grow through this experience to become a better person?"

If what we resist, persists, then continuing to resist the reality of our estrangement will simply produce more of the same in other places. If we focus on the unfairness of our estrangement and fight against it, we will begin to see unfairness in every aspect of our lives. When we begin to accept estrangement for what it is—a mystery that we can only partially explain, a choice by adult children who we cannot change, a problem that can totally deplete us and leave the situation no better—only then can we turn our attention to our own recovery.

Claiming Our Powerfulness

A good summary statement of this chapter might be that we must come to realize that we are powerless over parental estrangement. When we refuse to accept our powerlessness over anything we can't control, our lives become unmanageable. Why? Because we have invested so much time and energy trying to move the immovable stone, that there is not enough left for other important aspects of life.

A person who spends all their money trying to win the unwinnable lottery will likely end up penniless, homeless, and starving. Parents who invest all their mental and emotional energy focused on their estrangement will often end up damaging their health, their relationships, and their spiritual life. And all for something over which they have absolutely zero control. It's like taking their money and burning it, their energy and discharging it, their time and Rip van Winkling it. In an adaption of the words of Neil Young, "just like children sleepin', we could dream this life away." (Young, N. 1992).

Hidden in the sentiment that we have come to realize that we are powerless over parental estrangement is just how powerful we can actually be if we shift our focus. We must claim our powerfulness. If all the energy wasted on changing the unchangeable is redirected toward realizing the possible, the results can be stunning. A woman, estranged from three daughters, always wanted to live on a beach in California. She finally moves there from New England. Another, estranged from her son, always wanted to take a year and travel across Europe. She finally claims her powerfulness, and books the flight.

Whether we are claiming our own powerfulness, or the powerfulness of our Spiritual Source, both require refocusing away from what we cannot control, and toward the infinite potential of what is possible in the realm of our Spiritual Source.

Steps Toward Recovery

What steps does this chapter suggest are important for our recovery?
- Accept that we are powerless over the choice our adult child has made to cut off or seriously curtail their relationship with us. Yes, powerless.
- Conduct an inventory of how much time, mental and emotional energy, and money we are investing into trying to control something we cannot control.
- Engage our creative imagination. If our energies were redirected toward other possibilities in our lives, imagine what those might be.
- Pain can be seen as a deficit of Divine love, peace, and faith. Take some time to brainstorm how you can get more of those Divine energy sources into your life.

Questions for Reflection and Discussion

What makes it difficult for you as an estranged parent to accept your own powerlessness?

What do you think is the difference between powerlessness and hopelessness?

What difficult emotions are associated with your powerlessness (such as fear, weakness, sadness, failure, or anger)?

What positive emotions are associated with your powerlessness (such as relief, freedom, trust, or resolution)?

Where are you on this emotional scale with regard to powerlessness?

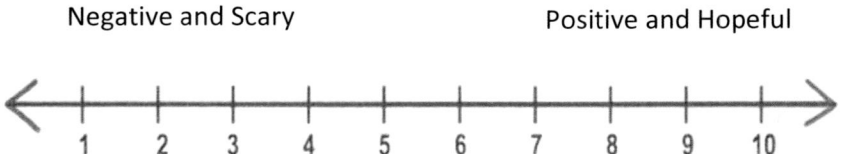

Chapter 16
Our Spiritual Source

In the last chapter, I looked at three aspects of powerlessness in the life of an estranged parent: the mystery of estrangement, a lack of control, and the finite parent. There is a fourth: the powerlessness of a parent to deal with all the impacts of estrangement on their own, and the powerfulness of God.

Our attempts to change the unchangeable is often a response to a bottomless pain. The solution to a bottomless pain is an infinite love, and nothing less. If there is not enough love God will provide it, if there is not enough peace God will give it, if there is not enough faith God will distribute it.

As we have seen, the impacts of parental estrangement can be profound. Sleeplessness saps energy. Confusion paralyzes decision-making. Self-doubt erodes confidence. Sadness overwhelms any sense of joy or purpose. Guilt and shame undermine the self-worth required to exercise, eat well, and take other measures of self-care. Physical symptoms such as headaches, stomach problems, or body aches become excuses to avoid important activities or relationships. At their most severe, estranged parents can feel like they are going crazy or losing control of their lives.

That's because they are. I have observed parents who are gifted, competent, and accomplished in every other aspect of their lives reduced to marginally functional adults in dealing with their estranged child. The realization that an adult child they have not seen in five years is going to show up at an event they also are attending can send them into an emotional tailspin. The same parent that competently and confidently helped their five-year-old navigate kindergarten, now can't eat, sleep, or work, (or can't stop eating, sleeping, or working) because of some situation involving the child that has cut off the relationship with them. To anyone witnessing this for the first time it is a stunning reversal.

Why this emotional runaway train? Because the qualities that served them and their children well when they were young—taking responsibility, meeting their children's needs, delaying or deferring their own needs, finding worth in their role as a parent—are now the sources of deep emotional distress. In spite of the pain associated with these patterns, these reflexes are deeply engrained and can't simply be shut down. Estranged parents often find themselves powerless to change them.

Powerlessness as Gift

This admission of powerlessness is actually a gift because it opens us to one of the most important junctures of life: discovering that we need the help of a higher power, a Spiritual Source, what many people choose to call God. In Chapter 11, I wrote about adopting a spiritual perspective on parental estrangement. In this chapter I will address our relationship to this Source and why our traditional use of religion and religious texts may fail us.

While many estranged parents may have been brought up in a religious community, or may currently be participating in the life of one, coming to a point of powerlessness where they must turn to a Spiritual Source in order to be restored to sanity is a new experience. It often comes after exhausting every other source, years of bargaining, even therapy with a professional counselor.

One might hope that the teaching of various world religions would be useful.

Many people who have grown up in traditional religions were raised to honor their parents. Honoring parents is one of the Ten Commandments. In the Jewish Talmud, the commandment to honor one's human parents is compared to honoring God. Jesus reaffirmed this responsibility and was particularly critical of adult children who found ways to renege on the responsibility to care for aging parents. The apostle Paul writes, "Children, obey your parents in everything, for this is your acceptable duty in the Lord."[94] The Qur'an frequently orders kind treatment for parents.[95] Buddha is quoted as saying, "Good is filial devotion to one's mother in the world, and devotion to one's father is good."[96] The Reformed theologian John Calvin also refers to the sacred origin of the role of human father, and comments that the commandment does not therefore depend on the particular worthiness of the parent.[97]

Adult children of estranged parents can counter all these references with other passages from sacred Scripture citing the responsibilities of parents. The instruction that a man should leave his father and mother to cleave to his wife is found in both Testaments, and on the lips of Jesus as well. The apostle Paul clearly instructs fathers not to provoke their children to anger. Estranged adult children would be able to cite numerous ways that a parent has made them so hurt and angry that they cannot remain in the relationship. The failure of parents to live up to the standards they espouse is a form of hypocrisy that Jesus railed against. In addition, Jesus counseled that an errant Christian who refuses to listen to the community should be excluded from the fellowship and treated as a Gentile and a tax collector, in other words, shunned. Surely, they might argue, we should expect no less from the behavior of a parent. Arguably, toxic parents would fit into one of those categories.

Since both estranged parents and their adult children can use the Bible to make a case supporting either connection or estrangement, religion is frequently of little help. In fact, religion can exacerbate the problem by appearing to provide a divine mandate that can be

---

[94] Colossians 3:20
[95] http://www.islamforchristians.com/honoring-parents/
[96] http://www.onenessofreligions.com/honor-thy-parents-2/
[97] http://www.religionfacts.com/ten-commandments/honor-parents

leveraged for or against parents, or for or against children. Older parents are at a disadvantage in that they tend to be more involved in faith communities than their uninvolved children. They are hearing sermons focused on their responsibilities as parents while their children are not being similarly challenged. In pastoral counseling, parents are similarly being instructed to bear all the responsibility for reaching out to the children who have cut them off.

Clearly, estranged parents need a different approach to their Spiritual Source than the religious rules most learned in their faith community. The approach I have experienced and found most helpful is one that is used in recovery groups for people dealing with a variety of issues (alcoholism, drug addiction, co-dependence, growing up in a dysfunctional home, and so forth). While groups don't adopt a particular religious perspective, they do find it important to be clear about several things when we speak of this Spiritual Source.

Qualities of Our Spiritual Source

First, it is both our belief and experience that this Spiritual Source's intention for our lives is goodness. Goodness means that our Spiritual Source intends for our lives to possess approval and esteem. This is critical because many estranged parents hold the belief that their estrangement means they are defective or inferior. They may subconsciously avoid activities or thoughts that make them happy because they don't feel that they deserve to be happy. If they have occasions where they feel positive and peaceful, they feel guilty that they have "forgotten" how bad things are with their children. There may be other voices reminding them of their estrangement, those of family members, ex-spouses, or well-

> *A few PEAK "pearls":*
> *parents are more attached to children than children are to parents. Through grace and forgiveness, we can stop searching for what we should have done as parents.*
> R.R. from Lansing, MI

meaning friends offering solutions. Empty seats at holiday tables and empty mailboxes at birthdays also become occasions for self-recrimination. Our Spiritual Source is kinder to us than we are to ourselves.

Second, this Spiritual Source is gracious and forgiving. No parent, or adult child for that matter, is perfect. We can all benefit from an exercise of self-examination to acknowledge specific areas where we have failed to be the parent we should have been. Some of those failures affected our children directly; other effects were the indirect impact of poor decisions affecting spouses, finances, or family reputation. Again, it is both our belief and our experience that our Spiritual Source is an inexhaustible source for grace and mercy for every failure we are willing to acknowledge. Our Spiritual Source is undoubtedly more willing to forgive us than we are ready to forgive ourselves and many times more willing to forgive us than other persons in our lives. Healing requires that we give greater weight to our Spiritual Source than any other voice.

Third, this Spiritual Source is wise and has a better understanding of how our recovery needs to unfold in our particular situation than anyone else. For this reason, we do best by asking our Spiritual Source for guidance rather than telling our Spiritual Source what we would like to have happen. For example, in some cases our Spiritual Source may work to quickly restore an estranged relationship with an adult child as we open ourselves to guidance. In other cases, that restoration may be delayed in order for us to realize the personal and spiritual growth that is more important. In still other cases, it may become clear that our Spiritual Source has plans for us that do not include reconciliation with our adult children. In those cases, our Spiritual Source can guide us through a process of grieving the loss and moving on with our lives.

Notice how different this approach to spirituality is compared to the perception of many faith communities where

- Religion is used to establish who is right and who is wrong, or to win a moral argument.
- Membership is understood to be an indication of virtue or positive standing in the broader community.
- God is conceived as a punitive judge holding the threat of hell as the eternal destiny for those who do not measure up.
- The faith community is an extension of God. If the faith community rejects us, God probably does as well.

Asking for Help

Key to the entire process is sincerely asking our Spiritual Source for help. Taking the step of asking for help implies an acknowledgement of powerlessness that has the effect of calming the mind from its relentless striving to find a way out of pain. It is the paradox of spirituality: the more we try to find peace, the further it eludes us. As we surrender to our Spiritual Source by asking for help, peace descends. It is easier to save a drowning swimmer once they have surrendered. As long as they are fighting to survive, they threaten to sink both rescuer and swimmer.

Estranged parents have many opportunities to ask for help from their Spiritual Source. They not only need help dealing with the emotional pain of estrangement, but guidance on how to handle an entire range of issues connected to their adult children. Those answers might come in the form of the 12 Steps, from a PEAK recovery group, or other resource recommended by the PEAK network. Sometimes we will misunderstand what our Spiritual Source wants us to do, but as long as our heart's intention is to discover and follow the guidance of our Spiritual Source, we can trust that we will eventually arrive where we are supposed to be.

Changing Our Minds

One of the mistakes we make on our spiritual journey is to equate our thoughts with who we are. This gives our thoughts incredible power. In fact, we become a victim of our own thinking and the emotions generated by our thoughts. We keep waiting for our thoughts and feelings to change, hoping that something we read, hear, or experience will suddenly make us think differently.

In reality, we are not our thoughts. We think our thoughts. We choose our patterns of thinking. The reason our thoughts seem to be "us" is that our choice of thinking patterns over years have actually rewired our brains into neural freeways. If every time I have a creative thought, I tell myself I am stupid (which I have done for years), it becomes easier and easier for that thought pattern to zoom through my brain. After a while, it happens so quickly and easily, it feels like me. I feel stupid.

Every spiritual tradition addresses this thinking process as an element in human transformation and healing. Recovery from the trauma of parental estrangement is no different. This generally requires several commitments:

- We must value the perspective of our Spiritual Source above our own or the opinions of others in our lives.
- We must become aware of our thinking patterns and the ways they diverge from the perspectives of our Spiritual Source.
- We must consciously work to conform our thinking to the perspectives of our Spiritual Source.
- We must make these internal changes in spite of how we feel, trusting that our feelings will eventually align with our new thinking. If I consistently think "I am bright and creative" I will eventually have positive feelings about myself.
- We must set an intention that in particular situations we will begin to behave in ways consistent with our new thinking inspired by our Spiritual Source. When I take steps to share my

creativity with others, my thinking about myself begins to change.

Parental estrangement tends to cultivate thinking patterns that are not only inconsistent with our Spiritual Source, but self-destructive as well. In some cases, estrangement may simply surface and intensify patterns that have controlled our thinking for years, perhaps from our childhood. I have tried to write this book in a way that is consistent with my best understanding of our Spiritual Source. It is an offering made to you, the reader. Like any offering, it is yours to embrace, amend, or discard. It is my hope that at least some of the content will resonate as true so that you might begin to bring your thinking more in line with your Spiritual Source as you conceive it.

Daily Bread

One biblical metaphor that I find of practical significance is that of daily bread. It goes back to the Jewish experience of manna, a kind of bread the Hebrews collected each day to survive in the wilderness. One characteristic of manna was that it could not be stored. If anyone tried to store it for more than a day it would become infested with maggots. The power of this metaphor is that it graphically illustrates our regular need for both physical and spiritual nutrition that is fresh and wholesome rather than stale and rancid.

We cannot live long on yesterday's dust-covered, sentimental religious dogmas. This is especially true for us as estranged parents. The narrow, idealistic perspectives we grew up with are partly to blame for our current quandary. If our spiritual formation had been more reflective of real life, including the many instances of family and parental estrangement found in various scriptures, we would not find ourselves adrift in religious communities that are wordless in their preaching and teaching about these relational breaks. Nor would we find ourselves under such inner assault for failing to live up to these misshapen ideals.

A daily updating of our spiritual perspective can help here, first by helping us unlearn what has been emotionally deadening, then by replacing those toxins with fresh, grace-filled, and life-affirming insights. Gradually we are able to absorb enough spiritual nutrition to give our souls the capacity to heal its wounds, and even to strengthen an emotional immune system than can help protect us during stressful times like holidays and special celebrations. Even when we take a hit, it does not lay us low for days, or leave us vulnerable to self-destructive thoughts and impulses. From an emotional standpoint, we still catch cold, but it doesn't go into pneumonia.

Again, this is rarely achieved by an occasional prayer, or reading a book or two. We need daily doses. There is a reason the Lord's prayer asks for daily bread. Research has demonstrated that even small amounts of time each day given to deep spiritual reflection can have significant positive impacts.[98] PEAK has developed resources to provide this daily bread, all available on the PEAK website.

Above all, our Spiritual Source can help us gain clarity about what lies within our power to change, and what does not. This then becomes the basis of the serenity prayer:

"God, give us the serenity to accept the things we cannot change, the courage to change the things we can, and the wisdom to know the difference."[99]

---

[98] Basso JC, McHale A, Ende V, Oberlin DJ, Suzuki WA. "Brief, daily meditation enhances attention, memory, mood, and emotional regulation in non-experienced meditators." *Journal of Behavioral Brain Research.* 2019 Jan 1;356:208-220.
[99] Attributed to Reinhold Niebuhr.

Questions for Reflection and Discussion

How difficult is it for you to ask for help? Write about a time in the last week or so when you asked someone for help.

How are the teachings of your faith community helpful, unhelpful, or irrelevant to your experience of parental estrangement?

Which of the thoughts about yourself or the estrangement from your adult children diverge the most from the perspectives of your Spiritual Source as described in this chapter?

What steps can you take to begin to conform your thinking to that of your Spiritual Source as described in this chapter?

What daily spiritual practice might help in your recovery?

If you are using this book in a group discussion, what did you gain from hearing others speak? From speaking?

Chapter 17
Forgiveness

In an American legal drama called *Suits*, the main character, Harvey, reconnects with his mother over dinner after years of estrangement. He has scheduled the conversation in order to let her know that he has forgiven her. As a child, Harvey had caught his mother in an affair which she required him to keep secret from his father. What follows is a condensed paraphrase of the dialogue.

Harvey begins, "I want you to know that I forgive you for what happened to me as a child."

His grateful mother replies, "Thank you, Harvey. And I forgive you, too."

The notion that Harvey might need forgiveness sends him ballistic. "What do *you* have to forgive *me* for?"

"For all those years you treated me as if you didn't care if I lived or died."

Harvey storms out, incensed by the suggestion that there is anything for which he needs to be forgiven. His decades of indifference do not register in his conscience as morally significant.

Some version of this conversation could play out between parents and their estranged adult children five million times in the United States. At the root is a critical question: Is indifference morally significant? In 1986, the Romanian-born American writer, professor, political activist, Nobel laureate, and Holocaust survivor Elie Wiesel wrote: "The opposite of love is not hate, it's indifference."[100]

What makes forgiveness different for estranged parents compared with others is the nature of the offence. It is not the rudeness or deceit

---

[100] Elie Wiesel, *U.S. News and World Report,* October 27, 1986.

of a stranger that must be forgiven, but the indifference of one who is beloved. It is not simply the breaking of contact that is so injurious. It is the indifference to the state of a parent's existence, or whether they exist at all.

Who Needs Forgiveness?

Given the human fallibility of parents, there will always be something they do, or fail to do, that will need to be forgiven by their children. Do estranged parents need to forgive their adult children as well?

The sins of the father are indeed visited upon the children, as the Bible says. The failures of a parent, especially when a child is young and powerless, can have a profound effect on that child decades later. Modern psychology joins in with Wordsworth's perspective that the child is father to the man, expressing the idea that the character we form as children under the influence of all-powerful parents stays with us into our adult life. The pervasive assumption of our culture is that a significant portion of any person's psychological issues is rooted in the way they were parented as young children. The result has been an explosion of resources for adults, tracing their problems back decades into their childhood. An internet search using the term "childhood trauma" returns 11 million hits. Most estranged parents are self-aware enough to admit these mistakes; they deal with a significant amount of guilt because of them, and many seek forgiveness.

However, any fair reflection must also point out some merit in a more balanced perspective which might be summarized as "the father is child to the adult son." The adult son or daughter of an aging parent may not be all-powerful to the same degree that a young child perceives a parent, but they are a potent force in a parent's psyche. As we have seen throughout this book, the indifference expressed through estrangement has the capacity to significantly impact the life of an aging parent. I have referred to the negative impacts of estrangement as parental trauma. If you do an internet search using the term "parental trauma," it will only return about 24 thousand hits compared to the 11 million for childhood trauma. However, none of these refer to the actual trauma experienced by an older adult from the treatment by their adult child. That concept of parental trauma is virtually non-existent in our culture.

That the suffering of a parent is even worth noting is a concept more ancient than modern. One does not need to accept the authority of the Old Testament as a religious document to appreciate its historical description of parental suffering. "A foolish man despises his mother."[101] The tense of the verb indicates an ongoing, continuous loathing. In my translation of the Hebrew found in a similar verse, this loathing brings a mother "grief and depression,"[102] words approaching a modern clinical diagnosis. A similar sentiment is expressed regarding the impact on a father that I would also translate as "grief and depression,"[103] combined with the ominous inability to feel joy. *Inability to feel joy.* Ponder that for a moment. A final verse observes that a son can be his father's calamity, his ruin and destruction.[104] This verse hits with particular force when an estranged father calls me up to say he is actively suicidal.

> *We have been estranged from our son for over two years. He is also keeping us from contacting our three grandchildren. We are looking for guidance and encouragement as we deal with this horrible situation.*
> L.B. From Rockford, IL

Going back to the question raised at the beginning of this chapter, does Harvey's mom, flawed as she is, need to forgive her son for the decades of indifference? Is the simple yet sustained indifference of an estranged child powerful enough to affect a parent in all these ways? The answer to both questions is "yes." If Harvey's mother is going to heal from the grief, depression, joylessness, calamity, ruin, and

---

[101] Proverbs 15:20
[102] Proverbs 10:1
[103] Proverbs 17:21
[104] Proverbs 19:13

destruction, accurately detailed 2500 years ago, she will need to forgive her son. In other words, forgiveness is essential to our recovery from parental trauma. In many cases it will be indifference, or a similar offence, that will need to be forgiven.

What Is Forgiveness?

Forgiveness is the release of hurt, anger, or resentment toward our adult children or others who may be factors in our estrangement, and the setting of a positive, heartfelt intention for their well-being and happiness. We are motivated to forgive in order to reverse many of the negative impacts of parental trauma. While most people think of forgiveness as only a religious concept, people like Dr. Fred Luskin of the Stanford University Forgiveness Project, have developed a step-by-step approach to forgiveness that doesn't require a religious framework at all.[105] Multiple studies have shown that forgiveness is associated with lower levels of depression, anxiety, and hostility; reduced nicotine dependence and substance abuse, higher positive emotion, higher satisfaction with life, and fewer health symptoms.[106] Estranged parents will recognize that these benefits of forgiveness mirror many of the crippling issues they began dealing with in the wake of the estrangement.

Friend and forgiveness expert, Lyndon Harris, correctly identifies the core of parental trauma as a profound, prolonged grief. The problem occurs when that grief becomes a grievance. The two words actually have the same root, but grief is focused on a loss, and grievance is focused on an offender. The feelings that arise from grief are part of a healthy healing process that ease over time. A grievance may result

---

[105] Fred Luskin, *Forgive for Good,* (Harper Collins, 2003).
[106] Toussaint LL, Worthington EL, Williams DR, eds. *Forgiveness and Health: Scientific Evidence and Theories Relating Forgiveness to Better Health* (Springer; 2015).

in many of the same feelings, but they never heal without forgiveness. Here are Lyndon's words from my interview with him:

> It is like battery acid. Battery acid is what gives the battery its energy to get us started moving forward. But outside of that battery, the acid destroys everything it touches. All the emotions of grief, shock, sadness, anger, depression, help move us forward in our healing process. But when grief decays into a "grievance" all those emotions can get focused on our adult children where they become corrosive. And the person most affected by that corrosion is ourselves.

What are some indicators that we have not yet forgiven our adult children who have cut off the relationship with us? Here is a check list.

- ☐ I am having physical symptoms that began with the estrangement which are not improving with the passage of time.
- ☐ I am feeling angry and resentful whenever I remember how the estrangement began and continues.
- ☐ I struggle with feelings of resentment that a relationship with my grandchildren has been taken from me.
- ☐ I find myself ruminating over the estrangement and unable to focus on other important aspects of my life.
- ☐ I don't want my child to be happy or successful without me.
- ☐ I secretly hope that my children will experience some of this pain with their own children so that they know what it is like.
- ☐ I want my child's relationships with those who encourage estrangement to come to an end. This may include spouses, partners, therapists, spiritual advisors, and others who are important to my child.
- ☐ I am engaging in coping mechanisms that are not the best that might include eating, smoking, drug or alcohol use, or excessive use of the internet.
- ☐ I feel like my adult child has robbed my joy, and any hope for future happiness.

- ☐ I find myself saying negative things about my children to other people that I later regret.
- ☐ I have thoughts of harming or killing myself as a way of letting them know how much they have hurt me.
- ☐ I find it difficult to pray for or direct positive energy toward my adult child.
- ☐ I am putting my child out of my mind as if they don't exist.
- ☐ I have never really gone through a process of forgiveness and I don't know how to do it.
- ☐ Something else that comes to mind suggesting I have not yet forgiven_____.

Some of these, like anger, are the battery acid of which Lyndon spoke. They have a temporary role to play in our grief process. But when we notice that they are becoming fixed features of our inner life, they have already begun doing damage. Forgiveness becomes the necessary acid clean-up.

What Forgiveness Is Not

Most of us have heard of forgiveness, but know relatively little about it. It may be important to pause and say what forgiveness is not.[107]

Forgiveness is not condoning irresponsible, hurtful behavior. A mother depletes her life savings to purchase a home for a son who then estranges her and refuses to make payments. Forgiveness does not require her to excuse his behavior or forget that it happened. Neither does it prevent her from taking legal action to secure her future.

While the aid of a Spiritual Source can be essential, forgiveness does not have to be an otherworldly or religious experience. A sacramental confessional process is not required to experience the benefits of forgiveness. In fact, the positive effects are so accessible that Dr. Tyler

---

[107] Fred Luskin, *Forgive for Good,* (Harper Collins, 2003), vii-viii.

J. VanderWeele, Professor of Epidemiology at Harvard argues that forgiveness should be considered a public health issue.[108]

Forgiveness is not forgetting that something painful happened. It does not deny that something wrong occurred. But it separates the memory from the pain, the bee from the sting. Forgiveness remembers what happened, but it lets go of the suffering. It also stops keeping score.

Forgiveness does not imply that we are perfect or without fault. No parent is. The process by which we conduct our own relational assessment and make amends where necessary is important. But it is a separate process from forgiving our children.

Forgiveness does not require that our adult child admit to anything wrong. In fact, they might find the notion that we need to forgive them for anything to be upsetting. Forgiveness is not about them. In most cases, it will be wise not to tell them at all. Forgiveness is what we need to do to heal.

Forgiveness is not reconciliation. Reconciliation involves a process of reestablishing a healthy relationship with the person who has injured you. It requires both parent and adult child to participate in constructing a cocreated narrative and a process of rebuilding trust. Reconciliation can never happen without forgiveness, but forgiveness is always possible whether reconciliation is offered or not.

The Process of Forgiveness

It is said that churches have many menus but few recipes. We are given a list of things we should do, but not much guidance on how to actually do it. Forgiveness is on that list. It is one thing to know that we should forgive or that forgiveness is important. It is another thing to know how to forgive.

---

[108] VanderWeele, T.J. "Is forgiveness a public health issue?" *American Journal of Public Health*, 108:189-190.

The first step is to get clear about what we as estranged parents are forgiving. In each of these areas, write down both the facts and your feelings. How did the estrangement happen? What was communicated? How was it communicated? Who encouraged or aggravated the estrangement? What holidays or celebrations have been missed? What times of vulnerability, illness, or loss have gone unacknowledged? What have you done for your child that was never acknowledged with a significant degree of gratitude? What hurtful things have been said to you, and how were they communicated?

The second step is to seek an understanding of why your child might have responded the way they have. Perhaps they were put into a loyalty bind by another person that they found impossible to navigate. Maybe they are dealing with a multi-generational tendency to cut people off that they are not even conscious of. Perhaps they have a mental health or addiction issue that is overpowering them. Sometimes people can get so stressed out in their own situations that they have nothing left for an additional relationship. In all cases, this will be a benefit-of-the-doubt guess designed to help you forgive, not a single cause of the estrangement that explains everything. Remember. An attempt to understand does not give you a reason to excuse them. It gives you a way of forgiving them.

Then explore where you might have done something similar in a different situation. This is the advice most of us have heard: Take the log out of your own eye before you take the splinter out of the eye of another. Have you ever cut off the relationship with another person rather than work through a significant issue? Have you ever failed to be grateful to another person for ways they have contributed to your life? Have you ever made a poor decision because you were stressed out? Have you ever allowed someone to put you into a loyalty bind where you felt you had to reject someone else? Did you answer all these questions with a "No"? Is your adult child also a person who always thinks they are right?

The third step is to release your adult child from any penalty for what you have experienced. I find this visualization helpful.

Take your adult child by the hand, and into the presence of your Spiritual Source. You might envision Jesus, Allah, Yahweh, a Light, etc. I will simply call it God. With your child at your side, tell God about all the pain you have felt and would like directed toward your child. Be as honest as possible. Say it all.

When you have finished, wait a full sixty seconds. Then say to God this, or something similar: "God, I have changed my mind. I don't want you to direct any of this pain to my child. I release them from it all." Turn to them, tell them you love them, hug them, and walk out alone. Let a few hours pass before taking the next step.

The fourth step is to make a list of all the good things you want your child and grandchildren to have instead of the pain. Either pray that God will send those blessings to them, or imagine them flowing out of the entire universe toward them. Accompany this with a visual image of love flowing from your heart to theirs.

The fifth step is to let others know that you have forgiven your child for the estrangement. Tell several people that you know well. Do not communicate this process to your adult child. Again, forgiveness is not about them. It is about you. Above all, do not weaponize forgiveness. Forgiveness is not a way of letting someone know how good you are in forgiving someone as bad as they are.

Forgiving one of our adult children can be especially difficult for an estranged parent because of the nature of the relationship. For many of us, the pain and the relationship have become fused. If we let go of the pain, it feels like we are also letting go of the relationship. In one sense, that is true. We are letting go of the relationship as it was previously constructed. As it was constructed, that relationship did not prove sustainable in spite of how fondly we may remember it. Forgiveness makes space for a new relationship to emerge. In our hearts, the relationship continues with our regular offering of positive energy and love in the direction of our beloved child.

Steps Toward Recovery

- Spend some time reflecting on your readiness to forgive. If we forgive too soon, we may simply drive our normal grief reactions underground. For example, we sometimes need our anger to give us the energy required to move forward with our lives. If you are not ready, set a fixed time (maybe a month) to revisit the question.
- At the other extreme is becoming so loyal to our pain that we can never let it go. The pain becomes woven into our life narrative in a way that both defines us and excuses us from the responsibility to move forward. Identify any long-tenured grievance you are hesitant to let go of. What are you gaining from your connection to the pain?
- If forgiving your child is too big a step, take a smaller one. Go through the process of forgiveness for an offence that feels more manageable, like a person who was rude to you on the phone or at the market.
- Ask for guidance from your Spiritual Source. Look for signs during your day, or even in your dreams, of who you are ready to forgive.

As you work through this process you may discover points of resistance within yourself. This is normal. You may need to go back and remind yourself of what forgiveness is and is not. Forgiveness doesn't condone or excuse. Neither does it make us a doormat or relational beggar. Forgiveness is giving up all hope of a better past,[109] so that we can have the best of all futures.

---

[109] Adapted from Lily Tomlin.

Questions for Reflection and Discussion

In what ways do you think the opposite of love is indifference, rather than hate?

Why do you think Harvey got so upset upon hearing that his mother forgave him?

Why do you think our society pays so little attention to parental trauma and the need to forgive our adult children?

What instruction have you had related to forgiveness? Where is it the same or different from the understanding of forgiveness in this chapter?

Which boxes did you check indicating you have yet to forgive your adult child?

What are the things you listed that you need to forgive?

What resistances do you experience as you think about going through a process of forgiveness?

If you are using this book in a group discussion, what did you gain from hearing others speak? From speaking?

PEAK: Parents of Estranged Adult Kids
A Resource for Recovery

Chapter 18
Getting to Acceptance

Dealing with loss is an aspect of being human that we all experience. While it is important to say that the ways we work through grief is unique to each of us and do not always follow the same set of linear "stages," they can provide us with a helpful way of thinking about the different aspects of the grief process. Whatever the precise order in which we experience them we normally work through all the stages of grief to one degree or another until we can finally accept the loss. Acceptance enables us to move forward.

Beginning in the pages of the introduction, I suggested that acceptance is not affirmation. This is one of the core beliefs of PEAK. Nothing will do more to impede our recovery than confusion of the two. Acceptance does not require us to affirm that estrangement is justified, reasonable, healthy, or the best solution to issues in the relationship. Acceptance *does* mean adjusting to the fact that the door behind us has closed whether we like it or not. We may stand for a time at the door hoping it will open again like a wayward puppy returning home. Eventually we realize at an emotional level that the door to the past is permanently closed. We turn around and walk forward into the future.

In the face of any change, acceptance liberates us to take next steps. It enables us to buy a home in a new community after leaving another community behind. It also enables us to hunt out coffee shops, register to vote, and make that first new friend. Without acceptance, we would sit homeless, voteless, and friendless in our new community hoping for the opportunity to simply return to life as we had known it.

There are few things sadder that observing an estranged parent who has been stuck for years waiting for the phone call, letter, or knock on the door that never comes. On the other hand, there are few things more inspirational than the transformation of an estranged parent from paralysis to incandescence as they begin to reclaim the divine glow of a soul who has risen from the ashes. In PEAK we are not called to judge. Instead, we bear witness to the breathtaking capacity of parents to take the most devastating blow of a lifetime, get up, and walk into the world with purpose and a head held high. That requires acceptance.

As mentioned earlier, getting to acceptance is difficult for estranged parents because it involves an ambiguous loss, much like a missing person who may show up any day. Acceptance does not mean that we give up hope for a future reconciliation. However, the door to the past is permanently closed. The previous relationship led to estrangement. A healthy reconciliation will require rebuilding the relationship on different terms. Relating in the same ways while expecting a different result is to knock on the door of more heartache.

The consequences of an estranged parent failing to move through their ambivalence to acceptance are significant, similar to the person above moving to a new community but so emotionally stuck in the previous one that they cannot move forward to do what is required to be safe and secure, let alone thrive. They become emotionally homeless without established roots, victims who surrender their personal power and thereby fail to take responsibility for their own well-being, isolated from relationships with others.

Here are some of the things that keep estranged parents from navigating through acceptance.

Guilt

One major obstacle to acceptance is guilt. A significant parental failure, either direct or indirect, can prevent parents from moving through acceptance. They may feel that they have no right to move forward with their lives. In one of the "PEAK Turning Points" that we review weekly, we state that "by learning that we deserve to play and have fun, we will discover or rediscover sources of joy and happiness in our lives." This is difficult to do when a guilty voice in the back of our heads keeps reminding us that we don't deserve it. Allowing ourselves to enjoy moments of happiness is key to our recovery. If we allow guilt for the situation to talk us out of positive feelings, who benefits? Not our family, not our friends, not the people we work with, and certainly not ourselves.

Guilt is universal. All major spiritual traditions deal with the issue of guilt, and finding closure often requires a spiritual solution. Jewish law states that the person who did wrong should ask for forgiveness up to three times, after which the person is no longer considered accountable for the wrongdoing. Christian teaching is that confession of sin brings assurance of God's forgiveness since "he is faithful and just to forgive us our sins and to cleanse us from all unrighteousness."[110] However, it is also realistic in acknowledging that the forgiveness of God does not guarantee the forgiveness of others, including our adult children.

> *I made MANY mistakes and I've taken full responsibility for them. Over and over and over. Told my daughter verbally and in writing every single thing and asked her to tell me what else could I do to validate her in any way I could. For years now. Nothing has changed.*
> A.E. from Sacramento, CA

Nor does it guarantee that we will forgive ourselves. It is a stubborn aspect of human nature to hold ourselves hostage to a guilt that the God of the Universe has long since forgotten. Reminders of the need to self-forgive abound in PEAK, including this one from our "PEAK Turning Points": "We will experience growth in our self-acceptance, forgive ourselves and others for mistakes of the past, and give ourselves approval on a daily basis." Forgiving ourselves is a choice we must make in the sacred space of our own hearts. Even God will not invade the sanctity of that process.

---

[110] 1 John 1:9

Sometimes estranged parents make the mistake of believing that apologizing for their failures will restore the relationship. While owning our failures and making amends is always a healthy step of self-awareness and spiritual growth, estranged parents may be disappointed at the response from their adult children. A parent's repeated apologies may be experienced as a boundary violation by an adult child who has asked not to be contacted. An estranged child may question a parent's sincerity. They may feel that the parent is not apologizing for the right mistakes. Or they simply may not be ready to forgive their parent. Their core values may prevent them from doing so. We sometimes must adjust to livin' unforgiven.

It is indeed possible that forgiveness will lead to reconciliation, but it cannot lead to a restoration of the relationship on the same terms. New conditions for the relationship will need to be negotiated; trust will need to be reestablished, and that always requires a new behavior consistently experienced over time.

Lack of Closure

A second obstacle to moving through acceptance is a lack of closure. A clear message has not been transmitted that the relationship is over. As I define it, estrangement is not a simple growing apart. It occurs when one or more adult children intentionally chooses to end contact with a parent. That message may be delivered in a written communication, a face-to-face conversation, or through a third party. Estrangement is too significant as a life event to be left to filling in blanks. Without closure there is always the possibility of misunderstanding. A closer relationship may be desired but neither party knows how to develop it.

What kinds of things do adult children say in giving closure?

- I don't want to see you again. Don't contact me.

- You are no longer my father. Other people in my life have taught me what a real father is like, and it is not you.
- I will make sure that your grandchildren do not know who you are.
- It is no longer possible for me to have a relationship with you.
- I am going to live my life as if you no longer exist.

In their response, it is important that estranged parents are equally clear and unambiguous. Their message is simple: I love you. I am always willing to reconnect. The ball is in your court. A clear message from an adult child, combined with this clear message from the parent provides the closure necessary for both to move forward.

Uncompleted Grief Stages

A third obstacle to acceptance is getting stuck in the previous stages. It is impossible to move through acceptance if you are still in denial about the reality of the estrangement. Anger serves a purpose in helping an estranged parent move away from the relationship. However, sustained anger can actually prevent acceptance because the parent knows that anger is something they might get over at some point in the future. Anger also prevents us from thinking clearly about the relationship and may lead us to jump to conclusions or causes that are not valid.

Depression is also a stage where we can get stuck. One of the hallmarks of depression is withdrawal and self-exile. This can look like acceptance. But the withdrawal of depression is quite different from growth into acceptance. Acceptance enables us to move forward in life with fresh engagement; depression works to separate us from life and other important relationships.

Inadequate attention to the bargaining stage can also make it an uncompleted work. Before we count a relationship beyond repair, we are going to want to assure ourselves that we have tried negotiating other solutions. Of course, that requires that our adult children are willing to enter into that process (and that we are willing to make that investment as well), which is not always the case.

Acceptance makes things possible. Acceptance not only allows us to move forward in our lives, it also sets the stage for a number of essential tasks that are impossible to address prior to acceptance. It is important to emphasize here that the steps below are not taken to punish or antagonize. Prior to these actions, I assume that the other stages of grief have been worked through, as well as participation in a basic relational audit that can help provide clarity of thought and refine motivations.

Acceptance enables you to repurpose your life. Since caring for children and grandchildren no longer occupies a central purpose in your life, you now have the opportunity to intentionally redefine what that purpose will be. This is an opportunity that many older adults do not have. Make the most of it.

Acceptance enables you to rethink how you spend your time. Parents typically spend a significant amount of time with their children and grandchildren. About 40 percent of adult children see their parents once a week or more.[111] In addition, 70 percent of grandparents see grandkids at least once per week, and 81 percent all or part of summer vacation.[112] That time is now available for other purposes IF you are intentional and don't simply sink into a chair in front of a screen! Spending several additional hours each week educating yourself or serving others can have a big impact over the course of a year. Plan it. Do it.

Acceptance enables you to reallocate financial resources. Nearly three in four (74 percent) parents with adult children say they

---

[111] https://www.ined.fr/fichier/s_rubrique/19095/pop.and.soc.english.427.en.pdf
[112] https://considerable.com/surprising-facts-about-grandparents/?gp-banner

help their grown kids with their finances.[113] Parents who are in retirement give their adult children $6,800 a year on average so they can live more comfortably, a new study has found.[114] There are organizations that could do wonders with that amount of money. In addition, grandparents on average spend $2,383 per year on grandkids.[115] One option is to put that money into a savings account for their college education. Alternatively, plan a trip abroad with them when they turn eighteen and are able to make their own decisions about a relationship with you.

Acceptance enables you to build a relational network that works for you. My therapist Azaria Akashi once posed a question to me: "Why do you keep choosing to put yourself in situations with people who will reject you?" It was a helpful question. My specific answer to that question is not as important as the new decision I made at that point in my life: as far as is within my power, I am going to choose to be with people who are good for my soul with the hope that I am good for theirs as well! People who are good for you don't have to be perfect; they just have to light up your soul!

When members decide to exclude you from the family, you now have the opportunity to choose who will be in your relational network. There are a variety of possible roles: friend, surrogate grandparent, mentor, coach, team member, spiritual director, support group member, lover, and so forth. Are there relationships you need to rekindle? Then go on a road trip and reconnect with people you haven't seen for years. Would some workshops help you learn to build stronger relationships or function in different roles? Learning how to listen, how to think through your reactions, how to negotiate conflict

---

[113] https://www.usatoday.com/story/money/personalfinance/budget-and-spending/2017/12/11/nearly-75-of-parents-help-their-adult-children-financially/108507432/
[114] http://time.com/money/4803331/retirement-adult-children-money/
[115] https://www.aarp.org/home-family/friends-family/info-2017/2017-grandkids-cost-how-much.html

pay big relational dividends. Start investing in people you care about and care about you.

Acceptance helps you stop rehearsing in your mind past or future conversations with your adult children. Some refer to this as a mental spin cycle where thoughts go round and round. Acceptance frees up psychic energy that you can apply toward being more creative, productive, and positively engaged with life. You can still view your children as beautiful gifts of God, though flawed just like the rest of us. Pray for them, bless them, forgive them—and let them go.

Steps toward Recovery

- Spend some time thinking about acceptance as adjustment to reality. Do some journaling about the reality of your situation with your estranged child, and the degree to which you feel you have adjusted to it. Give yourself approval for the positive steps you have taken in making those adjustments.
- Try to identify anything that is in the way of your getting to acceptance, things like confusing acceptance with affirmation, guilt, lack of closure, getting stuck in a particular stage of grief, or something else that might come to mind. Set a reasonable goal to deal with one or more of those obstacles.
- Reflect on all the things that acceptance might help you do. Make a list. Then circle one or two that might be reasonable steps for you to take in the near future.

This is important work, but it can be difficult. Find some understanding person or group who can support you in this process. Also, make sure you are taking other self-care measures as you engage in this work. If it becomes overwhelming, take a break from it for a week or two and come back to it.

Questions for Reflection and Discussion
After reading this chapter, where are you on the scale that follows with regard to acceptance?

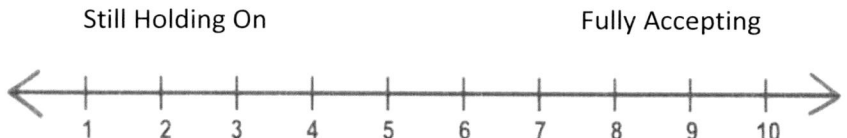

Which of the obstacles in this chapter present the biggest challenge in getting through acceptance? Are there other obstacles you struggle with?

Given your level of acceptance, how do you now understand the purpose of your life?

With acceptance, what new possibilities could present themselves that you might be willing to consider?

If you are using this book in a group discussion, what did you gain from hearing others speak? From speaking?

PEAK: Parents of Estranged Adult Kids
A Resource for Recovery

Chapter 19
Here There Be Dragons

"Here there be dragons" is a phrase designating dangerous or unexplored territories, in imitation of a medieval practice of putting illustrations of dragons, sea monsters and other mythological creatures on uncharted areas of maps where potential dangers were thought to exist. Such areas exist for estranged parents as well. I have observed that many, having ventured down these paths, become further disheartened or even retraumatized. It is worth a chapter to name some of those dangerous places that recovering estranged parents should avoid.

 I've marked the specific warnings with a dragon icon.

Misuse of Religion

Religion is at the top of the list because it can be one of the more powerful sources of healing, while, simultaneously, one of the most toxic and damaging. When I use the word "religion" I am referring to the institutional expressions of spirituality that take collective action through activities like worship, education, social engagement, administration, and pastoral care.

While a growing number of therapists are appreciative of the role that spirituality plays in positive outcomes for their clients, some continue to be wary, and for good reason. However, any field of knowledge can be misused, including psychology. We always have to be aware of the shadow side of any body of knowledge and practice.

To ignore the potential benefits of religion runs the risk of under-treating those who might benefit.

Let's start with the ways that religion can be useful. First, it is helpful to remember that the root of the word "religion" is the Latin *ligare* which means "to connect." We get our English word "ligament" from it. Assembled with *re-*, "religion" means "to reconnect." It's a beautiful concept, especially for those who are suffering from a trauma that tends to isolate them with feelings of disconnection. Much of the research indicates that the benefits of religion for people in crisis is in the connection they feel toward one another. The evidence suggests that it is not so much the doctrines or beliefs of a particular faith that are beneficial. The social connections are the protective factor. When religion lives up to its name as the reconnector, good things can happen.

Since parental trauma is so damaging to multiple dimensions of their lives, the healing ministries of different faith communities can be extremely helpful. No religion has a corner on healing. Rabbi Geoffrey Dennis notes that "Jews have been tremendously influential in the history of Western medicine and their reputation as formidable healers reaches back into classical antiquity."[116] In an article from *The Buddhist Review*, writer C. Pierce Salguero observes that "Just as some might refer to Buddhism today as one of the first 'world religions' in the sense that it expanded beyond its original cultural and linguistic context, one might similarly think of Buddhist healing as one of the first 'world medicines.'"[117] Multiple researchers have demonstrated that yoga, which originated in northern India, has benefits ranging from heart health to better sleep.

The healing ministry of Jesus has served as the basis for its replication through the Christian religion going back to its beginnings. It finds expression in healing services, sacraments, group laying on of hands, inspirational readings, and lay ministries. The fourth largest

---

[116] https://www.myjewishlearning.com/article/jewish-healing-magic/
[117] https://tricycle.org/magazine/paging-dr-dharma/

seminary in the country, Fuller Theological Seminary, offered a course in the 80's titled Signs and Wonders 101 in which students were offered teachings on miraculous healing, including the in-class practice of praying for the sick. Nearly every religious tradition has some form of healing ministry under its umbrella.

Healing takes many forms, and addresses many different aspects of the human condition, including mental, emotional, and physical suffering. It only makes sense that those estranged parents who are comfortable with spiritual healing in a religious setting take advantage of that offering. In my own experience, I have done just that. In times of particularly intense suffering, I have made it a weekly practice to seek out these ministries.

Nonetheless, many persons have had painful experiences with a particular religion in their past. This can result in its own form of trauma, which has been given a name, religious trauma syndrome (RTS). RTS occurs when an individual struggles with leaving a religion or a set of beliefs that has resulted in their indoctrination. It often involves the trauma of breaking away from a controlling environment, lifestyle, or religious figure. Persons who have had a bad experience with religion, including those with RTS, should never be pressured to take part in a religion-based experience, including those offering healing from the impacts of parental estrangement. This runs the risk of triggering, and layering religious trauma on top of parental trauma. In addition, members of a PEAK recovery group are allowed the freedom to pass on any spiritual exercise, including the PEAK prayer at the beginning and close of meetings.

This dragon is a cousin to the previous one. When asking for help in your recovery process, particularly in a religious setting focused on healing, be cautious in presenting the issue as a problem to be solved in the relationship with your child. This will invite an exploration into that relationship, which always has a long, complex history. It runs the risk of a well-intentioned, untrained person offering you advice. This can be retraumatizing, rather than helpful. Unless you want that advice, it is usually better to ask for healing of the trauma symptoms you are experiencing from the estrangement. Naming those symptoms can be helpful, especially if it shifts the practitioner from focusing on the relationship with your adult child to your recovery process.

At its best, religion establishes and reinforces the belief that a Spiritual Source loves us unconditionally. The alternative belief, that we are only loved, and can escape punishment, if we think certain things, act in certain ways, and feel certain feelings, makes it almost impossible for us to be honest with ourselves and others. The simple admission that our child has cut off the relationship with us is excruciatingly difficult if we believe the penalty for estrangement is being shamed, judged, and rejected. The self-awareness that is essential to our recovery can only expand when we believe we are loved regardless of our mistakes, that we are perfectly imperfect.

For many of us this requires a change in our concept of God from a punitive judge to a loving presence. Continuing with the legal analogy, we must free ourselves from thinking of God as a judge from whom we hide or minimize our wrongdoing in order to avoid punishment. Instead, we are invited to think of God as our counsel for the defense. Every time our conscience dredges up some failure from the past, and declares us defective and disposable, God rushes to defend and rescue us from our own self-accusations. Laws are useless in cultivating deep change and healing. They only drive us underground.

We must resist the temptation of using religious laws or rules as a means of convincing our estranged children that they are wrong. Quoting the fifth of the Ten Commandments, "Honor your father and your mother,"[118] will only invite someone to quote "…do not provoke your children to anger"[119] in response. Neither will provide the safe space for meaningful reflection that might lead to

---

[118] Exodus 20:12
[119] Ephesians 6:4

healing the rupture. It will only fortify defensiveness. This is a misuse of religion.

A final benefit of religion is the rebuilding of personal identity. Given the investment of love, time, and resources in parenting our children, it is natural that our role as parent might blur into our identity. This may not pose a problem for a time. But when we become estranged, the role of parent can evaporate. We are left with the question, "Who are we?"

As we saw in Chapter 11, a spiritual perspective restores our identity around a variety of affirmations that might include, I am a child of God, I am perfectly imperfect, I forgive and am forgiven, I am unique and gifted, I am a spiritual being having a human experience, etc. These kinds of affirmations, when kneaded into the deep heart by recitation or reflection, reestablish the foundation of who we are. Circling back to the root meaning of religion, they reconnect us to the identity given us by God. Without that identity, we feel like we are drowning in a sea of meaninglessness. If we just stop struggling, and put down our feet, we realize that we are only in four feet of water. We can stand easily on the spiritual foundation offered to us. Recognizing that this new identity on which we stand can never be taken away is key to our recovery.

We each must awaken to our spiritual identity in our own time and manner. Exerting pressure on others, including our children, to walk our particular path is a misuse of religion. Also, reducing all the issues in our role as parent, or their role as children, to a single spiritual solution is a similar misuse of religion. Sometimes, it is better to talk to God about children, then it is to talk to children about God. Becoming the best versions of ourselves is the most convincing testimony to the spiritual realm than any words we might string into a sentence. As St. Francis said, "Preach the Gospel at all times. If necessary, use words."

Group Rage

In the summer of 1987, a tailgater swerved up beside Rick Bynum's car on a Los Angeles highway and fired. His crime? His car was only going 65 mph in the fast lane. Road rage was born.

Today, we are dealing with group rage.

Dr. Ryan Martin, anger researcher featured on the website, All the Rage, suggests that anger begins with a provocation, like a driver going too slow in front of us. Then, we make a primary appraisal, like the thought that the driver is not a responsible person. That's when we start to get mad. But then, there is a second appraisal, like our spouse in the car commenting that it's just not that big a deal in the overall scheme of things. That calms us down, even a little. But when we are alone in the car, and really need to get somewhere, with no one to give us that calming secondary appraisal, that's when we get *really* mad.[120] That's when we rage.

Group rage is similar except for one key difference. The group makes the second appraisal worse. Instead of having a person next to us who can give us reasons to calm down, we have people in the group giving us even more reasons why we should be angry. The larger the group, the angrier we become. They throw gasoline on the fire, when water is called for. Instead of moderating the anger, the group inflames it to the point that it becomes something else: group rage.

I was a member of a cult for about thirteen years, and I have observed the pattern within myself. When we first join a group, and we hear something outlandish, we are confused. This can't be right. Or is it? We look around at people like us, maybe even people we respect. We don't trust our better judgement. We begin to adopt their thinking and feeling. We can't all be wrong, right? There are too many of us. When challenged with factual information, we don't really consider it. We fall back on the belief that we can't all be wrong. Group rage develops and is sustained in the same way.

---

[120] http://alltheragescience.com/

As estranged parents, we must resist the temptation of becoming caught up in the group rage of other estranged parents. It is a slippery slope. We begin with a provocation: our adult child cuts us off. We have the primary appraisal: our adult child has taken an unjustified action that is extremely painful. That hurts us, but it also begins to make us mad. Then a group we are in provides the secondary appraisal that goes something like this, kids today are all self-centered, thankless, spoiled brats. It ramps up our anger to group rage. We can't all be wrong. After a while, the anger develops its own neural pathways. Our brain rewires to support it. It becomes our go-to emotion.

It is one thing to get angry. It is another thing to live angry. Anger can be healthy when channeled into productive activities. Estranged parents have many options for turning that energy into something useful, not the least of which is helping other estranged parents. But living angry can make you sick. It has a range of negative health outcomes. It aggravates heart conditions. In ramps up your stroke risk. It weakens your immune system. It worsens mental health conditions like depression and anxiety. Above all, it can damage relationships that are important to you. Should an opportunity for reconciliation with your adult child come your way, an embedded anger that has been hard-wired into your brain will not serve you, or them, well.

The Cookbooks

After several years of research, and the same number working with estranged parents, I have come to believe that estrangement is extremely complex. My favorite measure of complexity is this: how many words does it take to say it? Knowing the four types of estrangement in Chapter 5 is just the beginning.

How many words would it take to describe the relationship with your adult child? You would have to start with your shared generational history, your individual history, their individual history, the stages of their development as you were parenting them, what was happening in the culture, their friendships, chance occurrences, etc. Then there is the estrangement, and all the factors surrounding that. There are all the effects of the estrangement, on both the parent and the adult child, and beyond. It would literally fill volumes.

In addition, there are a few things we know to be true about parental estrangement in general. It is almost always initiated by the adult child. In the great majority of cases, that adult child has little confidence that a functional relationship in the future will ever be possible. There is almost always a third party involved who instigates or exacerbates the estrangement. In contrast, the great majority of estranged parents believe the opposite, that a functional relationship in the future *is* possible.

So, what we have here is a failure to communicate. And that is creating a motivational gap. The adult child is highly motivated to move on with their life. The estranged parent is highly motivated to find a solution. There are a number of actors who step into that gap. In addition to therapists and journalists, we are beginning to see evangelical leaders who have read the signs of the times. They recognize the pain of estranged parents as an opportunity to expand their church's outreach.

What is often presented is a cookbook approach, including a recipe for reconciliation, with success stories focused on a particular method. That approach might be therapeutic in nature. A mother is helped by a therapist to see that she should stop interfering in her daughter's wedding plans, and the daughter is helped to forgive her mother. An estranged father accepts Christ, joins the church, begins reading the Bible, and is reunited with his daughter.

Why does this get a dragon? Why do I think it is dangerous for estranged parents to go off the map in this direction? (1) The cases presented are not representative of the ones I observe as typical. Simple arithmetic will get you by at the grocery story, but it won't get a person to the moon. Typical estrangements are much more complex than those presented. (2) Estranged parents are expected to function with a high degree of emotional intelligence when trauma is sometimes reducing their capacity to function in even the most basic ways. (3) It is never stated up front that the prognosis for a healthy, sustainable reconciliation is relatively poor. (4) The efforts outlined in the recipe fail to work for everyone, and, therefore, (5) The parent feels more demoralized than ever.

Thirty years ago, when I was a pastor, I walked into a patient's hospital room, only to be intercepted by a family member who immediately ushered me back out the door.

"We don't want her to see you. We're afraid it will make her think she is dying."

She actually was dying. I conducted her funeral the next week. She died alone in her thoughts, with no one to hear them, no one to sit with her, no one to help her grieve what she was leaving behind, and prepare her for what lay ahead. She died alone because no one would tell her the truth. I believe that it is a cruel mercy that does not name the suffering of parental estrangement, and help parents, as much as possible, heal and flourish, even if their children continue to choose estrangement.

The final warning is not to the estranged parent, but to those of us who are estranged parents trying to help other estranged parents. We are not therapists. We are not in a position to offer advice. Also, recovery is a process. What is helpful in one stage of recovery is not appropriate to another. Sadly, I have been estranged from my children, on and off, for twenty years now. On that first Father's Day when I received no cards and no call, my back locked up so badly that I literally could not get up and down from bed without help…and I had never had a day of back pain in my life.

I love and miss my children profoundly. Losing them is like the loss of a limb. An amputee never gets over that impairment, but they can learn to live with it, run with it, ski with it, even climb mountains with it. I have learned a lot about how to cope with loss. However, I also know that much of what I have learned would be totally inappropriate for an estranged father on his first Father's Day.

🐉 Don't give advice, don't evaluate, and certainly don't criticize or judge another estranged parent for how they are handling things. Even if you think you know a better way, allowing them to discover it on their own may be better in the long run. Just listen.

I first heard this story nearly forty years ago, but its lesson has stayed with me. A man found the cocoon of a butterfly. One day a small opening appeared. He sat and watched the butterfly for several hours as it struggled to force its body through that little hole. Then it seemed to stop making any progress. It appeared as if it had gotten as far as it could and could go no further.

So, the man decided to help the butterfly. He took a pair of scissors and snipped off the remaining bit of the cocoon. The butterfly then emerged easily. But it had a swollen body and small shriveled wings.

The man continued to watch the butterfly because he expected that, at any moment, the wings would enlarge and expand to be able to support the body, which would contract in time. Neither happened! In fact, the butterfly spent the rest of its life crawling around with a swollen body and shriveled wings. It never was able to fly.

What the man in his kindness and haste did not understand was that the restricting cocoon and the struggle required for the butterfly to get through the tiny opening were nature's way of forcing fluid from the body of the butterfly into its wings so that it would be ready for flight once it achieved its freedom from the cocoon.

Sometimes struggles are exactly what we need in our life. If we were allowed to go through our life without any obstacles, it would cripple us. We would not be as strong as we could have been. And we could never fly.

Sometimes we have to let folks struggle a little, even as we love and support them.

Steps Toward Recovery

In this chapter, the steps toward recovery might better be phrased as steps away from dragons! In reflecting on each item below, it is important to be both honest and self-compassionate. We all have our dragons.

- Make a list of any ways you may have used religion to deal with your estrangement that were not helpful in your recovery process or to your adult child. Exercise self-compassion and make some notes on how to avoid those in the future.
- Take some time to reflect on any religious experiences that were harmful to you. Also reflect on any religious experiences that were helpful to you. Reflect on any ways you may have thrown the baby out with the bathwater.
- Explore some sources of spirituality or religion that are healthy for your recovery process. These might be traditional religions, but could also be books, websites, videos, podcasts, retreats, etc. In addition to the daily readings, you may want to check out two other PEAK resources, *Absalom's Wounds: Parental Estrangement in the Bible*,[121] and *Relationsnip: Is there life after your adult child rejects you?*[122]
- If there are any situations where communication with other estranged parents has led to group rage, you may want to ease out of those situations without judgement of them or yourself.
- Become aware of how stories you hear are affecting you, especially on the Internet. Make a mental note of what you need to avoid.

Wise ones tell us it is easier to avoid temptation than resist it. Similarly, it is easier to avoid a dragon than it is to slay one. We do not possess the power to eliminate all the situations in life that make our recovery more difficult. However, in most cases we have the ability to avoid them.

---

[121] Fe Anam Avis, *Absalom's Wounds: Parental Estrangement in the Bible*, (Magi Press, 2021)

[122] Keli Rugenstein, Ph.D., *Relationsnip: Is there life after your adult child rejects you?* BookBaby, 2022

Questions for Reflection and Discussion

What experiences have you had since your estrangement that have been difficult for you to deal with? What are the dragons from your experience, roads you would recommend that other estranged parents not walk down?

What are some of the ways you have seen religion have a positive effect on people's lives? What are some of the ways you have seen religion misused in ways that were harmful to you or others?

Have you experienced an estranged parents' group where members were ramping up the anger to a level that was not healthy? How did that make you feel?

How does it make you feel to see articles on the Internet offering steps toward reconciliation? Hopeful? Discouraged? Something else?

As an estranged parent, what have been some of your best experiences where you felt listened to? What have been some of your worst?

What is your biggest challenge in listening to other estranged parents?

If you are using this book in a group discussion, what did you gain from hearing others speak? From speaking?

Chapter 20
For Adults Only

In the initial stages of our recovery, we are bewildered and confused by what is happening in the relationship with our adult child. There is a myriad of questions.

What are reasonable expectations? Is the adult child taking care of *us*? Are we taking care of *them*? For how long? Are *we* the caregivers, or are *they*? At what point do we cross the threshold where it all flips? When we retire? When we go into assisted living? When we are bedridden? When we are admitted into hospice? Never? Are we eternal parents?

Are we responsible for *their* emotional needs? Are they responsible for *ours*? Who gets to be angry, and who is responsible for silently absorbing the anger? Who takes the high road? Who makes amends? Who must be more understanding of the two, the parent or the adult child? A forty-year-old daughter becomes angry about a miscommunication over the timing of a weekend visit. The father writes a letter of apology. He sends a gift. She stops talking. Is he responsible to keep reaching out, keep offering an apology, be the understanding one, because that's what a 75-year-old parent is supposed to do?

Who should be grateful, the adult child for all that the parents have contributed to them? Or is it the parent who should be grateful for the adult child staying in touch with them? Are we supporting *them* financially? Are they supporting *us*? Are *we* paying for our past mistakes? Are *they* paying for theirs? Is there an emotional statute of limitations?

Who writes the parenting books that address these questions?

Where Are the Books? Where Are the Classes?

The market for parenting resources in the United States is immense, but only for parents of young children. It is estimated that young moms (ages 18 to 29) spend $231.6 million on parenting books and $141 million on parenting apps annually.[123] Today, Amazon returns 35,814 results in a search for parenting books. A Google search for "parenting advice blog" returns 104,000,000 hits.[124] Take a moment to scan through the list of the 100 best-selling parenting books of all time. Not a single one of them addresses the relationship between parents and their adult children.[125] Who writes the *Parenting Adult Children for Dummies* book? Who writes the how-to manual on being a good adult child to your parent?

Google the search term "parenting classes in my area" and you'll get about 130,000,000 hits, and a listing of numerous in-person and online classes on how to parent young children. But you won't find a single class on how to be the parent of an adult child, or vice versa. As a result, we have a broad, cultural understanding of how to raise young children, but virtually no education or shared perspectives on what the relationship between parents and adult children should look like. None. Do you understand why you might be bewildered?

As a society, we are crystal clear regarding the basic responsibilities of a parent for a two-year-old. In fact, we even have a specific word for a two-year-old: toddler. We have no equivalent word for a 50-year-old other than "child." Toddlers need to be protected and kept safe. They need to be fed, clothed, sheltered, read to, and given affection. They need the parent to patiently endure the tantrums when they are "acting like a two-year-old." Society is so clear about these

---

[123] https://askwonder.com/research/avg-amount-millennial-parents-spend-parenting-books-apps-field-great-break-down-xjjsxbcdl
[124] https://www.parent.com/blogs/conversations/how-parenting-advice-became-an-industry
[125] https://bookauthority.org/books/best-selling-parenting-books

responsibilities that a parent who consistently neglects them risks losing custody.

But what is a parent's physical, emotional, and financial responsibility for a 30-year-old adult child? On this point, there is almost total confusion. It's not that there are no expectations. The expectations are many, and the consequences of failing to live up to them are severe. But a parent may not discover them until it is too late. This is the estrangement experience.

A son in his late 20's asks his mother for ten thousand dollars to crew a sailing ship on its voyage around the world. His mother gently, but directly indicates that she won't give him the money, even though she has the resources. The adult child cuts off the mother, and hasn't spoken to her for three years. The mother is stunned and heartbroken. Was she wrong? It is a question that torments her. What is a reasonable expectation for the parent of an adult child? What is the appropriate penalty when a parent fails to meet that expectation? For some parents today, the penalty for getting it wrong is exile, and, unfortunately, it has become a life sentence for many.

A Model for the Evolving Parent-Child Relationship

Ellen Galinsky, chief science officer at the Bezos Family Foundation, is one of the few scholars to introduce a model for the development of the relationship between the parent and the child over the course of their lives. She identified the six stages shown in the table *Galinsky's Stages of Parenthood*. However, her model stops at "Stage 6: The Departure Stage," when the last child leaves home. At that point, the parent is, on average, 55 years old, and will live another 25 years or more. This is precisely the age at which we see the onset of parental estrangement. Her insights end where parental estrangement begins. How might we complete her model?

Our first observation is that a parent at this stage is facing almost as many development challenges as a young child. During these later years, parents deal with a threatened loss of identity due to retirement, but also an increase in freedom. There are end-of-life issues, and the likely deaths of their parents. There is the inevitable increase in chronic medical conditions, and the parent's entry into a stage of life where their reflection on the meaning of it all begins to dominate. How does the parent-child relationship continue to evolve in these later years? For estranged parents, it doesn't.

An estranged father sends me an email. He just lost *his* father. His mother had died the year before. He thought his daughter might show up at one of the funerals. She didn't. She has not reached out to him at all. Is this stage of loss for a parent not as significant as graduating from elementary school is for a child which, in Galinsky's model requires that "parents renegotiate their relationship with their children to allow for shared power in decision-making"? How many parents have suffered from the experience of a pandemic, either in isolation, or from contracting the actual disease, or faced some other life-and-death situation, but have not heard from their adult children to check in on them? Is there no model suggesting that adult children might adjust to the life-stage of a parent as a simple expression of compassion that even total strangers offer?

Laurence Steinberg, Ph.D., is a Distinguished University Professor and the Laura H. Carnell Professor of Psychology and Neuroscience at Temple University. Though he is one of the world's leading experts on adolescence, his clarity of thought evaporates when discussing the relationship between parents and their adult children. The ambiguity at this stage nearly jumps off the page when he writes:

"Many adults maintain an active relationship with their parents. As adults, they can now relate to each other as equals, although the feeling of one being the parent and the other a "child" (even though the child is now an adult) endures in some relationships. In some families, the adult children take care of their parents, much in the same way that their parents took care of them when they were younger. This situation has brought both stress and joy as parents and adult children struggle to redefine their relationship."[126]

Galinsky's Stages of Parenthood

Stage	**Age of Child**	**Main Tasks and Goals**
Stage 1: The Image-Making Stage	Planning for a child; Pregnancy	Prospective parents consider what it means to be a parent and plan for changes to accommodate a child.
Stage 2: The Nurturing Stage	Infancy	Parents develop an attachment relationship with the child and adapt to the new baby.
Stage 3: The Authority Stage	Toddler and pre-school	Parents create rules and figure out how to effectively guide their child's behavior.
Stage 4: The Interpretive Stage	Middle childhood	Parents help their children interpret their experiences within the social world beyond the family.
Stage 5: The Interdependent Stage	Adolescence	Parents renegotiate their relationship with their children to allow for shared power in decision-making.

---

[126] https://psychology.jrank.org/pages/472/Parent-Child-Relationships.html

Stage 6: The Departure Stage	Early adulthood	Parents evaluate their successes and failures as parents as their children become independent.
?	?	?

Dr. Steinberg's language is very tentative. "Many adults maintain," "some relationships," "some families." This is not a deficiency in his thinking. He is simply observing the current muddle. If you are an estranged parent feeling extreme confusion and frustration, you are not crazy. You are walking in a minefield of poorly defined, arbitrary, and largely unspoken expectations. That's not your fault. That's not your adult child's fault. It is the context in which we are living.

A Proposed Stage 7: Toward Adult-to-Adult Relationships

In PEAK, we seek to be as clear as possible about the desired relationship between parents and adult children. The goal is to evolve from parent-to-child relationships into adult-to-adult relationships as indicated by adding Stage 7 to Galinsky's model shown in the table *PEAK's Additional Stage*. The stage begins when the brain of an adult child has completed the development of their frontal cortex, about age 25. It ends at the death of the parent.

The work of Stage 7 requires a major adjustment on the part of the parent and the adult child. Since estranged parents have no access to their adult children, they can only take responsibility for making changes on their side of the relationship. It is in helping estranged parents make this adjustment that PEAK focuses its attention. Any significant recovery from parental trauma is impossible apart from the perspective of Stage 7.

PEAK's Additional Stage

Stage	Age of Child	Main Tasks and Goals
Stage 7: The Adult-to-Adult Stage	25 to the parent's death	Parents and adult children evolve together into a relationship characterized by mutuality, commitment, authenticity, and gratitude.

The underlying assumption of Stage 7 is that any adult-to-adult relationship is *voluntary*. This is what PEAK parents recite in each meeting: "The Way Forward is to live into the reality that relationships between parents and adult children are voluntary." In the United States, there is no law requiring adult children to stay connected to their parents, as there is in, say, China. A national law recently introduced in China requires the offspring of parents older than 60 to visit their parents "frequently" and make sure their financial and spiritual needs are met. Failure can result in a fine, or even jail time.[127] But is this what we want, compulsory visits?

Finding Peace in Transforming Obligations into Offerings

From one perspective, it makes sense that we as estranged parents might make some obligatory claim on our adult children. We have made deep, irreversible emotional investments in their lives. We were the first to look into their eyes when they were born, or claimed by our adoption. We sang and rocked them to sleep. We read to them, and then read with them their bedtime stories. We went to their schools, met with their teachers, and sometimes fought with their teachers, to make sure they were given a fair chance. We dried their tears when they

---

[127] https://www.cnn.com/2013/07/02/world/asia/china-elderly-law/

cried. We bandaged their skinned knees. We laid hands on their precious heads and prayed for them when they were visited by nightmares. We attended their games, plays, and concerts. We not only gave them our love. We gave them our hearts. So, yes, in all honesty, we now realize that we had an understandable, unspoken expectation that love would be returned, along with Paul McCartney's "grandchildren on your knee" (McCartney, P. 1967).

Understandable as those feelings might be, holding onto this obligatory expectation of our adult children is a major source of suffering for us as estranged parents. It not only contributes to a daily broken-heartedness, it can breed feelings of unfairness, resentment, and bitterness. It darkens our mood. It laces our conversations with a degree of cynicism, poisoning other relationships with a lack of trust.

> *All three of my children have decided they want nothing to do with me, all for different reasons. I'm trying to learn how to cope with this and move on.*
> C.U. from Bowling Green, KY

At its root, this is a spiritual issue. Buddha famously said that the root of all suffering is attachment. The Judeo-Christian tradition has its own way of expressing the same sentiment through the concept of offerings. Speak of an offering, and most Christians think of a felt-padded, brass plate passed up and down the pews. But the concept is so much richer than the collection of money. The Old Testament describes a complex array of offerings to God, but metaphorically, the insight is similar to Buddha's. Seeing our lives as an offering enables us to detach from their outcome in a way that brings peace.

Part of the work of Stage 7 is evolving toward an understanding of the past investment in our children as a spiritual offering. A spiritual offering makes a gift, while simultaneously releasing it from any obligatory strings. It gives with two open hands. In contrast, we sometimes discover that we have given love with the understandable, yet unspoken expectation that love will be returned. It is given with one hand, but we now realize that there is an expected return into the second hand. It begins as a blessing, but ends with great suffering. It keeps accounts while a spiritual offering liberates. Many of us as estranged parents have to do some work in transforming our early parenting contributions into spiritual offerings.

In the Old Testament, there is the additional concept of a burnt offering. A regular offering provided food for the priests to eat; it served a useful purpose. But a burnt offering took something valuable and destroyed it by fire. From a spiritual standpoint, a burnt offering is a gift we give out of love that is totally wasted by the recipient. In the case of a child, a burnt offering is money misspent, an education unused, or lessons totally forgotten. When these become an obligation that we throw up to our adult child in words or attitude, they harm both the relationship and our own souls. When we treat these like burnt offerings instead, we release ourselves from an attachment to unfairness and resentment.

A father spends tens of thousands of dollars on three different in-patient addiction treatment programs for his twenty-year-old daughter. She relapsed each time. After leaving the most recent treatment center, she cut off all communication with him. The last word he received was that she was living on the streets in San Diego. How does he deal with it? Being Jewish, he adopts an attitude toward the situation of an Old Testament burnt offering. He releases her from any resentment on his part. He has peace.

A ritual that enables you to let go of the suffering connected to the obligations owed by your adult child can be helpful. Take a piece of paper, and write on it a list of what you have given to your child that you want to become an offering. In a moment of sacred silence, set the paper on fire, and place the ashes at the roots of a beautiful tree, or spread it on the surface in a running stream. Alternatively, place it in an offering plate, or next to a votive candle in your faith community's worship service. This is the beginning of liberation.

On Mutuality, Commitment, Authenticity, and Gratitude

At Stage 7, an adult-to-adult relationship is characterized by four qualities: mutuality, commitment, authenticity, and gratitude. However, the evolution toward an adult-to-adult relationship generally begins at a parent-to-adolescent starting point. Parent-to-adolescent relationships tend to be unilateral, capricious, guarded, and entitled. When parents choose to enable relationships that are stuck in that phase, they are multiplying their suffering.

The first adult-to-adult quality is mutuality. In a mutual relationship, each carries responsibility for maintaining it. Here we move beyond the stage of offerings appropriate in adult-to-adolescent relationships. Now, we are equals, as Laurence Steinberg puts it. We take similar levels of initiative in terms of communicating, arranging to spend time together, and general support of the relationship. In a unilateral relationship, the burden falls disproportionately on the parent. The parent calls, invites, supports, pursues, and cajoles. The pleading of "Call your mom!" is appropriate when addressed to an adolescent. However, pleading is beneath the dignity of any person in an adult-to-adult relationship. It erodes confidence and self-esteem to have to beg.

If we have fallen into this pattern, recovery requires that we as estranged parents stop pleading. It doesn't work. If your child does not respond to your appeal, you will feel rejected. If they give in, you will feel worse about yourself in having to beg someone to care for you. In lieu of pleading, it is essential that estranged parents engage in activities and relationships that are interesting to them and build self-esteem. In the words from weekly PEAK meetings, "You will take responsibility for your own life and supply your own needs for relationships."

The second quality in an adult-to-adult relationship is commitment. In relationships characterized by commitment, both parents and their adult children benefit from the security of knowing that the other will stick with them, even when difficulties are encountered. The relationship is not capricious. Parents don't walk on eggshells for fear their adult child will abandon them. The threat of ending the relationship is not used as emotional blackmail, or as a regular way of expressing displeasure. Therapist Keli Rugenstein describes this pattern as the estrangement dance. The adult child moves in and out of the relationship based upon their emotional state. In many cases, this estrangement dance is a prelude to the crisis leading to a full, long-term cutoff.

Commitment is essential to any healthy relationship. Like any other person, a parent needs a level of commitment in order to develop trust. When that trust is broken by a cutoff, the parent has the right to negotiate a process that will reestablish trust over a period of time. A parent should settle this in their mind: "In the event of a reconnection after a period of estrangement, I will not jump back into the relationship without a commitment to a period of rebuilding trust." As estranged parents, we deserve as much.

Then, there is authenticity. Commitment is what gives persons the ability to feel safe in developing authentic relationships. Without commitment, and a fundamental acceptance, both parents and their adult children must remain guarded. They cannot share their deeper thoughts. The damage can go both ways. Adult children going through divorce, career issues, or financial struggles don't feel they can be honest with parents for fear of disapproval or rejection. A fifty-year old man has an affair and goes through a divorce. But when he tells his mother about it, she cuts off the relationship. While a reconnection eventually takes place, he remains guarded for the rest of her life. (This type of estrangement is actually rare. Only 5% of the time is the cutoff initiated by the parent.)

Parents struggling with depression, anxiety about their health, worries about their finances, or a conflict with their adult child are sometimes guarded and don't share their thoughts for fear of abandonment, or simply being a burden. They become isolated in their pain, or, worse, take actions that are self-destructive. I have observed that a large percentage of estranged parents are struggling with suicidal thoughts. The highest suicide rates in the country are among those in the estrangement years, usually guarding their secret despair until it is too late.

Authenticity is essential, especially for older adults recovering from parental trauma. "Our recovery begins when we risk moving out of isolation….by gradually releasing the burden of unexpressed grief, we join others in the journey toward gentleness, humor, love and respect." These are words we recite each week in PEAK recovery groups. Parents need authentic relationships, and when they can't experience them with their adult children, they need to engage in a serious effort to find them elsewhere.

The final characteristic of adult-to-adult relationships is gratitude. They contain healthy doses of appreciation expressed in conversations, notes, cards, letters, gifts, and public tributes. Their orientation toward the relationship is that of a gift. Entitled relationships and the benefits they offer are either taken for granted, or considered a right. Since gratitude is not valued, entitled relationships slowly rot from the inside out. Gratitude multiplies our blessings in both quality and quantity. What we feel entitled to is depleted and exhausted. Reflecting on the relationship with his adult children, a physician friend of mine who had become wealthy through his pathology practice confided, "My money has become the greatest curse of my life."

There are a number of indicators that a parent is in an entitled relationship with their adult children. One is found in the weekly recitation of "Our Common Experiences . . . We have adult children who either refuse to have a relationship with us or only relate to us when they are in need of financial or material assistance." In the United States, it is estimated that over 10% of those age 65 and older experience some form of elder abuse in a given year.[128] Included in that abuse is financial exploitation. Six out of ten times, it is a family member exploiting the parent. The root of the issue is entitlement.

Many of the perpetrators do not think of themselves as committing a crime or even doing anything wrong. They may see the older person's

---

[128] https://www.justice.gov/elderjustice/about-elder-abuse

savings as something they are entitled to because they are helping the person. For example, a child who helps her mother manage online bill payments may transfer a "little extra" to her own bank account as compensation for her time. "These situations can be nightmares for the elders who lose both their money and trusted family relationships," says Tim McNeil, a partner at The Elder Law Firm in Portland, Oregon.[129]

Estranged parents need the relationships with their adult child to evolve from entitlement to gratitude. Entitlement is a danger sign. Those who cannot say "thank you," cannot be trusted. It is an indication that an adult child is stuck in adolescence, and caution is always in order.

Steps Toward Recovery

Most parental estrangements are characterized by over-functioning parents and under-functioning adult children. As a result, parents are inclined to take too much responsibility for the relationship which can result in (a) violations of boundaries set by their adult child, (b) feelings of guilt on the part of the parent for not being able to repair the relationship, or (c) exhaustion as the parent attempts to carry the lion's share of the relationship on their shoulders. Recovery requires a realignment of the parent's thinking and feeling in the direction of an adult-to-adult relationship.

The following are steps in that direction.

- Spend some time reviewing your relationships with your adult children. Do they tend more toward parent-to-adolescent or adult-to-adult? Avoid guilt or judgement here. It is simply your starting point.
- Set an intention to work toward adult-to-adult relationships with all your adult children. Remember, they have likely had no

---

[129] https://www.drstaceywood.com/fraud-in-the-family/

training on how to do this, so be patient. Begin by taking concrete actions that model mutuality, commitment, authenticity, and gratitude in your relationships with them.

- In the case of an estranged adult child, do a review of how you may have over-functioned in the past, any boundaries you may have violated, and any unrealistic expectations you may have taken on yourself. Given the possibility of a reconnection in the future, give some thought to how you will communicate your need for an adult-to-adult relationship as a part of a healthy reconciliation.
- Create a Stage 7 mantra that you can repeat on a daily basis. Use the paragraph below as a starting point, amend it to fit your situation, print it off, and hang it somewhere that you will see it several times a day:

> I am a parent evolving toward an adult-to-adult relationship with my estranged child, even if I must evolve on my own. I will no longer plead for time or energy. I will match my child's investment in our relationship, meeting moment with moment, sentiment with sentiment. I will not exceed the commitment of my child. I will not walk on eggshells or distort my personality to temper the fear of abandonment. Should a reconnection be initiated, I will expect a commitment to rebuilding trust. I will seek opportunities to share deeply about things that matter. I will neither rejoice in silence nor despair in secret. I will not judge, as I expect not to be judged. I shall be alert to entitlement and flee it, however close it comes to me. I will offer gratitude, even as I expect gratitude. My abundance shall become a gift to the world.

Finally, if all adult-to-adult relationships are voluntary, we want to be the best versions of ourselves that we can be. As a seminary professor once said, "If you are going to talk to someone about God, make sure you are fun to be with!" As estranged parents, we don't have to be fun all the time, but the world needs for us to take our recovery seriously. No one benefits from our staying stuck in our trauma.

Questions for Reflection and Discussion
The beginning of this chapter speaks about the confusion that exists in the expectations between parents and adult children. Where have you experienced this confusion in the relationship with your estranged child?

Why do you think that virtually no books have been written for parents and adult children on how they should relate to one another?

Why do you think it is difficult for estranged parents to accept that the relationship with their adult child is voluntary? What suffering does this resistance introduce into their lives?

When you think of the relationship with your adult child prior to the estrangement, how would you describe it in terms of

        Mutuality

        Commitment

        Authenticity

        Gratitude

Do you think you deserve to have an adult-to-adult relationship with your child? How afraid are you to ask for that?

How might your recovery make you a better partner, friend, parent to others in your life?

If you are using this book in a group discussion, what did you gain from hearing others speak? From speaking?

Part III
Bringing Life Back Online

Chapter 21
Living in the Estranged Parents Community

One of the greatest miracles to witness is the degree of healing that can take place in a group of estranged parents who choose to be in community with one another. The damage caused by feeling alone, confused, and powerless begins to be reversed before our very eyes as people experience companionship, insight, and potential. In PEAK it is safe to be where we are, afraid, sad, angry, and, yes, still not over it. It is truly beautiful.

That said, we are not always the easiest folks to deal with, and for a number of reasons. In this chapter I want to address a core issue: how do we sustain our relationship to this estranged parent community that is so essential to our recovery, and theirs.

At the top of the list is tolerance and flexibility.

It helps to understand the process of adult development. The community of estranged parents is one of the most diverse groups we will ever encounter. This is largely because of our age and life experience. If you ask someone what they were doing at 9:00 am on the third Thursday of October when they were 10 years old they would likely have the same answer as everyone else: in the fifth-grade learning reading, writing, history, math, etc. But if you were to ask someone what they were doing at 9:00 am on the third Thursday of October when they were 50 years old, all the answers would be different. As we age, we have increasingly different experiences. As someone said, we are born into uniformity; we are aged into particularity.

What estranged parents share in common is their agony. Everything else is likely to be different. Some of us are black, some white, some

Asian, some Latino. Some of us are Republicans, some Democrats. Some of us are Evangelical Christians, some progressive, some Jewish, Buddhist, some Muslim, some are spiritual but not religious, and some have no spiritual perspective at all. Some of us have a college degree, some have not finished high school. Some of us are wealthy, some scrape by.

These differences in life experiences come into play whenever we are engaged in a shared process, like a PEAK meeting. We have differing preferences regarding how things are worded, what should be read aloud and what should be read in advance, what needs to be repeated and what is becoming tiresome, what is too much sharing and what is too little, when is a meeting too long and when too short, when should we require a commitment and when should we give people freedom, what pushes my buttons versus what pushes yours, what's too late for a meeting and what is too early, etc.

> *I found PEAK by accident. I enrolled and went to my first meeting. The camaraderie, nonjudgmental attitudes, and love has started my journey of reclaiming my life.*
> Q.D. from Little Rock, AR

This amount of diversity requires a high degree of tolerance and flexibility. The gift of PEAK is that it can help us remember that we all share a common humanity, that pain is pain regardless of our particular beliefs, and that a broken heart feels the same to each of us. As Shakespeare put it, "If you prick us, do we not bleed? If you tickle us, do we not laugh? If you poison us, do we not die?" (TMOV.3.1.) If we become too focused on a particular way of doing things, we have probably hitched our wagon to a footnote, and are avoiding what is most important: our recovery.

We need to be sensitive to the severity of estrangement, and the stage of recovery in the persons we are with.

First, severity. As we saw in Chapter 5, the mother of a college senior who has stopped communicating is struggling just like every other estranged parent. But she may be more annoyed than traumatized as she wrestles with whether to keep paying her daughter's cell phone bill. In reality, a college student's brain is still developing, and the estrangement may self-correct with maturity. That possibility in no way minimizes the struggle. Any estrangement introduces a painful degree of uncertainty and ambiguity into the relationship with an adult child. Compassionate support is essential.

In contrast is a father who hasn't spoken with his daughter in 20 years and is facing the prospect of dying without ever seeing her again. This can be deeply traumatizing in a way that may be difficult for a younger parent to comprehend. In fact, the stories of a parent who has been estranged for 20 years may be anxiety producing for a newly-estranged parent. And vice versa. In both cases, it will be important to listen for where parents are coming from, without anxiety blocking compassion, no matter how severe their situation.

Then there is the stage of recovery. When parents are first estranged, they are generally feeling shock and bewilderment. They are not sure how long the estrangement will last. They are holding out hope for reconnecting. Other estranged parents are at a different stage. They have fully accepted that estrangement is a long-term prospect for their lives. They have worked through much of the pain and are focused on how to rebuild their lives. As we say in our weekly meetings, "We are each at different points in the recovery process. Some of us are feeling shock and anger that this has happened to us. Others of us are searching for ways to restore the relationship even as we try to move forward with our lives. Still others have accepted that estrangement may be a long-term aspect of their situation, and are working toward lives with purpose and zest."

It is tempting for us to project our stage of recovery onto others. However, to those in the early weeks of anguish, hearing how much better life is in the later stages can feel a little like being shut in by a blizzard in Maine, and receiving a post card from a friend vacationing in Hawaii with the words "wish you were here." It is extremely important that we accept and support everyone, no matter what their stage of recovery without trying to shoehorn them into ours.

Listening is important in every respect. Listening is always important, but especially when dealing with persons as vulnerable as estranged parents.

One of the simple things I learned in graduate school is that there are two ways of listening: listening to analyze and listening to understand. As a former engineer, which of the two do you think I did better?

When we listen to analyze, our goal is to evaluate the person speaking, their situation, how they are handling it, and how others are behaving as well. With regard to the estranged parent, we may get focused on the mistakes they have made, the things they did right, or even the behavior of their adult child we judge to be unfair.

When we listen to understand, our goal is to get as close as we can to the experience of the person we are listening to. What is it like to be them? What do they feel, and why? This is best summarized by a statement like, "Sounds like Carol is feeling _(a feeling word)_ because of _(a fact from the situation)_." This may seem canned and mechanical, and without authenticity, it is. But when combined with authentic care, this kind of listening can be one of the most powerful ways we show love.

Since estranged parents are typically carrying a great deal of inner pain, it is likely that this pain will surface with anyone who cares and is truly listening. They may begin weeping, sobbing, shaking or venting their anger. The more intense their reaction, the more important it is for us to stay present to them without yielding to the temptation to calm them down. They will likely apologize for "losing control." Reassure them that they are doing fine.

Alternatively, a parent can choke up, and stop speaking at all. They may be trying to get back into control of their emotions. Or they may be trying to find a way to say what they are feeling. Again, stay present to them. Say something permission-giving like, "Take all the time that you need. We are right here."

People who are in a lot of pain sometimes act out. They can be irritable about different things, meetings starting a little late, something in the script they don't like, or in response to something another person says. They can show up late. They can be distracted by their stress or lack focus on what is going on around them. They can be withdrawn and non-participating. Or they can begin to talk over people.

We need to forgive one another when we behave in these ways. But if it is really disruptive, or we have a genuine concern for them that needs to be addressed, we can say something like "Bill, you don't seem to be yourself today. What's going on?" Wisdom will dictate whether to do this in the group or one-on-one.

One of the most important ways that we care for another, and our relationship with them, is to keep our commitments and show up. Eighty percent of the success in our recovery will be showing up whether we feel like it or not. As an estranged parent, you are going to have good days, bad days, too tired days, too hurt days, I'm-fine-don't-need-it days, and I-got-nothing days. You'll never recover if you are driven by your emotions to the point that they dictate your life. Show up.

A soldier was wounded on the field of battle. His friend went after him, but in the process was mortally wounded himself. As he was dying, his commanding officer said, "Now look what you've done. I've lost both of you."

The solder replied, "It was worth it, Sarge. His last words to me were 'I knew you'd come.'"

Showing up begins with just bringing your body into the presence of others. But it also requires showing up emotionally, participating in the conversation, and taking the risk to let others know how you are feeling. These also are acts of true courage.

Finally, showing up can provide creative opportunities to enter the lives of others in ways they don't expect. Sending someone a note of encouragement, a text, or a brief surprise phone call can sometimes land at just the right moment in their lives. I have a cousin who lives by an interesting principle. When a thought comes to mind about doing something for others, she just does it. She doesn't overthink it.

She drops what she is doing at the moment and takes action. That is also showing up.

Developing and maintaining trust is essential to all our relationships, but especially with estranged parents. We have just gone through one of the most trust-shattering experiences of our lives. We may need to help other parents rebuild their ability to trust—and rebuild ours at the same time. How do we build trust?

Building trust takes time; there are no shortcuts. All relationships start with the minimal amount of trust required to get the conversation going, a kind of relational ante. They grow from there.

Trust grows by acting in a trustworthy manner. That includes showing up and keeping our word. It also means consistently staying within the guidelines of the group. It means listening without judgement or critique. It means maintaining confidentiality and not having side conversations about another who is not present.

Trust ultimately cannot grow without someone mustering the courage to take risks. We take a risk when we let someone know that we care about them or when we honestly share something about ourselves that scares us a little. Trust is developed when someone shows us something about themselves of which they may not be proud and discovers that we do not go away.

This leads to another key element of maintaining a healthy relationship with our estranged parent community: vulnerability. The word *vulnerable* finds its root in the Latin word *vulnus* which means "wound." The word has a double impact. It means letting others know we are wounded. It also exposes ourselves to be wounded further should someone choose to do so. That's the irony of a wound. Only at the risk of further wounding can a wound be healed.

The invitation to vulnerability begins early in a PEAK recovery group when a member is asked to read "Our Common Experiences." Anytime we sound our voice before a group, it's a small, but important step. As most people have experienced or learned, people are more afraid of speaking before a group than death itself. The invitation to vulnerability increases step by step with a self-introduction, then sharing some aspect of one's story. Without vulnerability, silence locks up the entire conversation.

The final act of vulnerability is actually leading a PEAK recovery group. Ordinary people step into this role. They are usually not therapists or highly skilled facilitators. They are trusting the group to give themselves to the process, and the group is trusting them to keep things moving forward in healthy ways. There is vulnerability and trust on both sides.

The entire process hangs on a feeling of safety, and safety requires boundaries. At the top of that list are the ground rules for the group. These include treating one another with respect and accepting every person no matter where they are in their process. Because most of us are not professional therapists, we are careful *never* to give advice.

Finally, one of the most important components of maintaining a healthy relationship to our group is gratitude. Some aspects of gratitude can be built into our groups through ritual. After each person speaks, we say "thank you," and at the end of the meeting, we thank the group leader. But other expressions of gratitude are essential. Pick any of the paragraphs in the list and you will find a possible opportunity for expressing gratitude to someone.

"Thank you for always showing up."
"Thank you for having the courage to be vulnerable with us."
"Thank you for listening to me and understanding how I feel."
"Thank you for helping me feel safe when I shared today."
"Thank you for forgiving me when I went off the rails."

Gratitude is the only true inoculation against the disease of entitlement, and the one virtue that violates the laws of physics. It creates more of the very thing that created it in the first place: abundance.

Steps Toward Recovery

- Set your intention. The only requirement for joining a PEAK Recovery Group is a desire to recover. It is a simple choice, but no one can make that decision for you except you.
- Commit to unity with your fellow estranged parents and a focus on recovering from parental trauma. There are groups of every kind that address political, religious, educational, financial, and ethnic concerns. We are here only for estranged parents.
- Open yourself to growing as a person in all the ways mentioned in this chapter. If you become more tolerant, more committed to showing up, a better listener, more trusting and trustworthy, more courageously vulnerable, more compassionate, and more grateful, you will become the happier, better person the world needs.
- Put some faith in the guidance of your Spiritual Source to bring you into relationship with people who can help you fulfill your destiny, and you theirs.

Questions for Reflection and Discussion

What has been your past experience with small groups of any kind? Was it positive, negative, mixed, or non-existent?

What were you doing on the third Thursday of October at 9:00 am when you were 10 years old? Fifty years old?

What was the most emotionally healing experience of your life? What happened? Where were you? Who was there?

How is parental estrangement different from anything else you have experienced in your life?

Of the characteristics below, which do you think you have already nailed? Which one will require some growth?

    Tolerance and flexibility

    Listening

    Accepting the imperfections of others when they are upset

    Being committed/showing up

    Developing trust

    Being vulnerable/taking risks

    Staying within boundaries

    Expressing gratitude

What has brought you to the intention of recovering from parental estrangement?

If you are using this book in a group discussion, what did you gain from hearing others speak? From speaking?

PEAK: Parents of Estranged Adult Kids
A Resource for Recovery

Chapter 22
An Estranged Parents Bill of Rights

Remember the story of my broken ankle in Chapter 8? Here is the rest. Twenty-five years ago, I was fulfilling an item on my bucket list: I went skydiving. Unfortunately, I landed incorrectly, and hit the ground with such force that I badly fractured my left ankle. It was splinted at a trauma center, and two days later a sports medicine surgeon installed a pin on one side of my ankle, and a plate with screws on the opposite side. For a couple of years after the accident, I couldn't watch any kind of collision on television or in a movie without an uncontrollable flinch, as if I were hitting the ground over and over again.

I have gone over the mistakes in my landing approach many times. But more than that, I have found an accusing inner voice telling me how stupid I was for letting it happen. If I hadn't broken my ankle, those mistakes would have faded from my memory beneath the storyline of a courageous leap from a perfectly good airplane! But the injury to my body affected how I think about myself. That physical trauma baked in a negative feeling of incompetence.

That's one of the impacts of parental trauma. It bakes in low self-esteem, but at a much deeper level than a physical accident. It is common for us as estranged parents to believe that if we had just been wiser, smarter, more loving, more attentive, less attentive, more demanding, less demanding, or simply better people, none of this would ever have occurred. But we weren't, and it did. Now, we are left with all the negative consequences, a loss of dignity, a beggar mentality, shame, self-doubt, and, sometimes, even self-hatred. Often, we experience an inability to assert or advocate for ourselves in other situations.

Recovery is impossible if we do not find a way to deal with our tattered self-esteem. According to the research, one of the best ways to accomplish this is through repeated self-affirmations of one kind or another, things like

- I am perfectly imperfect.
- I forgive and am forgiven.
- I am unique and gifted.
- I have companions on this journey.
- I deserve to play and have fun.
- I am worthy of friendship and love.
- I am becoming whole.

This often requires an intentional thought-swap. When we have a negative thought about ourselves, we swap it out with a self-affirming one, like those on the list above. This is an important part of our recovery process, and I urge every estranged parent to engage in this inner work.

But there is even better news. Research suggests that self-transcending values and goals may be even more powerful in building our self-esteem.[130] In other words, instead of a self-affirming statement like, "I am a good friend," a more powerful statement would be "Friendships are important and are essential to my happiness." This is a more universal affirmation, and while it is about me, it also goes beyond me.

Another way of making a powerful self-affirmation that is universal is by affirming rights that belong to all of us, but find specific expression for estranged parents. What are the rights of estranged parents that really apply to everyone?

To answer that question, I developed The Estranged Parent Bill of Rights. Before diving into these, I want to be clear on three points.

---

[130] https://depts.washington.edu/anesth/edi/_resources-docs/Cohen_annurev-psych-010213-115137.pdf

First, these are for your own internal work of rebuilding your self-esteem. Do not weaponize them by foisting them upon your estranged child. Second, I consider these to be universal. They apply to all parents of adult children, but have particular force for estranged parents, since, in many cases, they are being violated. In addition, these rights are reciprocal. With only slight modifications in language, these could just as easily become The Estranged Adult Child Bill of Rights, and they would be equally valid. Finally, the research suggests that affirming these values for ourselves and others helps relieve the depression and anxiety brought on by self-reproach.

The language of each of the twelve rights listed below is in the first person. There is a reason for this choice. They are designed to be repeatedly read, perhaps aloud, as a form of self-affirmation. In the descriptions below each right, the language switches to that of an external voice speaking the affirmation to you. To be affirmed by ourselves, but not by others, feels like we are crazy. To be affirmed by others, but not by ourselves, feels like we are phony. We need to hear both affirming voices.

Right #1 - I have the right to expect, but not compel relationships with my children that evolve from adult-to-child, to adult-to-adult, to finalist-to-adult.

You have the right to expect that the relationship with your child will change over the years. During the first two stages, you will be doing most of the adapting as your child grows from infancy to young-adulthood. You will need to learn to treat him or her like an adult, instead of like an adolescent child. During the finalist stage, roughly the final quarter of your life, you have the right to expect your child will be responsive to you. You will be the one going through massive changes. These are the years when you are reflecting on the meaning of your life. In those years, you will also be faced with a number of major life events, death of parents and some friends, the onset of medical issues, some acute, some chronic, retirement, relocation, and, frequently, divorce. Eventually, you will experience physical decline and death. You have the right to hope that your child will be engaged with you as you walk through those finalist years, and increasingly involved as you physically decline.

The 2002, 79-page Report of the Second World Assembly on Aging, put it this way: "We recognize the need to strengthen solidarity among generations and intergenerational partnerships, keeping in mind the particular needs of both older and younger ones, and to encourage *mutually responsive relationships between generations.*" [131]

You have the right to expect a mutually responsive relationship with your adult child. However, it is a voluntary relationship. You do not have the right to compel it. If it is not freely offered, you have the right to grieve it, with all the components of grief, shock, anger, guilt, depression, and final acceptance. You do not have the right to harangue your adult child, which will only drive them further away. With that loss, you have a responsibility to the world and your own life to spiritually evolve in a different direction with your precious life. Spiritually, you do not have the right to quit.

Right #2 - I have the right to form relationships characterized by mutuality, commitment, authenticity, and gratitude rather than relationships that are unilateral, capricious, guarded, and entitled.

You have the right to form relationships that enrich, ground, and even extend your life. Within the family, these are often called "loved ones." Outside the family, these are called "friends." You have the right to form both, along with the responsibility to make the investments that these require. The best way to make good friends is to be a good friend. There is no adage more true or essential.

---

[131] https://documents-dds-ny.un.org/doc/UNDOC/GEN/N02/397/51/PDF/N0239751.pdf

Right #3 - I have the right to assert the legitimacy of my thoughts, feelings, and motivations, rather than being told what I think, feel, and intend.

You have the right to be free from gaslighting. Gaslighting is a form of emotional abuse that says you don't think what you believe you think, you don't feel what you believe you feel, and your motives are not what you believe they are. You have the right to reject gaslighting, to express what you think, feel, and intend, and to have that heard.

About twenty years ago, I was chairing a board meeting of the non-profit I had founded. There was a disagreement about an issue I have long forgotten, but I still remember an interaction between two board members that left a lasting impression. Let's call them Tom and Bob. Tom made a statement that Bob disagreed with. But, instead of saying he disagreed, he jumped to a conclusion about what Tom was "really" thinking.

"You think the board can't be trusted with this decision."

Tom said, simply and respectfully, "Please don't tell me what I think."

There was an awkward silence.

Bob, was undeterred. "Well, it's pretty clear to me that you don't trust the board."

Tom responded, simply and respectfully, "Please don't tell me what I feel."

A longer, awkward silence.

Finally, Bob said, "OK, tell me again."

I have repeated those words, "Please don't tell me what I think," many times. I'm not trying to be difficult. I find it usually slows down the conversation, and eventually makes for a richer communication.

In tense conversations, we regularly tell other people what they are *really* thinking, feeling, or motivated by. It happens so often that we don't even notice. What we end up doing in the process is not hearing their thoughts at all. We end up hearing the thoughts we have created, and then planted in their heads. This can be especially tempting for people who think they know each other well, like parents and their estranged adult children. When a person says something like, "I think of you every day," or how they feel, "I miss you so much," or what is motivating them, "I came to support you," the other counters with, "You don't really think that," or "You don't really feel that," or "That's not why you really came." That includes the presentation of factual information, and being told it is not real. There is a name for the condition where people do not know what they think, do not know what they feel, do not know what their true motivations are, and do not know which facts are real: psychosis.

You have a right not to be told you are psychotic.

Right #4 - I have the right to individual relationships with children, grandchildren, friends, and associates that are not complexified by issues from other relationships.

You have the right to individual relationships that have their own qualities and nuances, joys and sorrows, and, yes, even conflicts and resolutions. Except in cases of outright abuse or neglect, you have the right to have challenges or even failures in one relationship, that do not spill over into multiple relationships. You have the right to engage in a relationship with a person, without having to deal with the influence of a shadow figure who is working surreptitiously behind the scenes to undermine the relationship.

I have already pointed out that in at least 90% of the cases, there is a third party instigating or aggravating the estrangement. That third party can be an ex-spouse, the adult child's spouse or partner, a friend, or even a well-meaning therapist or spiritual advisor. You have the right to deal with your adult child as an individual without the pressure of a loyalty test weighing on the relationship.

Estrangement can become more difficult to repair or contain when something known as emotional fusion is at work. Emotional fusion is a dysfunctional mechanism that binds people together to the exclusion of their individuality. In fused relationships, individual choices are set aside in the service of achieving harmony within the system, whether that system is a family, a couple, or a therapist-client bond. One of the characteristics of emotional fusion is group speak. Individuals speak in the first-person plural. *We* think. *We* feel. *We* have decided. Another one of the characteristics of emotional fusion is the tendency for individuals to be cut off, or to cut themselves off from the fusion in order to achieve some degree of individuality. This is often the source of parental estrangement.

You have the right to individual relationships with each of your children, your grandchildren, and other persons, without intentional efforts of those in the system to expand the cutoff. Even if that happens, in spite of your best efforts, you at least can claim this right to what a system would offer you if it were healthy. Asserting that right within the sanctuary of your own inner life is a source of self-esteem.

Right #5 - I have the right to closure on past failures, real or perceived.

You have the right for failures of the past to be settled, either through forgiveness, restitution, or a period of relational exile and time served. In cases where there has been a breach of trust, you have the right to know the actions that are needed to rebuild that trust, over what period of time, and with what accountability. Beyond that, you have the right not to be reminded of past failures, as you have the equal responsibility not to remind others of theirs. Estranged parents have often lived with the indication that their children did not care if they lived or died. This, also, requires closure.

Right #6 - I have the right to be told directly when closure on past failures is not possible, and to know the limitations that lack of closure will place on our relationship.

You have a right to know when forgiveness, restitution, or a period of relational exile will not be sufficient for closure on a past failure. This can occur when the past offense was so egregious in the eyes of your adult child that it is unforgiveable, because the issue is an irreconcilable difference in core values, or because the adult child is not convinced the behavior will not occur again. Estranged parents join the majority of Americans who are livin' unforgiven. In a 2001 study of 1,423 Americans conducted at the University of Michigan, nearly three-quarters say they feel they've been forgiven by God, but only 52 percent say they have forgiven others. This means that over half of us have at least one person in the world who has not forgiven us for something significant. In many cases that person is our adult child.[132] As painful as this is to face, you have a right to know whether a functional relationship is possible at all. You have the right to move forward with your life.

Right #7 - I have the right to live without abuse, neglect, or exploitation.

You have the right to live without the trauma that is caused by

- *Physical abuse*. Use of physical force that may result in bodily injury, physical pain, or impairment.
- *Sexual abuse*. Non-consensual sexual contact of any kind with an elderly person.
- *Emotional abuse*. Infliction of anguish, pain, or distress through verbal or non-verbal acts.
- *Financial/material exploitation*. Illegal or improper use of an elder's funds, property, or assets.
- *Neglect*. Refusal or failure to fulfill any part of a person's obligations or duties to an elderly person.

It is estimated that approximately 1 to 2 million Americans age 65 or older are abused, neglected, or exploited, most often by their adult children.[133] Parents are often too embarrassed to ask for help, for fear of losing the relationship with their child.

---

[132] http://ns.umich.edu/Releases/2001/Dec01/r121101a.html
[133] https://www.apa.org/pi/prevent-violence/resources/elder-abuse

Right #8 - I have the right to recover from the trauma of estrangement, and to develop a positive identity and purpose for my life.

You have the right to recover from the multiple symptoms of complex trauma that accompany parental estrangement. You have the right to become mentally, emotionally, physically, and spiritually healthy. After honestly admitting your own human mistakes, you have the right to be liberated from the debilitating effects of guilt, shame, fear, and regret that can haunt us all. You have this right even though your adult children may wrongly interpret your return to health as a testament to your indifference. No words can convince them otherwise.

Among others, there can be a tendency to resent those who excel, including those who have found a path out of the depths of suffering and into abundant living. The Roman King Tarquin was said to have cut the heads off the tallest poppies in his garden as a sign to his son that he should set about secretly assassinating those of achievement around him to ensure his own success. This phenomenon, now referred to as the tallest poppy syndrome, leads to a tendency in people to self-sabotage in order to avoid punishment by those who are less accomplished—or more miserable. The tallest poppy syndrome, also called the crab-bucket effect, was confirmed in research with university students where it was found that test scores improved by 18% when the exam results were anonymous, rather than posted with names.[134] If you thrive, there will be those who resent it. Thrive anyway.

Right #9 - I have the right to develop new relationships that are mutually beneficial.

It is sometimes the case that parental estrangement only affects the individual relationship between a parent and an adult child. More likely

---

[134]Simon Spacey. "Crab Mentality, Cyberbullying and 'Name and Shame' Rankings". Waikato University, New Zealand. S2CID 38442243. Retrieved April 19, 2015.

is that the loss will also involve one or more grandchildren. Occasionally, there will be multiple adult children who are estranged from the same parent, along with their children. The total loss can range from a single relationship to twelve or more. The impact of these simultaneous losses of multiple relationships is difficult to overstate. For some parents, the estrangement can wipe out half of their support system. You have the right to grieve these losses as some of the most significant of your life.

Sometimes adult children need their parents to feel isolated, especially if they are angry. Social isolation has always been an instrument of punishment in society going back to the beginnings of civilization. After a divorce, one estranged child said to her mother, "What makes me mad is that people still want to be your friends." And, ironically, adult children who feel threatened by the children in a second marriage, and fear they will be replaced, often make that a self-fulfilling prophecy. In order to protect themselves from feeling rejected, they do the rejecting. They take control and make the break total and irreversible. These losses make parenting mistakes a capital offense. They lead to illnesses of all kinds, and the likelihood of an early death.

People are irreplaceable, but support isn't. You have the right not to be isolated. You have the right not to die an early death. You have the right to rebuild the relational network in your life, including people of all ages and in different roles. You have the right to re-partner or remarry. You have the right to form relationships with persons who become surrogate children and grandchildren. You have the right to friends. You have the right to a good life with people you love and value.

Right #10 - I have the right to celebrate the contributions I have made to the world over the course of my lifetime without repeated reminders of my deficits.

According to a theory called peak-end,[135] we do not remember everything that has happened to us in the same way. Research has discovered that we tend to remember two things about an experience (a) it's intensity, positive or negative, and (b) how it ended. Our memory of a great vacation can be spoiled by a bad flight experience on the way home. We tend to remember the frustration of the trip home, rather than the fun at the beach.

This is a problem for us as estranged parents. There are undoubtedly many positive experiences that we had over the years with our children, but these tend to be minimized by the way the relationship ended. And because estrangement occurs in the last quarter of our lives, it tends to diminish the positive memories of every other aspect. This characteristic of memory formation impacts the way our estranged children remember as well. They tend to view their entire childhood through the negative events leading to estrangement. In some cases, they are inclined to remind us of that.

You have the right to recount the positive contributions you have made to your adult child's development, and to rescue those memories from the downward drag of the estrangement that came later. Once you have acknowledged your imperfections, you have the right to refuse being reminded of your failures to the exclusion of your contributions. You have the right to conduct a life review and to celebrate your other lifelong contributions through your relationships, vocation, volunteer activities, hobbies, and other interests.

Right #11 - I have the right to make plans for my future that provide for my financial and physical security.

According to the Pew Research Center, half of parents with an adult child provide them with at least some financial support, about $1,000 per month on average. Ninety-five percent of parents indicated they would do so if their adult children needed help. Where would they find

---

[135] https://positivepsychology.com/what-is-peak-end-theory/

the money? The most commonly mentioned adjustment was living a more frugal lifestyle, followed by pulling money out of savings, delaying retirement, or taking on debt. Roughly three-quarters of parents who support their adult child financially indicate they are somewhat or very stressed about their ability to live comfortably in retirement.[136] Since the best predictor of future behavior is past behavior, it is unlikely that estranged children, who have demonstrated an indifference to the well-being of their parents over weeks, months, and years, will reciprocate that level of commitment.

This trend worries financial planners, especially those who are familiar with parental estrangement.[137] They observe a tendency among parents to withhold information about their estrangement out of guilt or family loyalty. Even when they are willing to discuss it, there is an inclination to view the future through the lens of a likely reconciliation. It can be difficult to face the fact that your adult children will not be available to provide any support in your declining years. Feelings of guilt may make it difficult to plan for a future where financial resources are all retained for one's care rather than shared with children and grandchildren who could use the money.

You have the right to disclose your parental estrangement to an experienced financial advisor. You have the right to conserve your financial resources to provide for your own security in the final years of your life. You have the right to make financial distributions to persons other than family members who are committed to your long-term well-being. You have the right to appoint persons other than family members to make decisions in the event of your incapacity. You also have the right to disclose your parental estrangement to an estate attorney, and to make distributions consistent with your values rather than dictated by guilt or sheer duty.

---

[136] https://www.savings.com/insights/financial-support-for-adult-children-study
[137] https://www.cnbc.com/2021/05/05/parents-are-sacrificing-their-own-financial-wellness-to-support-their-adult-children.html

Right #12 - In any eventual reconciliation, I have the right to establish boundaries in a process that gradually redevelops trust.

A number of years ago, I spoke with a woman who coached the trainers of Olympic athletes.

She said, "I can teach a person how to listen in a single day. Assertiveness and confrontation take two days. Personality and vocational assessment, three days. But developing trust takes time. There is no shortcut to regaining someone's trust."

Estrangement breaks a fundamental trust. Since it is almost always initiated by the adult child, an estranged parent is generally shocked to realize that the relationship, in which they assumed an equal and unconditional investment, is both conditional and one-sided. While adult children generally indicate that they have made the estrangement decision in a thoughtful process over a period of time, the break comes as a complete surprise to most parents. To be fair, estranged adult children almost always indicate trust issues with their parents. Whatever those might be, the breach of trust that totally ends a relationship is qualitatively different. It takes time to trust that a misstep on the part of a parent won't result in another painful cutoff over which they have no control.

As an estranged parent considering an adult child's initiative for reconciliation, you have the right to insist on a process of rebuilding trust. You have the right to negotiate steps in that process that also take into consideration the trust needs of your reconciling child. You have the right to slow down the process as a way of gaining confidence in the strength of the commitment. You have the right to decide that rebuilding a significant degree of trust is impossible. Instead of a reconciliation, you will have a reconnection, but without a deep, emotional investment. You have the right to decide if even that is a possibility for you.

Steps Toward Recovery

Integrating these rights into our lives requires focus and intention.
- Go through the twelve rights of estranged parents and put a checkmark beside those which you believe have been violated by others. In the sanctuary of your own heart, offer them compassion and forgiveness.
- Go back through the same list, and circle the numbers of those rights which you may have violated in relationship with others, including your adult child. In the sanctuary of your own heart, offer yourself compassion and forgiveness.
- For one week, read aloud the Estranged Parent Bill of Rights found in Appendix D each day, and journal how your feelings have changed at the end of the seventh day.

Do not communicate these rights or any of your reflections to your child without first consulting a therapist or spiritual guide who is trained to deal with parental estrangement.

Questions for Reflection and Discussion

In what ways has parental estrangement changed the way that you feel about yourself? What feelings about yourself have not changed?

How difficult is it for you to think of yourself as having rights?

Turn to Appendix D. Read through these rights aloud. How does reading through them affect how you view yourself?

Which of these rights are the most important for you to claim? How would claiming the rights you identified change how you view yourself? How you view your situation?

Which of these rights do you need to respect in the life of your adult child? How difficult or easy is that for you?

If you are using this book in a group discussion, what did you gain from hearing others speak? From speaking?

PEAK: Parents of Estranged Adult Kids
A Resource for Recovery

Chapter 23
Rethinking Family

One of the primary challenges in recovering from the trauma of parental estrangement is dealing with the perception that even talking about it violates some deep fundamental law of the social universe. It just feels wrong. It's not a problem like your car breaking down, needing a crown on your tooth, or a leaky faucet. It is easy to picture a social setting with other parents where talking about any of those problems would feel appropriate and natural. The fact that the others in the conversation had cars that were running fine, teeth that passed their last dental examination, and washerless faucets wouldn't make you uncomfortable to talk about your car problems, or any of the rest.

Contrast that with a group of parents having a conversation about their adult children, what they do and where they live, complete with photographs. They turn to you and ask, "Do you have children?" You say, "I do, but they stopped communicating with me five years ago." The room falls over the cliff of an awkward silence. No one knows what to do or say; their eyes dart here and there like those of high school students looking for an answer on the exam paper of the student next to them. Someone takes a stab at the awkward beast with something like, "Oh, I'm sorry to hear that." It is said in a way that leaves you certain that she and her husband will exchange their sentiments about the appropriateness of your statement a few minutes after they walk out the door.

Stigma and the Definition of Family

What just happened? Well, you have just run straight into the buzz saw of the stigma of parental estrangement.

What is a *stigma*? Stigma is a mark of disgrace associated with a particular circumstance, quality, or person. A stigma is not simply a problem; it is a problem that should not be talked about.

At the core of this stigma is the way society understands family. Family is generally defined by biology and law as the social arrangement whereby parents bear or adopt and then nurture children. Except in cases of mistreatment, this social arrangement is buttressed by the legal responsibility assigned for parents to care for their children. It is involuntary both for parents and children.

This definition works fine until children come of age. At that point the relationship becomes purely voluntary; there is no legal requirement for parents and adult children to have any relationship at all. Society, on the other hand, does not make this adjustment. It assumes that the involuntary nature of the family remains intact for parents and their adult children until death, and that any deviation from this standard raises the suspicion of faulty parenting, defective adult children, or both.

It is not simply that society imposes a standard on parents that is impossible for them to meet. Parents also imbibe these expectations and weave them deep into their own self-understanding. When problems arise in the relationship with their adult children, they feel ashamed. The combination of social stigma and personal shame on top of feelings of loss is extremely painful.

Implied in this problematic understanding are elements of shared identity, exclusivity, and permanence.

The Fallacy of Shared Identity

Because family members partake of a common genetic lineage and years of shared experiences it is assumed that this shared identity should help the personalities of family members "click." How many times have we heard struggling parents say, "I don't understand. I didn't raise him this way," or "She isn't anything like me—or her father"? In fact, the research converges on the remarkable conclusion that environmental influences make two children in the same family as different from one another as pairs of children selected randomly from the general population, and children are nearly as different in personality from their parents.

From a personality perspective, there is little reason that parents and children should get along any better than two randomly selected adults from different generations. To state it a different way, there is little reason to believe that two parents and their two adult children will have compatible personalities any more than four adults randomly selected from a crowd walking down the sidewalk. We would never expect to be able to pour such a randomly selected crowd into a van (along with their children), travel to a one-week stay at a beach house, and enjoy a great vacation.

> *Parental estrangement should no longer be stigmatized and kept silent. We need to share and help each other....*
> D.D. from Baton Rouge, LA

Kitchen table wisdom claims that opposites attract. The reality is that they don't. When researchers Barbara Barron-Tieger and Paul Tieger studied the personality type of several hundred couples, they found that the more type preferences a couple had in common, the more satisfied they were with their relationship.[138] There is no reason to believe that people of widely different personalities in a family

---

[138] https://www.truity.com/story/compatibility-and-your-myers-briggs-personality-type

should get along any better, even when those are personality differences between parents and adult children.

Here is the truth: personality differences *can* play a significant role in parental estrangement.

The Fallacy of Exclusivity

Related to the fallacy of shared identity is the assumption of exclusivity. Exclusivity means that the functions of family members are unique to the family and therefore irreplaceable by anyone outside the family. Exclusivity has several ramifications.

First, the tribal nature of families can react to close, nonfamily friends as intruders and work to push them out. Ironically, this can happen at the same time that adult children are withdrawing from the family. The result can be parents who not only have lost the relationship with their children, but also with close friends, or after a divorce, the spouses their children married.

The second ramification of exclusivity is an exaggerated family loyalty. Estranged parents feel guilty talking about problems that they believe should be kept in the family, even in confidential situations where they are trying to get help. Added to the impact of stigma and shame, this demand for loyalty further isolates estranged parents in their pain and confusion.

The final impact of exclusivity is that it deepens the sense of hopelessness in estranged parents. If children and grandchildren have cut off communication, and no other relationships can help fill that space in their lives, then they are left with nothing less than a complete, tragic loss. Faced with this lifelong prospect, parents are often inconsolable.

As we have seen, these losses have significant impacts. However, it is also clear that friendships can provide relationships that are both rewarding and protective against the physical and emotional problems that accompany parental estrangement. In a study involving more than

270,000 people in nearly 100 countries, author William Chopik found that both family and friend relationships were associated with better health and happiness overall. But at advanced ages, the link remained only for people who reported strong friendships.[139]

I can say from personal experience that nothing is more wrenching than the memory of a grandchild you adore and may never see again in this earthly life. However, a surrogate grandparent website that connects older adults with young children is headed with the words of founders Charles and Ann Morse: "A child needs a grandparent, anybody's grandparent to grow more securely into an unfamiliar world."[140] Amy Morin, a social worker and foster parent in Lincoln, Maine, argues that offering children positive relationships with adults who are not blood relatives can be positive for everyone: "If you don't have people lifting you up, find support elsewhere. It's empowering to know you can choose your family," says Morin.[141]

Here's the truth: no one and nothing can take the place of an adult child or grandchild lost to estrangement. However, families are not exclusive. Other relationships can provide meaningful experiences that are mutually beneficial and protective against the ravages of isolation.

The Fallacy of Permanence

Implied in the fallacies of shared identity and exclusivity is the assumption of permanence: families are for life, and the involuntary nature of families with younger children automatically transfers into positive and permanent relationships that are "till death do us part."

---

[139] http://time.com/4809325/friends-friendship-health-family/

[140] Meera Lester, Carolyn Dean, Susan B Townsend, *Happiest You Ever: 365 Ways to Invite More Love, Sex, Fun, Friendship, Fellowship, Community, and Career Satisfaction into your Life - Each and Every Day!* (Simon and Schuster, 2011)

[141] https://www.yahoo.com/lifestyle/tagged/health/parenting/close-friends-substitute-family-154200498.html

Also implied is the assumption that as parents age, adult children will reciprocate the care given to them as children and support parents in their decline and journey toward death. This simply does not mesh with reality. Whether we like it or not, a large percentage of marriages that are characterized by public vows of permanence will end in divorce. In addition, one-third of estranged parents are seventy to eighty years of age, and face a future without their children.

Here is the truth: most relationships between parents and adult children (and grandchildren) will be permanent. Many will not.

All these fallacies can be traced to a definition of family that is primarily biological and legal. It is not the only way to look at family.

Family as a Spiritual Reality

In PEAK, we hold that while biological and legal families should be honored as the instruments of our existence, our true family is that body of people with whom we have relationships characterized by mutuality, commitment, authenticity, and gratitude. I addressed these four qualities in Chapter 20, and will say more about them in Chapter 25.

Here I will simply note that while spiritual texts from various traditions advocate for respect and care of parents by adult children, they also recognize the limitations of defining family in strictly biological terms. A spiritual definition of family expands to include those who seek the guidance of a Spiritual Source, who demonstrate their love through respect and practical concern, and who engage people who are broken and hurting with a nonjudgmental attitude.

Benefits of Redefining Family

This expanded understanding of family has a number of benefits:

- It helps estranged parents form a more realistic set of expectations for their biological family that potentially reduces shame and strengthens a positive view of themselves.
- It encourages estranged parents to adopt a perspective that views their adult children as independent persons responsible for their own choices rather than measures of success or failure in their parenting.
- It gives permission to estranged parents to seek support through relationships outside the family that are no longer excluded by a false sense of loyalty.
- It renews hope for estranged parents that they can find meaningful surrogate relationships that are fulfilling and mutually supportive.
- It provides an avenue for estranged parents to experience spiritual renewal by observing how their Spiritual Source is working to relieve their suffering and build meaningful connections.
- It invites some estranged parents to grieve their loss and move forward in making concrete plans to deal with holidays, birthdays, anniversaries, weddings, funerals, illnesses, and grandchildren, as well as legal issues concerning wills, estates, powers of attorney, and final arrangements.

The concept of family is deep seated and powerful. The painful emotions take time to subside. Your brain has been formed over decades of thinking about family in a particular way. It will not change overnight. Readers often expect to simply read a book like this one and find that it quickly alleviates their suffering. It generally won't. You will have to knead your new thinking into the contours of your mind. If you have ever kneaded dough, you know that is work.

Steps Toward Recovery

It might be helpful to create a concise statement like this one and repeat it to yourself:
> I am a child of God and my children came from God as well. I was the biological instrument of their birth and development [or in the case of adoptive parents, the custodians of their care and development]. My children were created with distinct personalities both resonant and dissonant from my own. I have the power and privilege of expanding my family by choosing those relationships that are mutually enriching and good for the world, which may or may not include my adult children. Every relationship has its seasons, a time to be born, and a time to die. In eternity, I belong to the universe, to everyone and everything.

Reading this statement is a start but only the beginning. I encourage you to make it your own. Amend it. Memorize it. Journal it. Sing it. Turn it into poetry. Romanticize it. Court it like you would a lover who has the power to transform your life. Frame and hang it on your walls. Explain it to someone you trust. Find sacred Scripture that supports it. Read authors that say the same thing in different words.

I believe that as we come together with other estranged parents, maintain an open mind, share honestly our own experiences and feelings, and open ourselves to the care and leading of our Spiritual Source, we will gradually find relief from our suffering, clarity regarding our path forward, and a more positive perspective on our lives and those of our adult children.

Questions for Reflection and Discussion

Tell about a time when you experienced the stigma of parental estrangement.

Which of the three fallacies (shared identity, exclusivity, and permanence) is most likely to trip you up?

From this chapter, what do you think is the most important change you could make in your thinking about family?

What are the potential benefits in your life of redefining family?

How difficult is it for you to claim those benefits even if your decision is not popular among others you know?

What help do you need from your Spiritual Source?

If you are using this book in a group discussion, what did you gain from hearing others speak? From speaking?

PEAK: Parents of Estranged Adult Kids
A Resource for Recovery

Chapter 24
Seeing a Larger Life

According to Pew research, parents spend a total of about twenty-two hours a week on childcare, about 1,100 hours a year or roughly 20,000 hours over an eighteen-year lifespan, or about 10,000 hours per parent. That's a lot of time.[142]

What happens when we do anything for 10,000 hours? In his book *Outliers,* Malcolm Gladwell argued that it takes about 10,000 hours of practice to become an expert at just about anything.[143] So the typical parent could have instead become an expert at early American history, a crack fighter pilot, or a rock guitar player. At retirement a person would be able to look back on these accomplishments as a source of pride.

Contrast this with the experience of estranged parents who make a similar investment only to find that it seemingly evaporates into thin air. It is not like a guitar you can always pull out and play a riff from "Stairway to Heaven." There is nothing but silence except for the nagging question: What did it all mean?

What happens to the human brain when we do something for thousands of hours?

Hawaii native Craig Smallwood is suing NCSOFT South Korea, claiming that the developer of the game *Lineage* should pay an unspecified amount of money due to the addictive nature of the game. The suit states that Smallwood played the game between 2004 and 2009 for 20,000 hours, but would not have played if he were aware of

---

[142] http://www.pewresearch.org/fact-tank/2018/06/13/fathers-day-facts/
[143] https://www.newyorker.com/news/sporting-scene/complexity-and-the-ten-thousand-hour-rule

the addictive nature of the game. He claims that it is so addictive that for five years he apparently lost all measure of self-control and became "unable to function independently in usual daily activities such as getting up, getting dressed, bathing or communicating with family and friends."[144]

When the brain focuses on a particular activity for long periods of time, it actually rewires to define reality through the lens of that activity. It loses its ability to function in a larger reality or even to feel that a different reality is possible. Fleas confined to a jar for a number of days will not escape when the lid is removed. Fish in an aquarium divided in half by a clear piece of glass will continue to turn at that point and swim back even when the glass is removed. A sustained focus on a small part of the universe traps us in that universe, and makes other universes invisible.[145]

Craig Smallwood became an expert in the universe of the game *Lineage*, but lost his ability to function in other arenas. He is an extreme example of what happens to any of us when we focus on a singular activity for thousands of hours. Through a similar process, parents can become so focused on the universe of parenting that it defines who they are. Fifty-seven percent of parents say that parenting is extremely important to their identity.[146] This is necessary for a season of life. However, for those who cannot move beyond their identity as a parent, it is difficult for them to conceive *emotionally* of an identity that goes beyond that. Therefore, when estranged parents are asked to think about what they have accomplished in life, it is natural for their minds to gravitate toward what they perceive as a failed parenting experience. This can dominate their perspective to such a degree that they are unable to see any other significant achievements without help.

---

[144] https://www.digitaltrends.com/gaming/gamer-sues-developer-after-spending-20000-hours-playing-game/
[145] https://www.makeavisionboard.com/self-limiting-beliefs/
[146] http://www.pewresearch.org/fact-tank/2018/06/13/fathers-day-facts/

In 2006 a researcher named David Haber published a paper on the positive effects of what he calls a *life review*. He defines a life review as the recall of memories typically structured around one or more life themes. This review not only includes family themes, ranging from one's own childhood, to the experience of being a parent, to being a grandparent, but also work themes from first job, to major life's work, to retirement, to significant turning points. In addition, other themes include: impact of major historical events; role of education, health, holidays, music, literature, or art in one's life; experiences with aging, dying, and death; and meaning, values, and purpose. In other words, it expands a person's mind from a focus on parenting to a more comprehensive review of life.

The positive impact of such a review in older adults is remarkable including:

- The emergence of a healthy unifying philosophy and the wisdom learned from experience no matter how dearly the price paid for it.
- An increase in life satisfaction with the individual feeling more vital, balanced, and whole in relation to the self and the world.
- A significant reduction in depression without the use of expensive medications and their side effects.
- An increase in the sense of control over their life story even as other factors may be decreasing their control (lack of independence, medical issues, and living situation).

There are a number of other advantages to a life review. A life review is a more appealing and less threatening activity than most counseling interventions because it invites older adults to discuss their past and to uncover positive life experiences and inner strengths. It requires few resources and modest training.

It can be done by oneself, but more often it is guided by a partner or by a facilitator as part of a group experience. Group sessions add the benefit of helping older adults establish new peer relationships that are critical to the recovery from the trauma of parental estrangement.

For a life review to have substantial impact on the participant's mental health, it should involve a sufficient investment in time (six weeks or longer), scope (birth to present), and intimacy (listening by others). The ideal length of a single interview session is unknown, but sessions often last between one and two hours, unless physical frailty requires a shorter time period.[147]

Inspired by Haber and other researchers, I have created a life review process with questions formulated specifically for estranged parents. A full listing of the questions in a PEAK life review are found in Appendix B, but here are a few of the summary questions:

1. If your life were a book, what would be the title? What would be the titles of some of the chapters?
2. As you remember those you have loved in your life, even those who broke your heart, how would it change your perspective on life to consider that they were each sent for a purpose?
3. If you were sent to earth on assignment, which actions you have taken in your life have best fulfilled that assignment?
4. If the purpose of life is to help you fully experience a balance of joy and sorrow, strength and weakness, and love and loneliness, how balanced has your life been?
5. If your life has been a school and you are a student, what are the most important lessons you have learned?
6. If part of our life's purpose is to be negative teachers who help other people learn what not to do, what have been those lessons you have given others?
7. If life must be lived looking forward, but understood looking backward, what do you now understand about your life that you did not perceive as you were living it?

---

[147] https://jshellman-reminiscence.wiki.uml.edu/file/view/Haber_LR_Rem_200.pdf

8. If the secret to life is making things the right size and putting them in the right places, what are the things you need to make smaller? What are the things you need to make larger?
9. If there is a life to come that solves problems we cannot solve in this life, what do you look forward to?
10. If every gift is a test, given to us with the hope that we will succeed by being grateful rather than suspicious, proud, or inferior, what gratitude are you ready to offer for your life?

A life review is one way of accomplishing a profound and necessary expansion in one's perspective, the movement from an understanding of life as accomplishing a set of rule-based, narrowly defined, tribal tasks to participation in a grand cosmic order full of paradox and mystery. There are other experiences and spiritual practices that can accompany this expansion including meditation, contemplative prayer, spiritual readings, artistic expressions such as painting and poetry, near-death experiences, pilgrimages, and transformative mission experiences. Anything that expands the mind beyond the years of habit-driven mental ruts can be healing for the trauma of estrangement.

Even though they have no relationship with me, my estranged children are making important contributions to the world. Through PEAK, I came to realize that as a source of meaning for me.
K.G. from Duluth, MN

Parental estrangement can ultimately be a gift if it helps us take this critical step in our spiritual journey. Again, this does not simply happen by the reading of a single book, but by the integration of a new way of thinking about the significance of your life. There is a sense in which your life is the accumulation of all your decisions, right, wrong, and in between, combined with the impact on your life of all the decisions made by others. In another sense, your life has been exactly as it had to be in order for the universe to evolve toward the expressions of love and justice carried in the heart of our Spiritual Source.

Steps Toward Recovery

Here, again, is an affirmation you might find helpful to weave into your thinking:

> I am a child of God. My life has unfolded in precisely the ways that were necessary for the Universe to evolve more fully into love and justice. The ripples of goodness from my life are unseeable, and the greater purposes of my mistakes are unknowable. Some of my life accomplishments have arisen from my conscious contributions to the good of others. Some of my life accomplishments have arisen from simply surviving great hardships that I might continue to bear witness to the strength of Divine endurance wrapped about by my human body. For whatever wisdom I have acquired, and at whatever price, it has all been worth it. I give thanks for my life.

Questions for Reflection and Discussion

How do you think your substantial investment of time in parenting has impacted the way you view your life?

Has there ever been a time when you became aware of a part of yourself that you did not know existed? What did you discover? What brought it to your consciousness?

From what you know of a life review, does it seem like something that would be helpful? Why or why not?

What new thought do you now need to weave into your thinking as you recover from the trauma of parental estrangement?

Based on this chapter, if someone says to you, "Family is the most important part of anyone's life," how would you respond?

If you are using this book in a group discussion, what did you gain from hearing others speak? From speaking?

PEAK: Parents of Estranged Adult Kids
A Resource for Recovery

Chapter 25
On Friendship

I had a conversation with someone about friendship that has stuck with me. A statement at the end of it echoed a sentiment I have heard hundreds of times: "Friends are fine, but family is what really counts." While I have no interest in demeaning the value of a healthy, supportive family, I think it is important to be reminded of the reality that families can be the locus of some of the most painful experiences of our lives, both for children and adults. By far, the most common causes of abuse and neglect happen at the hands of those who are supposed to love us. While this is a tragic reality for young children, it is no less true for the parents of adult children. Approximately one in ten Americans aged sixty or older have experienced some form of elder abuse or neglect, and two-thirds of those responsible are adult children or their spouses.[148] Sometimes a family is what really hurts and friendship is what really counts.

A chapter expounding on friendship might seem misfit to a book on parents estranged from their adult children. I am including it for four reasons. All four are admittedly a reflection of my biases.

First, in a book focused on one of the most painful of parental experiences, I would like to end on a positive and promising note. Sometimes a significant trauma in one relationship can cast doubt on the value of all relationships including friendship. I am firmly convinced that Thomas Aquinas was right when he wrote: "There is nothing on this earth more to be prized than true friendship."

Second, in an ideal world, children develop into adults who are able to become friends to their parents. I believe this because I have

---

[148] https://www.ncoa.org/public-policy-action/elder-justice/elder-abuse-facts/

observed over the decades that the happiest parents and adult children are those who call each other friends—and act that way. I acknowledge from the outset that dependency in some parent and adult child relationships is ingrained so deeply that friendship will never be a real possibility. Many non-estranged parent and adult child relationships fall short of this ideal. On the other hand, I think friendship in many parent and adult child relationships could be a possibility were it not for the fact that they simply don't have a good understanding of what friendship looks like or how to develop it. Think about it. Who teaches us how to be friends?

Third, in the absence of relationships with their adult children, expanding their network of friends becomes even more important for estranged parents. Family researcher Kristina Scharp points out that the phrase "blood is thicker than water" is often misunderstood to emphasize the importance of biological relationships. In its older meaning, it refers to the fact that the blood shed in battle is more significant than the water of the womb. "The phrase was meant to say the people who you'd give your life for are more important than your biological relations."[149] It is reminiscent of the words of Jesus of Nazareth: "No one has greater love than this, to lay down one's life for one's friends."[150]

The final reason is purely personal. I discovered in the early nineties that I didn't have a single friend. As a pastor all my relationships were vertical; I had people for whom I was responsible and I had people to whom I was accountable. The journey to the love of friendship was rewarding and I made mistakes along the way, but it has been worth it no matter the price. Willa Cather wrote: "Only solitary men know the full joys of friendship. Others have their family, but to a solitary and exile his friends are everything."[151]

---

[149] http://usustatesman.com/family-estrangement-usu-professor-finds-lack-research-shocking/

[150] John 15:13

[151] Willa Cather, *Shadows on the Rock* (Vintage Publishing, 1995).

We live in an interesting time where people don't seem to know what to make of friendship. An article in the *Washington Post* tells us that "smart people are better off with fewer friends."[152] Then we are also told that smart people are more likely to have more mental illnesses,[153] that those with writing or artistic ability are more prone to suicide,[154] and then that a major factor in suicide is, wait for it, not having friends (social isolation)! My assumption is that many of us would find life richer if we were better friends. To do that, we need to have a better understanding of what friendship is.

The Four Components of Friendship

I was profoundly influenced by Robert Roberts who wrote the book *Taking the Word to Heart*. Inspired by his thoughts on friendship, I have concluded that friendship has four essential components. You will recognize these components from other pages of this book, but they bear repeating in the context of friendship.

The first component is *mutuality*. I define mutuality in a friendship as sharing responsibility for sustaining the relationship. Mutuality means that both friends feel an equal responsibility for staying in touch, taking initiative to see each other, and reaching out to one another in times of need. You know mutuality is lacking when you hear someone say, "I'm always the one who has to call my friends, plan get-togethers, or send notes." Mutuality also means that both persons take responsibility to care for the needs of the other. A relationship where one person is always listening to the crisis *du jour* of the other, and never asked how they are doing—and listened to—is not a friendship.

---

[152] https://www.washingtonpost.com/news/wonk/wp/2016/03/18/why-smart-people-are-better-off-with-fewer-friends/?noredirect=on&utm_term=.0a30cf08f8b7
[153] https://bigthink.com/design-for-good/why-highly-intelligent-people-suffer-more-mental-and-physical-disorders
[154] http://highability.org/161/high-ability-giftedtalented-suicidal/

Mutuality was one of my major friendship shortcomings. Sometimes friends have to ask for more mutuality. A friend once said to me, "Look, I need you to call me occasionally, too." So I did. And I do.

The second component of friendship is *commitment*. This simply means that you have set an intention to make the relationship a priority in your life. Friendship is like other important relationships, like marriage, employment, or membership in a faith community in that you act in a manner consistent with its importance in your life. I don't think that friendship contracts, covenants, or ceremonies are required, but I believe both parties in the relationship need to be clear that it is, indeed, a friendship that is important to them.

Commitment assures people that their relationship can endure stresses and even conflict. I know someone who says that she doesn't count a person a friend until they have survived their first fight. I think that must make me one of her best friends!

Friendships, like any other important relationships, take time. In a research article published in the *Journal of Social and Personal Relationships*, researcher Jeffrey Hall found it took between 40 and 60 hours to move from an acquaintance to a casual friendship, and from 80 to 100 hours to call someone a friend.[155] People often say that they haven't seen a friend for years and connect instantly when they do, but that's not a friendship that has much substance when it comes down to everyday living. Friendship requires a commitment to spend time connecting.

The level of commitment will vary from one relationship to another. Some people are contextual friends. The current circumstances of their lives are the container that holds the relationship together. Contextual friends may be friends because they are neighbors, work together, attend the same faith community, or are in the same service organization. When they move to another community, the friendship gradually dissolves.

---

[155] https://journals.sagepub.com/doi/full/10.1177/0265407518761225

Other folks are soul friends. They may start out as contextual friends, but when the context changes they realize that the relationship is important enough that they are willing to make a substantial commitment to maintain the relationship no matter what the geographic challenges.

The third component of friendship is *authenticity*. Here I am speaking of the ability to share honestly with one another matters of concern. Friends would find it almost impossible to struggle deeply with something in their lives without speaking to one another about it. There will be certain boundaries, of course, but friends generally feel that they can and want to talk with one another about things that are important in their lives. They feel safe, respected, and listened to.

When I discovered PEAK, I was really suffering with estrangement from my brother and two step-daughters. It was a relief to be in the group and admit this without fearing judgement!
L.S. From Greenville, SC

Bowling team members talk about bowling, work associates talk about work, neighbors give one another tips on lawn care, but if that is all the deeper it goes, it's probably not friendship. Friends are able to talk about what weighs heaviest on their hearts as well as what makes their lives worth living. The privilege of a lifetime is to have a circle of friends with whom you can become who you truly are.

The fourth and final component of friendship is *gratitude*. I confess it is my favorite. Gratitude in friendship is a readiness to show appreciation for the relationship. Using John Mayer's song for inspiration, say what you mean to say. (Mayer, J. 2007). Gratitude in a friendship is what keeps mutuality from deteriorating into a transactional tit for tat: I send you a card, you send me one; I give you a birthday gift, you give me one. Gratitude expresses, in one way or another, that the relationship has an ultimate value that goes far beyond a simple utilitarian exchange. In absence, gratitude says, "I miss you. I am not the same without you." In presence, gratitude says, "Thank you for being my friend."

Gratitude is particularly important in the parent and adult child friendships that remain unestranged. As we have already noted, adults over sixty enter a stage of life where they are reflecting back in time and asking what it all meant. Gratitude expressed by an adult child can help make the difference between meaning and despair in the life of a parent. Gratitude from a parent for an adult child can help fulfill basic affirmational needs that are important to all of us.

In many cases, you can make a relationship ten times better just by saying "Thank you for being in my life." Say it face to face; say it on a card; say it through a text, tweet, or email. Say it. They need to hear it. We need to say it. Nothing haunts us like the things we don't say.

Missing Ingredients

Mutuality, commitment, authenticity, gratitude. Think of them as the four ingredients of a cake. Without any one of them, it's simply not much of a cake. Take away gratitude and you have an engine without a sparkplug. Take away commitment and you have a life of leftovers. Take away authenticity and you have loneliness over coffee. Take away mutuality and you have Sisyphus always bearing the burden of the relationship up the mountainside of life.

If you take away all these qualities from a relationship, then you have to seriously wonder what you have. In some cases, ending the relationship may be the best option and the closest you can come to a happy ending. This is the reality that every estranged parent must face squarely. Every person deserves to experience the rich blessing of friendship. Every person deserves the opportunity to grow into the responsibilities that friendship requires.

Steps Toward Recovery

Take some time to conduct a friendship audit for your life.

- Think of your most significant relationships. List their names in the table that follows. Then reflect on whether these relationships demonstrate mutuality, commitment, authenticity, or gratitude. If so, place a checkmark in the column.

Name	Mutuality?	Commitment?	Authenticity?	Gratitude?

- Decide if you need to take steps to strengthen your friendships. If the best way to make a friend is to be a friend, think about the changes you need to make in that direction.
- Consider copying the pages of this chapter and giving it to one or two friends. Then talk about it.

Questions for Reflection and Discussion

The number of friends people say they have is declining.[156] Why do you think that is?

Compared to 20 years ago, do you have more friends, fewer friends, or about the same?

---

[156] https://www.americansurveycenter.org/research/the-state-of-american-friendship-change-challenges-and-loss/

What books or articles have provided you with guidance on how to develop friendships?

Think about the best friendships you have ever had. What made them so good?

While friends can never replace our children, do you think that having good friends is an important part of a recovery process? Why or not?

If you are using this book in a group discussion, what did you gain from hearing others speak? From speaking?

Chapter 26
A Fearless Relational Audit

This chapter leads us through a process of reviewing how we deal with the important relationships in our lives. I placed this chapter near the end of the book rather than the beginning for three reasons. First, I wanted to avoid the impression that the purpose of a relational audit is to discover reasons for the estrangement. The goal of self-awareness is growth, not guilt. Second, I wanted to give time for the recovery process to lay a foundation of love, acceptance, and self-compassion. It is impossible to become self-aware with the gun of judgement to our heads. Finally, I expected that the chapters of the book would lead to some discoveries that would contribute to the relational audit. For example, now that you know a little more about friendship, you might realize some steps you could take to be a better friend.

Let's begin by focusing on three of the questions that require a significant amount of courage to contemplate:

- If you were going to live your life over again, what would you change?
- Everyone has had disappointments. What have been the main disappointments in your life?
- What was the hardest thing you had to face in your life? Please describe it.

These questions will likely surface some uncomfortable memories, tragic events, difficult circumstances, and the actions of others that have impacted us negatively. In addition, there are likely to be memories of our own shortcomings. There will be examples of poor judgment that we wish we could change, disappointments in the way we handled certain things, and hardships we have had to face as a consequence of some of our actions. Some of those failures will be in our relationship with our adult children.

It is important that we not try to avoid these insights. This may seem counterintuitive. After all, we are already feeling badly about ourselves as it is. Why focus on our mistakes in a way that only makes us feel worse? Besides, these are now all in the past. Isn't it time to let bygones be bygones? In addition, I'm not the one who broke off the relationship with my adult children. That's the problem here, and that clearly is not my fault.

The Benefits of a Fearless Relational Audit

There are five reasons why it is helpful in our recovery to engage in a fearless relational audit that explores the ways we have failed to be our best selves.

1. By conducting a fearless relational audit, we can assure ourselves that we have done everything within our power to address the estrangement of our adult children.
2. By conducting a fearless relational audit, we can address problematic patterns in our lives and improve our relationships with others in the future.
3. By conducting a fearless relational audit, we can find relief from guilt feelings through our Spiritual Source.
4. By conducting a fearless relational audit, we may find it easier to forgive others including our adult children for the ways they have hurt us.
5. By conducting a fearless relational audit, we are less likely to engage in problematic behaviors involving food, money, sex, or consumption of drugs or alcohol.

Obstacles to Move Out of the Way

Before going further, it is important to discuss some misconceptions that get in the way of a relational audit. Here are some of them.

I am loved because I don't make mistakes. Admitting them means I won't be loved. This is a big one. For many of us, the love we have experienced has been highly conditional and threatened to be withdrawn when we fall short of the highest or most arbitrary of expectations. Remember, our Spiritual Source is gracious, forgiving, and intends goodness for us. This is the essence of an unconditional love that is unbounded.

Fortunately, there are people in the world who reflect this love, however imperfectly. They don't need us to be perfect. In fact, it is generally the case that people are easier to love when they can own up to their frailties than when they try to achieve a perfection that makes the rest of us mortals look bad!

Here's the truth: owning up to our faults generally makes us more lovable not less. As for those who cannot handle the real us, warts and all, it is better to know that sooner rather than later.

If I admit I am wrong, it makes them right. This is another big one, especially in relationships. It turns relationships into a contest of egos with winners and losers. If I am in a relationship with someone who unintentionally flaunts their successes, and I find myself envious of them, my admission doesn't excuse them from examining their pride and insensitivity. They may or may not choose to do that, but that's their business. My admission of failings in relationship to my children doesn't justify their ending the relationship with me. It simply puts me in a healthier place to move forward in my future.

Thank you for your courage in telling your truth in order to help parents like me!!!
J.D. from Washington D.C.

Here's the truth: admitting where I am wrong is an act of courage that others may or may not reciprocate.

My faults are the cause of our estrangement. This bears repeating. The mystery of estrangement was discussed in a previous chapter. It is impossible to say with any certainty what causes estrangement. At most we can say that there are risk factors. Undoubtedly, there are certain genetic predispositions that are risk factors. Some adult children of divorce end up estranged from one or both parents, but not in every divorce. At most we can say that divorce is a risk factor for estrangement. Some adult children who were physically or emotionally abused at home end up estranged from one or both parents, but not in every case. The most we can say is that abuse is a risk factor. We can't say that workaholic parents, or alcoholic parents, or inattentive parents, or wayward parents, or moody parents, or virtually any other kind of parent is the cause of estranged adult children.

Here's what we can say: admitting the ways that I could have been a better parent will probably make me a better person but it's not the cause of the estrangement from my adult children.

Admitting my failure makes my whole life a failure. This is the all or nothing fallacy. Admitting a fault does not negate all the good qualities of your life. In fact, every gift has a shadow side. If you are a visionary, you probably are not great at details (meaning you might forget some birthdays). If you are an adventurer, you are probably not great with routine (meaning you might introduce an element of chaos into people's lives). If you are great at thinking about things deeply, you are probably not as good at being spontaneous and lively (meaning you might feel a little stiff at parties). Only God is the "fount of every blessing" as the song goes. For the rest of us human souls, we are a mixed bag.

Here's the truth: our strengths are not negated by our failures.

Correction is rejection. This one is last for a reason. A few of us are fortunate enough to have people we trust who will challenge us when we go off course. Many of us have experienced correction as a form of rejection. People point out what is wrong with us as a way of justifying their pushing us away. There are people who are important exceptions to that experience. If you have found one or two, make sure that you keep your heart open when they challenge you. The pain of parental estrangement can cloud our best thinking. Having a couple of people who can help us find true north when our compass has gone haywire is one of the greatest gifts we can ever find.

Here's the truth: there are a few people who love us enough to tell us the truth. Listen to them. Correction is not rejection.

It is critical that you absorb what has been written above before moving on. If you find the remainder of this chapter emotionally threatening or discouraging, you may need to pause, go back to the obstacles, and do some more work with them.

Indirect and Direct Faults

I want to make the distinction between indirect and direct faults. Indirect faults are those that impact others, including children, by creating a difficult environment for them to grow up in. For example, problems in a marriage relationship have a negative impact on children even though the parent may be attentive to the needs of their child. Indirect faults can range from physical/emotional spousal abuse to marital infidelity to poor communication or conflict management skills.

Indirect faults also include modeling problematic behavior like drug or alcohol abuse, lack of self-care on the part of the parent, or failure to take responsibilities seriously. Indirect faults can also include failure to maintain a safe and ordered physical environment or introducing children to other adults who are not physically or emotionally safe.

The consequences of unaddressed issues in the life of a parent can also erupt in children. Failing to deal with mood disorders or other mental health issues can also be indirect faults. In addition, children need to see parents successfully negotiate relationships with other family members, friends, and neighbors.

Direct faults are those that involve behaviors in relationship to a child that impact them negatively. These range from a lack of parental involvement to harsh or inappropriate discipline. Direct faults can also include a failure to communicate in healthy ways, failure to adequately shelter or nourish, or failure to see that a child is provided with adequate educational opportunities.

Some faults are subtler. Parents can sometimes over-function in a way that fosters unrealistic expectations of them and other adults in their lives, including teachers, coaches, bosses, work associates. They can also shield their children from age-appropriate challenges to a degree that arrests their development.

The Process

I call the process a "fearless relational audit." It is *fearless* because the entire process is grounded in the love and grace of our Spiritual Source rather than fear of a punitive God. Before you begin, it is important to establish your confidence in this love and grace through prayer.

This is also a *relational* audit. Focus particularly on the most important relationships in your life. Think about how you have related to yourself. Physically, do you eat a healthy diet, exercise regularly, get enough sleep? Do you have regular checkups with doctors, dentists, and eye doctors? Mentally, do you work on having positive thoughts about yourself? Do you protect yourself by setting appropriate boundaries in your relationship with others?

Think about your relationship with your Spiritual Source, who many call God. Do you have a clear set of values that guide your life? Do you have a purpose statement? Do you have a set of spiritual practices to nourish your relationship with God? Have you developed an understanding of your Spiritual Source that is good and loving rather than harsh and punitive?

Thank about your relationship with others: friends, family, work associates. Do you keep your word, communicate honestly, really listen to them, spend appropriate amounts of time with them, and give them reason to trust you? Do you assume innocence when something goes wrong? Do you bring out the best in them? Do you support them in their dreams and forgive them for their faults?

Steps Toward Recovery

Now with pen and paper in hand, reflect on the questions at the beginning of this chapter.

- If you were going to live your life over again, what would you change?
  a. What would you change in general?
  b. What would you change in the environment you created for your children including your marriage?
  c. What would you change in the way you related to your children?
  d. What would you change in the way you related to other significant persons in your life?
- Everyone has had disappointments. What have been the main disappointments in your life?
  a. Where specifically have you been disappointed in yourself?
  b. Who has disappointed you that you need to forgive?
- What was the hardest thing you had to face in your life?
  a. What sense of unfairness or bitterness has taken root as a result?
  b. What grudges or resentments do you hold?
- What mistakes had the biggest impact upon the lives of your children?
- What mistakes had the biggest impact on other important relationships?

Put the list aside and return to it a few days later. Make notes of anything you would add or change.

Find someone that you trust: a pastor, a counselor, a sponsor, or a special friend. In a spirit of prayer, read through the list. Ask your Spiritual Source for forgiveness; then receive that forgiveness. Leave the list with your helper or burn it as a symbol that you are letting it go.

In some cases, you may feel the need to make amends, that is, go to those you have wronged and ask forgiveness. This should only be done with the guidance of a counselor, pastor, or sponsor.

Questions for Reflection and Discussion

In your own words, why was it important for this chapter to be near the end of the book?

Which benefits of a relational audit seem most important to you?

As you review the list of obstacles, which one or two is the biggest hurdle for you to overcome?

What is an example of an indirect fault that you now realize has affected your relationships?

What is an example of a direct fault that you now realize has affected your relationships?

If you are using this book in a group discussion, what did you gain from hearing others speak? From speaking?

Chapter 27
Practical Concerns

Once you have addressed some of the emotional, physical, and relational aspects of parental trauma, there are some practical issues to begin to consider.

Legal Issues

You will need to name an executor for your estate. The last thing in the world you want to do is have a will naming an estranged adult child to the responsibility of selling your property, paying creditors, bringing lawsuits, reviewing medical records, and distributing your assets to others. They may have totally lost track of what is important to you by the end of your life. They may also end up in conflict with those folks you have built positive relationships with over the years. Or they may simply refuse to carry out the duties. There are a number of good sites on the Internet that can help you make this decision.[157]

In the event of your incapacitation, you will need to appoint someone as durable power of attorney who has the legal authority to handle your affairs. In addition, you will need a healthcare power of attorney who can act on your behalf to make decisions regarding your healthcare. Guidance for your healthcare power of attorney is provided in documents you have prepared such as a living will and an advance directive. Again, you will want to make these decisions in consultation with knowledgeable resources that provide expert guidance.

---

[157] https://www.kiplinger.com/article/retirement/T021-C032-S014-7-tips-for-choosing-the-right-executor.html

There are implications for where you will live in the later years of your life. You'll want to consider a number of factors including relationships and your personal preferences for geography, climate, interests, and activities. However, it will be critical that you live near enough to those whom you have appointed to help manage your affairs for them to be able to do so without extensive travel to where you live. This will not only be an inconvenience for them, it may compromise their ability to advocate for you when that need arises.

If you use an attorney in any of these roles you will need to be prepared to compensate them for their work. However, even if you appoint friends to these roles, you should be prepared to compensate them for their time as well. This compensation should be agreed upon in advance and specified in legal documents.

Financial and Estate Issues

This brings us to the topic of estate planning and distributions specified from a will. The considerations exceed the scope of this book and should be discussed with an estate attorney. Broadly, there are several things to consider:

- A will should reflect your priorities including charitable causes, improvement in the lives of people you care about, and acknowledgement of the contributions that others have made in your life. Such decisions should be made carefully and with due regard for long-term consequences. They should not be made in anger or haste.
- Take a long-term view of reconciliation that exceeds the bounds of this life. If distributions to children do not seem appropriate, consider the future needs of grandchildren with gifts protected by a trust and trustee.
- Give consideration to those who have stood with you through the years even if they are not blood relatives.

- If children are totally disinherited or their share is significantly reduced, it raises the prospect of a lawsuit that could significantly deplete the estate and the benefits that others receive from it. Think it through before taking this step.

You will also need to make decisions about final arrangements and document those directives. Is it important to friends or relatives beyond your children that there be a grave to visit? What do you want in terms of services? What do you want included in them? Who will provide the leadership?

In the event of your incapacitation or death, what information do you want to have communicated to your children, and how do you want it communicated? At minimum, it is generally important to inform adult children of a parent's death. How they choose to respond to that information is left to their best judgment.

Grandchildren

Grandchildren can be a particularly heartbreaking aspect of parental alienation. They have generally not played a role in the estrangement process. In cases where there has been a close relationship between grandchildren and an estranged grandparent, the loss can be painful on both sides. What we don't want to do is put grandchildren in the middle of a conflict for which they have no responsibility. While seeking to maintain contact with them may be emotionally beneficial to us, it can inadvertently heighten the tensions in their environment. Sending them cards and gifts can reassure them that you have not forgotten them, but it may also create a desire to see you, which may put them at odds with parents. In some situations, it may be best to wait until grandchildren are eighteen when they will have the

As PEAK materials relate, financial, emotional, psychological and spiritual wellness becomes compromised when relationship problems remain in limbo.
B.D. from Miami, FL

right to make their own decision in relationship to you. In extreme cases, you may want to pursue the relationship using legal means. Some states have laws guaranteeing grandparents access to their grandchildren. There are no easy answers, and solutions will have to be developed on a case-by-case basis.

Holidays and special occasions are often difficult for estranged parents, and feelings of sadness at those times may never go away. Don't avoid those feelings or thoughts of those you miss. On the other hand, don't leave your own well-being to the whimsy of nature. Plan and practice self-care. Make arrangements well in advance of the holiday for activities that are both meaningful and connecting. Some of my best holidays have been celebrated on sightseeing tours. Establish your own traditions with people you love and who love you. If you are in a PEAK group, plan a holiday get together. On special days like your birthday or Father's/Mother's Day, fill up your schedule with things that will be good for you, such as a day trip, a dinner out, a massage, or time with friends. If there is a portion of this book that you have found particularly helpful, read it again. Above all, ask your Spiritual Source for help.

How to Talk about It

One of the larger challenges with parental estrangement is knowing what to say to people who ask about your children and grandchildren. Here's the reality: there is sufficient stigma around parental estrangement that attempts to talk openly may not be fruitful for either you or them. On the other hand, you don't want to feel that you must totally deny your own reality in order to fit in. What you feel comfortable sharing will vary from one situation to another. Certainly, you will want to share your estrangement journey with those who are closest to you. Even these people may need help understanding parental estrangement and how to best support you without trying to fix the situation or violating boundaries. You might want to give them copies of this book so they can learn how to do that.

In casual conversation with others, there are a variety of possible responses depending on how deep you want to go:

- I have three children: one's a lawyer, one's a nurse, and one's a musician. (Talk about their career rather than current activities.)
- I haven't talked to my children for a while, so I'm not sure what they are up to these days.
- I don't have a close relationship with my children right now so I can't fill you in on what's happening in their lives.
- We've discovered that our family is horrible at relationships, so getting away from each other works well for us!

Social Media

In an age of social media, it is easy to make the mistake of sharing personal information in a public forum that could create problems. Be vigilant in not sharing information about the estrangement that could be unnecessarily harmful to children and grandchildren.

Also, be careful about the degree to which you use social media to learn about your estranged children. This can almost become an obsession that takes you through the following cycle: 1) you are overcome with a sense of longing to connect with children/grandchildren; 2) you use social media to view posts and pictures of them; 3) the sight of their happy faces—aren't they all happy faces?—causes more pain; 4) you exit the program because it hurts too much; 5) after a few hours or days the pain subsides and the longing intensifies, and it all begins again.

Many estranged parents find it necessary to temporarily shut down their social media accounts until they have progressed further in their recovery.

Steps Toward Recovery

Many of the issues in this chapter require the services of professionals in a variety of specialties. This will require some research and planning.
- Make a list of the issues that you will eventually need to address. Then go back and write down an approximate time frame for addressing them, e. g. five years from now, next year, this year, etc.
- Identify and list the professional resources you will need to help you with these issues.
- Spend some time thinking about how you will respond to those who ask questions about your children or grandchildren. What response works best for you?
- Evaluate the impact of any social media accounts on your recovery. Make decisions about which accounts to keep, close, or limit.
- Remember to practice self-care during this part of your recovery. This is difficult emotional work. If it becomes too difficult, set it aside for a while.

Questions for Reflection and Discussion
Professionals in various fields observe that parents often hesitate to talk with them about their estranged children which makes it difficult for them to realistically plan for their future. Why do you think that is the case?

If there are estranged and unestranged children in the same family, should an estate be divided evenly among them?

How much pressure should estranged parents exert to stay in touch with grandchildren?

If you had a medical emergency today, who would be there for you?

What have you found works best in responding to questions about your children or grandchildren?

How has social media impacted parental estrangement in general?

Are there other practical issues you need to address?

How do you feel after working through this chapter?

If you are using this book in a group discussion, what did you gain from hearing others speak? From speaking?

PEAK: Parents of Estranged Adult Kids
A Resource for Recovery

Conclusion

An article titled *"8 Genuine Reasons Why the World Needs You Today"* lists them in this order:

1. The world needs you to do your duty.
2. The world needs you to realize your potential.
3. The world needs you to spread love.
4. The world needs you to be your own self.
5. The world needs you to truly live before you die.
6. The world needs you to share your gifts.
7. The world needs you to exercise self-care.
8. The world needs you to make it a better place to live.[158]

Here's the thing. It is going to be difficult for you to do any of those things very well if you have been in a serious accident when you were T-boned by another car on the driver's side.

It is also going to be difficult for you to do any of these things very well as a traumatized, estranged parent who is not moving forward in recovery. It's going to affect your work, limit your potential, make it harder to love others, tarnish your self-image, attenuate your passion for life, cast doubt on your gifts, make you more likely to get sick, and turn your attention toward your pain and away from the world that needs you.

Many people think it is selfish or self-centered to seek ways to grow through the pain of parental estrangement into recovery of a life that is vital and vibrant. This is especially true of those parents who have clearly failed in one way or another: became addicted, had an affair, been arrested, placed career or public image over family, walked out, or any one of a number of other significant failures, perceived or otherwise. There will be those who believe that you should suffer the

---

[158] https://medium.com/the-mission/8-genuine-reasons-why-the-world-needs-you-today-81234f610c11

emotional consequences of those failures until your dying breath, though they would never admit that to others or even to themselves.

And as an estranged parent, you have the option of doing exactly that. But make no mistake about it. Continuing to live in that misery is really the selfish choice. You will be stealing from the world what it needs from you. Finding a pathway to recovery is the unselfish choice. It makes you and your emotional, physical, and financial resources more available to a world in need.

Included in that world are other estranged parents who are living in pain and isolation. They need someone in recovery to reach out to them with a message of hope. Tell them your story. Give them this book. Pray for their Spiritual Source to walk them through this season of their lives. Have the courage that reaches out in love. Don't worry what people think of you.

While I regret the pain my children are experiencing, I can say that the collapse of my life with them has pushed me into the world in ways that would not have happened otherwise. This seems to be the pattern of God's working. When the nation of Judah was exiled to Babylon in 586 BCE, they were torn out of a familiar and navigable community and thrust into a world that was alien to all their previous experiences. In the face of a temptation to resign themselves to a victim mentality, God says, "But seek the welfare of the city where I have sent you into exile, and pray to the Lord on its behalf, for in its welfare you will find your welfare."[159]

I have indeed found my welfare in seeking the welfare of the world in which I now find myself. I have been exiled into a world of characters that I have been enabled to creatively love and serve, and who have given me a sense of community and purpose I never would have believed possible: Honduran children with HIV; women abused by their intimate partners; libraries trying to get levies passed to better serve their communities; pastors on the verge of suicide; gay and transgender champions of compassion and human rights; churches

---

[159] Jeremiah 29:7

trying to find their way into a fruitful and vital future; steadfast, transformative friends; and an incredible wife.

I began this book by writing about the pain of parental estrangement. Thanks to you, the reader, for journeying through that pain. I hope you can stay with me to hear one final thought. At the end of the journey, you may find a deep gratitude that can give thanks, not for the estrangement from your adult children, but for a working of God in that estrangement to bring a better you into the service of a better world. That is the ultimate healing.

Author Shannon L. Alder puts it this way: "Sometimes, you will go through awful trials in your life and then a miracle happens—God heals you. Don't be disheartened when the people you love don't see things like you do. There will be Pharisees in your life that will laugh it off, deny that it happened, or will mock your experience based on righteousness they think you don't possess. The only people that really matter in life are the people that can see your heart and rejoice with you."[160]

Questions for Reflection and Discussion
Based on the perspective of this chapter, define selfishness.

Which ideas in this book hold the greatest promise for your recovery?

How has your perspective on parental estrangement changed as you have read and discussed this book?

---

[160] https://www.goodreads.com/quotes/1223035-sometimes-you-will-go-through-awful-trials-in-your-life

What changes have you made since you began reading this book? What change do you need to make next?

If you are using this book in a group discussion, what did you gain from hearing others speak? From speaking?

Appendix A: Key Affirmations of PEAK

Our Common Experiences

We have adult children who either refuse to have a relationship with us or only relate to us when they are in need of financial or material assistance, or have set conditions for the relationship that render our lives physically, emotionally or financially unsustainable.

- We are bewildered by the decision our children have made to cut off the relationship with us. We waste precious time and energy focused on who to blame or what went wrong.
- We live in a capricious cycle of connect/disconnect with our adult children over which we have no control. Because we focus on what we cannot control, we feel weak and powerless.
- Given the investment in our children over many years, we are plagued by a loss of meaning. We get stuck in anger and feelings of unfairness.
- We have grief reactions that catch us by surprise. The smallest reminders can trigger feelings of loss, sadness, guilt, and depression.
- The intensity of our feelings sometimes boils over into behaviors that we are not proud of. We feel, and sometimes act, crazy. We use coping mechanisms that are not the best.
- Our minds go round and round trying to find a way of fixing things. We spend time replaying past conversations or rehearsing future ones.
- We are paralyzed by uncertainty about the future, whether to accept the estrangement as permanent and move forward, or hold out hope for reconciliation and look for positive signs.

- We have tried to follow the well-intentioned advice of books and articles, clergy and counselors, who offer suggestions for healing the estrangement. We are now exhausted.
- We are isolated from other estranged parents who might serve as sources of insight, support, and guidance. We feel alone.
- When we try to make amends to our estranged children our efforts are either ignored or the admissions used against us. Our best efforts to care or connect are consistently misunderstood or interpreted in a negative light.
- Our adult child's estrangement adds stress to other relationships, including spouses, friends, and siblings who feel conflicted, caught in the middle, and confused about appropriate boundaries.
- The fact that we are parents of estranged children leaves us feeling that we do not deserve to be happy, and we postpone opportunities to enjoy life and serve others.
- Because we see ourselves through the lens of our estrangement, it may be difficult for us to believe that we can be loved by others.
- The unrealistic expectation that our estranged children will change delays important financial and legal decisions, including plans for our eventual decline and passing.

We get stuck in these patterns of reacting that are detrimental to our lives and from which we need to recover.

The Way Forward

The Way Forward is to live into the reality that relationships between parents and adult children are voluntary. They are sustained by decisions made by both parents and their adult children who must take responsibility for their own well-being. In PEAK, you will be reminded that your adult children were shaped by a number of factors: your parenting, genetics, society's influence and pressures, factors unique to them and largely outside your control, and the choices they made along the way.

- Our recovery begins when we risk moving out of isolation. We discover that parental estrangement is not rare. By gradually releasing the burden of unexpressed grief, we join others in the journey toward gentleness, humor, love and respect.
- Many faith traditions share the insight that we are spiritual beings having a human experience, and that we are all children of a Spiritual Source. As human parents, we are the agents of our child's physical birth and custodians of their development. This Spiritual Source, whom some of us choose to call God, is their true parent. Our Spiritual Source is the beginning of healing and vital living, both for us as parents and for our adult children.
- Recovery from the trauma of parental estrangement requires that we do the work of rebuilding our identity, renewing our purpose, and reaffirming the meaning of our past. To accomplish this, we open our minds and hearts to fresh perspectives. We learn to restructure our thinking one day at a time.
- We find that we can recover, even if our adult child continues to choose estrangement. When we release our adult children from responsibility for our actions today, we become free to make decisions as actors, not as reactors. We progress from hurting, to healing, to helping.

- We all make mistakes that affect other people including our adult children. It is always important to be willing to examine ourselves. However, parental estrangement affects even the best of parents. Through PEAK you will be reminded that parental estrangement is not a reliable measure of your love, your mental health, or your competency. Everyone deserves to recover.
- You will also be encouraged to see parental estrangement for what it is: a choice made by adults taking responsibility for their own well-being. You will learn to keep your focus on yourself in the here and now. You will take responsibility for your own life and supply your own needs for relationships.
- You will not do this alone. Through the PEAK movement you will discover others who know how you feel. We will love and encourage you no matter what. We ask that you accept us just as we accept you.
- By following this spiritual program based on love, and exercising faith in our Spiritual Source, there is every reason to believe that recovery is possible. Parental estrangement negatively impacts many areas of life. However, our recovery has far-reaching, positive benefits that we cannot currently imagine.

The PEAK Turning Points

1. By changing the way we view ourselves and our children, we will gradually replace our feelings of hurt, anger, and unfairness with serenity and peace.
2. We will experience growth in our self-acceptance, forgive ourselves and others for mistakes of the past, and give ourselves approval on a daily basis.
3. Our mental turmoil will subside as we turn our thinking away from remembered conversations of the past or imagined conversations of the future, and refocus on the potential for beauty in each moment.
4. As we engage a plan of self-care for body, mind, and spirit, we will experience healing from the trauma of our estrangement and find a greater sense of wholeness.
5. We will find feelings of isolation and defectiveness easing as our ability to share our struggles openly and honestly grows.
6. As we release our children and ourselves to discover the relationship that is best for each of us, our preoccupation with fixing the estrangement will give way to patient acceptance.
7. By making plans that address our future needs, we will enjoy feeling stable, peaceful, and financially secure.
8. As we choose to invest resources in our adult children and grandchildren, we will make those decisions in a way that reflects our values and legacy desires.
9. As we become more secure in our own worth and dignity, we will find it easier to relate to other parents as they celebrate their relationships with children and grandchildren.
10. As healthy boundaries and limits become easier for us to set, we will discover ways to reduce the impact of estrangement on spouses, siblings, and other relationships.
11. By learning that we deserve to play and have fun, we will discover or rediscover sources of joy and happiness in our lives.

12. As we progress along the road of healing, our sensitivity to estrangement in the lives of others will increase, and we will experience the fulfillment of reaching out to them with confidence and compassion.

Appendix B: PEAK Life Review

Given their age, all parents of estranged adult children have entered a stage of life where they begin to reflect on the question "Did I live a meaningful life?" Psychologist Erik Erikson suggested that one of life's ultimate achievements is to authentically answer "yes" to that question and settle into a sense of accomplishment, fulfillment, and peace.

Parental estrangement threatens that process. Since parents invest heavily in the development of their children and tend to derive a great deal of meaning from those relationships, they can perceive the estrangement as a negation of their lives. "What was my life about?" is a frequent question of estranged parents, and the inability to answer that question can pose a major obstacle to their recovery.

Of course, parents do not spend their entire lives with children at home. They had a life BC (Before Children) and have a life AD (After Departure). Even during the years past infancy when their children were occupying a major part of their lives, parents had other interests, activities, and experiences. Estranged parents can take a positive step in their recovery by reclaiming those other chapters of their life story and giving them appropriate weight.

That process can be aided through a life review. The process and benefits of a life review are described in Chapter 24.

A number of formats have been developed for a life review, and a variety of questions can be used. Any of these can be fruitful. Most important is the quality of the listening and the openness of the person to move beyond the narrow definition of themselves as a parent to also include the lover, the actor, the experiencer, and the learner.

Since some questions in this review will be more relevant than others, I recommend the lists that follow be considered a menu. A sensitive listener will be able to discern which questions help mine the richness of a parent's narrative given the flow of the conversation. In all cases, a therapeutic life review will require several sessions, with time between sessions for the parent to reflect on what they have shared.

Since I believe that the aid of a Spiritual Source, however defined, is essential to the recovery from the ravages of parental estrangement, I structure this process around several assumptions.

First, I believe that every person is a spiritual being having a human experience. Our core identity is not located in our physical attributes, material possessions, or biological processes. We are on a journey through this world that is a necessary part of our spiritual development.

Second, as spiritual beings, we come from a Spiritual Source and will return to a Spiritual Source, what many people call God. This Spiritual Source is our true parent. Our human parents are only the biological instruments of our existence.

Third, we have come into the world for specific purposes that can be broadly described in four categories: someone to love, something to do, something to experience, and lessons to learn. Many spiritual traditions affirm that these purposes were assigned before we were born. In some traditions, it is believed that we participated in deciding what these purposes should be. In virtually all spiritual traditions, the ultimate purposes for our lives flow from a universal consciousness that is good and loving.

Finally, our Spiritual Source has worked throughout our lives to help us achieve these purposes in ways that may not be immediately obvious, but become clearer upon reflection. With this perspective, even regrets and traumas may have meaning and result in post-traumatic growth.

The questions of this life review are structured around this spiritual understanding of life. They are intentionally focused on aspects of life beyond bearing and raising children. Instead of arranging them under headings of age or function (family, job, hobbies), I ask the reader to reflect in terms of purpose: love, actions, experiences, and learnings.

Who and What Have You Loved?

1. When was the first time in your life that you felt truly loved?
2. Over the course of your entire lifetime, what persons or creatures have you helped care for (children, stepchildren, foster children, aged or disabled persons, pets, and so forth)? What were their names? How many were there?
3. Do you think caring for others mostly out of a sense of duty is love? Why or why not?
4. What properties (homes, land, cars, boats, and so forth) did you own? What did you do to take care of them?
5. What have been your most prized possessions? What made them important? Did you ever lose something, other than a person or pet, that made you sad?
6. Who have been the people in your life you always looked forward to spending time with? What was it about them that attracted you?
7. What persons from your past, deceased or living, do you miss?
8. "I would not have been the same without you." Who are the people you could say that to without any hesitation?
9. Over the course of your lifetime, would you say that you needed more friends, needed fewer friends, or had just about the right number of friends?
10. How many times have you fallen in love? If you fell in love, did it feel like something happening to you or something you were in control of?
11. How many times did someone break your heart?
12. "Some people would be surprised by how much I care." Do you think that statement is true or false? Why?
13. Overall, do you think you have had the right amount of love in your life? Where have there been shortages either in giving or receiving love?
14. Going back to your childhood, what groups have you been part of?

15. What role did you play in those groups? For example, if a sports team, what position or event; if a musical group, what instrument; if a faith community or nonprofit, what committee(s) did you serve on?
16. Of the groups listed previously, which ones would you say you loved being part of? What made them special to you?
17. During your time in those groups, what particular occasions stand out in your memory?
18. If your participation in some of those groups continues, what has kept you involved?
19. If your participation in those groups came to a close, how did it end?
20. Tell about a time you did something to help a total stranger.
21. Tell about a time a total stranger did something for you. How did that affect you?
22. What organizations have you supported that help people you will never meet?
23. What organizations have you supported that help people who have made mistakes, such as the addicted, the imprisoned, those who have been fired for misconduct, and so forth?
24. Has there ever been a time when you showed love to someone who had mistreated, misrepresented, or neglected you? Tell about it.
25. What are the most important times you have forgiven someone? Been forgiven by someone?
26. What lessons has life taught you about love?
27. Looking back over all your reflections about love, how often were you in control of what was happening, and how much does it now seem that something was unfolding that was bigger than you?

What Did You Do?

1. Did you have chores assigned to you when you were growing up? What were they?
2. How did you spend your summers, your holidays, and your free time?
3. Going back as far as your childhood, what was the first job you were paid to do?
4. List the different jobs you have had, including those in your childhood. How did each of those jobs contribute to your development as a person?
5. Did you serve in the military? What were your responsibilities? How did the military change you?
6. What have you done (paid or unpaid) that helped people directly, that is, people you came into contact with?
7. What have you done (paid or unpaid) that helped people indirectly, that is, helped people you never met?
8. Think of the things you loved doing and did well. Let's call this your sweet spot. What activities or work did you do that were in your sweet spot?
9. Has figuring out what you were supposed to do come relatively easy to you, or has finding the right activities or work been difficult and stressful?
10. Tell about a time when you finished a day's work with the feeling "I love my job."
11. Tell about a time when you finished a day's work with the feeling "I hate this job."
12. What did the money you earned enable you to do for others?
13. What work did you do that was significant for which you were never paid?
14. If you could have done anything in the world and money was no object, would you have done anything different? What?
15. Were you ever let go from a job? How did that affect you? How did you recover?

16. Have you ever pursued a dream or didn't get a job you really wanted? How did that affect you? How did you recover?
17. What would you say are the greatest achievements in the work that you have done, either for pay or as a volunteer?
18. Think back to where you were in life when you were twenty years old. What have been some of the biggest surprises in what you ended up doing with your life?
19. Did you ever rescue someone from a dangerous situation?
20. Did you ever feel guided by a power greater than yourself to make an important change in your work? Tell about that.
21. How many people in the world have a good understanding of what you have accomplished in your life?

What Have You Experienced?
1. What is your earliest memory as a child?
2. How many different places have you lived? Where were they?
3. Have you traveled internationally? Where? How did that change you—or not?
4. How many different climates have you experienced? What was your favorite?
5. What is your favorite season of the year? What makes it your favorite?
6. Other than sight and hearing, what is your favorite sense: smell, taste, or touch? Why?
7. Going back to your childhood, have you ever been in a physical fight with another person? How did that affect you?
8. What are the times in your life you were most afraid?
9. What are the times in your life you were most happy?
10. What was the biggest injustice you experienced in your life?
11. Do you carry any guilt that you haven't yet been able to let go of? What would it take to let it go?
12. How important were sexual experiences in your life? How did those change over the years?

13. Have you been comfortable with your gender identity? Sexual orientation?
14. When it comes to taking risks, do you think you have taken too many, not enough, or just about the right amount of risk?
15. What are some of the most beautiful things you have experienced? Most beautiful people?
16. Have you ever felt lonely in your life? How lonely were you?
17. What have been your mountaintop experiences?
18. Have you ever gotten angry in a way you regretted? In a way you didn't regret?
19. Who made you feel like your life mattered? What did they do?
20. Whether connected to an organized religion or on your own, have you ever had a deep spiritual experience? How did that happen?
21. Have you ever had a near-death experience, out of body experience, or deep mystical experience? What was that like?
22. Have you had other spiritual experiences that you don't talk about because you are afraid people will think you are crazy? Do you want to talk about them now?
23. How have the difficulties of life affected you overall?
24. How have the joys of life affected you overall?

What Have You Learned?

1. Did anyone read to you as a child? Who did the reading?
2. What was the name of the first teacher you can remember? What was that person like?
3. Who were your favorite teachers or coaches? What did they do that made them a favorite?
4. When did your parents stop helping you with homework?
5. What part of your educational experience did you like best? What was the worst?
6. Did you ever fail a subject? How did that affect you? How did you recover?

7. In school, what were your favorite subjects?
8. What has been your favorite way of learning: lecture from an expert, hands-on experience, or group discussion?
9. What were the positive lessons you learned from your parents or other family members (qualities you inherited or want to imitate)?
10. What were the negative lessons you learned from you parents or other family members (qualities or behaviors you want to avoid)?
11. What was your highest level of formal, educational achievement?
12. In school, were you an overachiever, underachiever, or just about right?
13. Were there any times when you learned the wrong lesson from an experience, for example, that loving is a mistake, that you are a defective person, or that talking about feelings is weakness?
14. Which persons taught you the most about how to succeed in your work?
15. Which persons taught you the most about how to live a meaningful life?
16. Who are your favorite authors? What makes them your favorite?
17. If regrets are lessons learned for another time and place, which regrets have taught you the most?
18. What life lessons have you learned the slowest and you need the lesson over and over?
19. What life lessons did you learn the fastest and you only needed something to happen once or twice for you to get the message?

Summary Questions

1. If your life were a book, what would be the title? What would be the titles of some of the chapters?
2. As you remember those you have loved in your life, even those who broke your heart, how would it change your perspective on life to consider that they were each sent for a purpose?
3. If you were sent to earth on assignment, which actions you have taken in your life have best fulfilled that assignment?
4. If the purpose of life is to help you fully experience a balance of joy and sorrow, strength and weakness, and love and loneliness, how balanced has your life been?
5. If your life has been a school and you are a student, what are the most important lessons you have learned?
6. If part of our life's purpose is to be negative teachers who help other people learn what not to do, what have been those lessons you have given others?
7. If life must be lived looking forward, but understood looking backward, what do you now understand about your life that you did not perceive as you were living it?
8. If the secret to life is making things the right size and putting them in the right places, what are the things you need to make smaller? What are the things you need to make larger?
9. If there is a life to come that solves problems we cannot solve in this life, what do you look forward to?
10. If every gift is a test, given to us with the hope that we will succeed by being grateful rather than suspicious, proud, or inferior, what gratitude are you ready to offer for your life?

PEAK: Parents of Estranged Adult Kids
A Resource for Recovery

Appendix C: Letter to Friends

Dear friend/supporter,

I am assuming that you are reading this because it was given to you by a friend who is an estranged parent of an adult child. Thanks for taking the time to read this, but especially for your offer of support during this season in your friend's life.

You may not have heard much about parental estrangement, because it is very difficult to talk about in a society where one of the first things that people share with one another are stories and photos of children, grandchildren, or other family members. Nonetheless, parental estrangement is not rare and it is occurring with increasing frequency in our society.

Your friend is going through one of the most excruciating experiences in a parent's life. Parental estrangement is an emotional trauma that is more difficult to deal with than the physical trauma of an accident. Like any significant loss, parental estrangement plunges us into a grief process. Your friend may be experiencing shock, denial, anger, guilt, bargaining, and depression.

In addition, parental estrangement raises questions about the meaning of life: If my adult child has ended the relationship with me, what was the point of all those years of care and nurture? Did it mean anything? It is also likely that your friend is isolated and has found little help from friends, doctors, clergy, or even counselors. Parental estrangement can have many secondary impacts including mental health issues, medical issues, and difficulty trusting other relationships.

Like any good friend you may be wondering what you can do to help. Here are a few things to think about.

First, do a little research on parental estrangement. There are an increasing number of resources online. You might want to read a copy of the book from which this letter was taken, *PEAK: Parents of Estranged Adult Kids,* what we refer to as our R4R.

Second, encourage your friend to talk by being a good listener. Remember, a good listener doesn't judge, offer advice, try to fix it, or keep looking at their watch!

Third, don't try to figure out the cause of the estrangement. Even if you are aware of failures in the life of your friend, don't jump to conclusions. What seems to estrange one adult child has little effect on another, sometimes in the same family.

Fourth, maintain healthy boundaries. Keep conversations confidential. If you happen to also have a relationship with the adult children of the estranged parent who is your friend, don't get caught in a triangle—don't talk to the parent about what the adult child said or did, and don't talk to the adult child about what the parent said or did, even if they ask you to!

Fifth, don't assume that your friend is an infinite source of emotional energy who must assume the full burden of reconciling the relationship with an adult child. Parents are human. They have limitations. By definition, adult children are, well, adults! Reconciliation is also partly their responsibility.

Sixth, be where your friend is. If your friend has hope of reconciling the relationship, support them in that effort. If your friend is working to accept the fact that the relationship as he/she has known it is over, support them in the effort to move forward.

Seventh be especially tuned in to your friend on birthdays, celebrations, and holidays when others may be connecting with children and your friend is not. Support during that time is especially important.

Eighth, watch for signs that your friend is getting into trouble, things like increased use of alcohol or other drugs, withdrawal, depressed mood, poor hygiene, or engaging in risky behaviors. Don't hesitate to encourage your friend to get additional help if you think that is needed. Call a hotline if you need additional support.

Finally, realize that love and perseverance as what are most important in caring for your friend. By being present in this time of recovery, you are offering a gift of inestimable value that will never be forgotten.

As an estranged parent, I would have benefited greatly from having you as a friend.

Soulfully,

Fe Anam Avis, author
PEAK
Parents of Estranged Adult Kids

PEAK: Parents of Estranged Adult Kids
A Resource for Recovery

Appendix D: Estranged Parent Bill of Rights

Parents, have rights. Given the fact that they began their journey with full responsibility for their child, they tend not to think in terms of these rights. This carries a host of negative consequences including an increased sense of powerless, a loss of dignity, a beggar mentality, a fragile reconciliation when it occurs, and an inability to assert or advocate for themselves in other situations.

These parental rights do not include the right to compel, manipulate, or financially leverage a relationship with their adult child. Neither does this list imply that adult children do not also have rights.

Reciting these rights aloud on a regular basis can be a helpful element of recovery.

1. I have the right to expect, but not compel relationships with my children that evolve from adult-to-child, to adult-to-adult, to finalist-to-adult.
2. I have the right to form relationships characterized by mutuality, commitment, authenticity, and gratitude rather than relationships that are unilateral, capricious, guarded, and entitled.
3. I have the right to assert the legitimacy of my thoughts, feelings, and motivations, rather than being told what I think, feel, and intend.
4. I have the right to individual relationships with children, grandchildren, friends, and associates that are not complexified by issues from other relationships.
5. I have the right to closure on past failures, real or perceived.

6. I have the right to be told directly when closure on past failures is not possible, and to know the limitations that lack of closure will place on our relationship.
7. I have the right to live without abuse, neglect, or exploitation.
8. I have the right to recover from the trauma of estrangement, and to develop a positive identity and purpose for my life.
9. I have the right to develop new relationships that are mutually beneficial.
10. I have the right to celebrate the contributions I have made to the world over the course of my lifetime without repeated reminders of my deficits.
11. I have the right to make plans for my future that provide for my financial and physical security.
12. In any eventual reconciliation, I have the right to establish boundaries in a process that gradually redevelops trust.

*"finalist stage" refers to roughly the final quarter of a parent's life. These are the years when adults are reflecting on the meaning of their lives, including their investment in raising children.

About the Author

J. Russell Crabtree earned a degree in engineering physics from the Ohio State University in 1972. He worked for three years in research and development at the Eastman Kodak Company before earning a master of divinity degree from Fuller Seminary. He served as a Presbyterian minister until 1998 when he left pastoral ministry and began working full time to develop a home for children with HIV in Honduras, Montana de Luz. His experience in Honduras, combined with his own spiritual development, led to such a period of transformation that he adopted his pen name on May 5, 2005 (5-05-05): Fe Anam Avis.

In the aftermath of three suicides in his community, he and Linda Karlovec, PhD., founded the Community Response Team, a cross-professional coalition representing parents, schools, churches, medical professionals, and mental health experts. He was recruited by Melinda Moore to serve as the chief operating officer of the newly formed Ohio Coalition for Suicide Prevention, which wrote the suicide prevention plan for the state of Ohio and created cross-professional suicide prevention coalitions at the county level.

He received suicide intervention and awareness training in 2002. Soon afterward, he founded a company called BestMinds, LLC, aimed at "helping persons find their best minds in times of personal crisis." He began working with county coalitions in southeast Ohio, developing suicide prevention plans and conducting awareness training. Since beginning that work, he has trained thousands of people across the United States.

In 2003 he worked with Dr. David Litts who was heading the Surgeon General's effort at suicide prevention in the United States and developing guidelines for clergy conducting memorial and funeral services for those who had died by suicide.

In 2003 he also became engaged in the issue of domestic violence. He was asked to write an intervention training curriculum by the Columbus Coalition Against Family Violence to be used in faith communities. Using that curriculum, *Breaking the Silence*, he has trained hundreds of people in scores of churches to deal with family violence.

In 2013 he created Soul Shop™, a one-day training experience designed to help church leaders equip their congregations to minister to those impacted by suicidal desperation. Soul Shop™ has become an international movement with specific trainings now developed for youth workers and collegiate ministries.

In 2019 he created PEAK, a support network for parents of estranged adult kids.

Fe has authored numerous books. He lives with his wife, Shawn, in Hendersonville, North Carolina.

For further information about PEAK contact:
Keli Rugenstein, PhD.
518-210-2486
peakrecoverytogether@gmail.com

818-954-5525